Investing in People

To Pino
whose investment has been priceless

Investing in People

Towards corporate capability

Peter Critten

Butterworth-Heinemann Ltd
Linacre House, Jordan Hill, Oxford OX2 8DP

PART OF REED INTERNATIONAL BOOKS

OXFORD   LONDON   BOSTON
MUNICH   NEW DELHI   SINGAPORE   SYDNEY
TOKYO   TORONTO   WELLINGTON

First published 1993

British Library Cataloguing in Publication Data
Critten, Peter
    Investing in People: Towards corporate
    capability
    I. Title
    658.3

ISBN 0 7506 0646 0

Composition by Genesis Typesetting, Laser Quay, Rochester, Kent
Printed and bound in Great Britain by Redwood Press, Melksham,
Wiltshire

Contents

Preface

At a time when redundancies are a daily item of news and companies are cutting back on any form of investment the publication of a book on 'investing in people' may seem an unlikely if not unfortunate choice of title. It was chosen to reflect a theme that was central to a course I had developed for MBA final year students to encourage them to take a strategic view of training and development which embraced the wide range of initiatives that had emanated from Government over the past five years.

It just so happens that one such initiative is the 'Investors in People' award on offer to companies through their local TEC – but there are others, like the movement towards competence-based assessment, which have seemingly appeared out of nowhere and companies and trainers have had to brief themselves and respond to them as best they can before another 'scheme' emerges. But from my perspective there are some very radical changes happening in the world of training and development whose significance we are in danger of missing. In my view they have to be embraced in a holistic way – which is what this book attempts to do.

Having spent a number of years with a major ITB I am only too aware of how national initiatives on training and development are kept at arm's length by companies. The argument I am proposing is that they offer companies a framework within which to reappraise themselves and their staff as a single entity. However, this also entails some 'upside-down-thinking' to put them into perspective. The process is not unlike turning round a kaleidoscope full of brightly coloured but separate fragments of prisms which at the flick of the wrist can be brought together to make a perfect pattern; with another turn of the wrist they disseminate and then come together again in another pattern.

The creation of new patterns and order to meet a continually changing world is a process that is unique to each company. A key message of the book is that there are some exciting initiatives available but they can only be fully grasped and maximum benefit derived from them if an organization has *first* looked at itself from inside out. Then and only then is it in a position to put a unique package together utilizing all that is available. However, it is also true that the initiatives can assist in the process of that review. They provide a framework within which the organization can break itself down and then put itself together again.

There will, of course, be other initiatives – some will be flavour of the month, others will be longer lasting. The hope is that this book will give you the stomach to face such initiatives from a new perspective – *your own*. In fifteen years with a major Industry Training Board I was always amazed that so few organizations took a proactive and strategic approach when dealing with the ITB. In the book I put this down to the rather British characteristic of, on the one hand, liking to complain about bureaucracy and systems and procedures that are imposed, but on the other actually preferring to *have* such rules to follow rather than having to create our *own* system; worse still having to create a *strategy* to shape such systems.

Another assumption we tend to harbour is that such systems, emanating from Government and/or professional bodies, *have* to be right and are unchangeable. Having worked for an ITB and over the last two years been closely associated with a number of Government agencies, in particular NCVQ and TECs, the only thing that is constant is change. A message of the book is not only that you can but that you *should* influence the way such initiatives are shaped in the future; and in the meantime you *can* negotiate with such bodies to ensure they serve your purpose *now*.

With another hat on, running courses for students at a business school, it has struck me that students also make assumptions about the system, that it is there to make it as difficult as possible to get their qualifications (another British characteristic – if it's not hurting it's not working). Having now sat in on umpteen examination boards I am equally amazed at the trouble to which the institution goes to *get* students through the system – but why don't we share this message with the students?

Equally there are thousands of potential students who would never dare pass the college gates because they believe they haven't got the necessary pre-qualifications and/or that they could never cope with an 'academic' course. Happily, this situation is rapidly changing as more young people recognize that to succeed they *do* need some kind of professional accreditation. But a large proportion of these potential students are *not* young people, they are adults in or out of work, who last studied decades ago. How do colleges and universities get the message across that they too are rapidly changing and that there are now opportunities for everyone to study, develop skills and get accreditation in courses and schemes of study/ learning adapted to meet the students' needs?

This book seeks to get these messages across to both industry and educational institutions alike. It may be that you are already familiar with initiatives like NVQs and Investors in People. This book aims to help you look upon them in a new light so that, if you haven't done so already, you can *use* them for your own ends. To do this and to deal proactively and strategically with all the other initiatives that are sure to follow during the 1990s, I believe you need to understand the background from which they have come. You will find, therefore, that in introducing the initiatives I put them into historical context and suggest sources, associations and follow-up references. This is not to make the book unnecessarily 'academic' but because I believe such 'underpinning knowledge' will help you come to your *own* considered opinion about the value of such an initiative. But more importantly, that it will enable you to anticipate developments for the future. I would also argue that you and your company/training/educational institution should be in a position to *influence* such developments.

This then is what the book is about. Finally, to return to the question posed in the opening paragraph – what is the justification of a book on 'investing in people' at a time of deep recession when companies are folding daily? The stock trainer response would be that it is just at such times that a company needs to build up its skills to capitalize on growth opportunities once the recession is over. However, as you will soon realize, this is anything but a stock book on training. My response to what is a very valid question, and dilemma, indulges in some 'upside-down-thinking' which will become very familiar to you; just to let you know when we revert to upside-down-thinking mode the text appears in italics. If you are in the unhappy position of seeing your external market evaporate and the jobs of your staff diminish in relevance, this is for you:

Now that you have exhausted all leads in the external market and all the experts have given you their gloomy forecasts, perhaps it is time to look at your internal market, at your staff. In trying to relaunch the business were they consulted? Do you know what the business looks like from their perspective? Maybe it looks better! Do you know what skills and resources they have to contribute?

By staff, I don't just mean your management team – I know you've been in close touch with them – I mean all your staff. For example, what do you know about Ada, one of the clerks in your Accounts Department? Did you know that staff from other departments regularly contact her to sort out their financial returns? They find she's a natural finance whizz kid – you might find out that she's got a very good working relationship with your supplier Clarks and could help you extend your credit there in ways that you couldn't imagine. Then there's Craig, the young servicing engineer you've just taken on from college. Did you know he's come up with a new way of cutting down servicing costs? Not only that but he'd like to get into design – just for the record he's just recommended a modification to his boss that's a potential market winner. Why haven't you heard about it? Well, you'd better discuss that with his boss; you'll find Craig's typed recommendation at the bottom of his supervisor's pending tray under all those memos from accounts.

Need we go on? The prime investment in people you need to make is your time. If you had only spent as much time with Ada and Craig as you did with that firm of consultants . . . but it is still not too late. Remember it is not just that you are as good as the people that work for you; you are also capable of being that much better because so are they, with a little help from you. This book will help you combine the new found release of ideas and energy in your staff with outside initiatives like NVQs and Investors in People which will in turn give them an incentive to invest their skills in your/their company. So read on . . . .

I am not so naive to believe that such an approach is going to bring about an economic miracle; but in the absence of anything better, I believe companies need to be reminded of the fact that though they may seem to have exhausted all their assets there are still assets that remain that never appear on the balance sheet. The irony is that at a time of economic gloom there is, and has been for some time, evidence of a radical review of the value of people at work together with issues of how they are managed and their capacity for transforming the organization of which they form an organic part. This book, I hope, will contribute to this debate and help organizations use the infrastructure and network of initiatives available to them from outside to build a new organization capability from within. I hope you enjoy it.

Peter Critten

Acknowledgements

I am very grateful to a number of people and institutions for assistance in commenting on the text of certain chapters and for permission to reproduce material. In particular I would like to thank: Dr Alex Lord of Henley Management College and the Chief Executive of Somerset TEC for comments on Chapter 2; Paul Ellis of NCVQ for comments on Chapter 3; David Slater of the Employment Department for comments on extracts related to the Investors in People initiative; Chris Hills of MCI for comments on Chapter 4; HMSO for permission to reproduce extracts from Crown copyright publications; Sutcliffe Catering Group for permission to reproduce extracts from the 'Learning from Experience' project quoted in Chapter 7. Finally I am very grateful to Peter Dixon of the Training and Development Department of British Gas for comments on the first draft of the text and for suggestions for revisions.

1 Introduction

This book has its origins in a 'one term' programme I have been running for
MBA students at Middlesex Business School. I was faced with the challenge
of designing a curriculum for business strategists of the future based around
traditional subjects from the past like 'The role of training departments',
'Systematic training', 'Validation and evaluation' etc. My response was to
propose a programme that was based more around integrating themes and
trends from today than on discrete subjects that might be found in a Training
Officer's Course.

The course gave me the opportunity to bring together key themes that
have excited me in different roles in training and development over the past
25 years. The reader should be warned from the outset, therefore, that this
is anything but an 'objective' primer on good training practice. It reflects
ideas and issues that have dominated my thinking over the years. But it is
only *now*, it seems to me, that a combination of factors present in our
economy and approach to the world of management and work make it
imperative that companies (not to mention Business Schools) take a fresh
look at what 'training and development' implies for them. My hope is that
the book can contribute to the national debate about training and
development by helping companies and colleges take an essentially *strategic*
view of these issues.

The title I gave to my course deliberately included no reference to training
and development. 'Investing in People', I felt, more properly described the
contribution training and development should make to the organization. (I
should add that at this time I had no idea the Government was to launch a
programme called 'Investors in People'.) This remains the main title of the
book.

The issues the book tackles are contemporary (as at the time of
publication) but I believe their implications go far beyond a particular
scheme that happens to be the flavour of the month. The one underlying
issue is that of 'corporate capability' which I believe will be the dominant
issue facing Human Resource Managers over the next decade – hence the
sub-title of the book.

The book is aimed at anyone in an organization who is fired by the idea
of 'investing in people' and has the power to do something about it. Though
not a 'How-to-do-it' book, there are plenty of suggestions for action and

examples of what I have called 'upside-down thinking' taking my cue from Charles Handy.[1] These examples paint a picture of how organizations in the future might manage the development of their staff and how the consequences of such development can have an impact on the organization as a whole. (Such examples and suggestions for action are signposted in the text – they appear in italic.)

Training and development have always seemed to me to be a *means* towards an end, that end being literally to add *value* to the organization as a whole. This goes beyond helping 'organizations and individuals to achieve their objectives', which is the overriding 'purpose' of training and development promoted in the National Standards for Training and Development.[2] A prime motivation for writing this book is to help those directly involved in development within organizations to see the wider picture, in short to develop a *vision*.

My formative development was in the 1960s and 1970s when training and development grew as a profession but when, in my view, they also got trapped within the 'systematic training cycle'.[3] During the same period management education and development was driven by 'strategy' and 'planning'. What was missing was a vision that could integrate individuals and organization alike into believing that their development actually made a difference.

In the 1990s the concept of 'vision' has suddenly become very popular in management thinking. It is no longer fashionable to describe management as a science; strategic planning is more akin to a craftsman's art which is shaped by a very different vision.

> What springs to mind is not so much thinking and reason as involvement, a feeling of intimacy and harmony with the materials at hand developed through long experience and commitment. Formulation and implementation merge into a fluid process of learning, through which creative strategies evolve.[4]

But how do you *get* a vision? You can learn about strategy but how do you acquire a vision and, even more mysterious, how do you *share* that vision with others so that 'you and I have a similar picture and are committed to one another having it, not just to each of us, individually, having it'?[5]

Trainers and developers have done a very good job over the past two decades helping individuals acquire knowledge, skills and maybe even visions *as individuals*. The key to success in the future is how to help organizations become *committed* to the *process* of sharing the vision, the knowledge, the skill so that it becomes as much the possession of the organization as of the individual and is able to shape its future. In short, I believe the key role for trainers, developers, facilitators (call them what you will) in the future is to help their organization become a *learning organization*. The concept of the learning organization is one that underpins this book. But at the same time as we are able to share a vision we must not lose sight of the reality of which we are still part (what Senge calls the necessary precondition of 'creative tension'[5]) and through which the vision will be achieved. This book seeks to help training and development practitioners and managers to recognize the realities and opportunities that confront them today not as unchangeable events to which they can only react but as initiatives which can be a focus for their own development and that of their organizations.

Before you can recognize their development potential, however, I believe you also need to understand the source from which these opportunities have come and the process whereby they have evolved. You will therefore find that each chapter spends time on the background of each initiative (for example, the emergence of competences) and tries to put it into a context within which we can review it and identify themes and patterns which depict the 'larger picture'.[5] This is particularly true of Chapter 6, which is an in-depth analysis of the concept of evaluation which in my view is not just a concept but a process in its own right and one which is at the heart of the learning organization.

This book is also the story of a personal journey and identifies stages in the way my own thinking has developed. This is the only way I could share *my* vision with you. I hope it does not get in the way of the key themes which are the centrepiece of the story which is about *investment* in people. All the titles of the chapters, therefore, in some way allude to the notion of investment.

Chapter 2, 'Unlocking the national training bank', sets the national scene by alluding to TECs (Training Enterprise Councils) as local clearing banks for human capital. It then goes on to explore how current initiatives like NVQs (National Vocational Qualifications), the British Standard BS5750 and the recently launched 'Investors in People' scheme can *together* be used by companies as a framework for both investing in people and capitalizing on this investment.

Chapter 3, 'Converting training needs into performance credit', focuses on the notion of competences and looks at the National Vocational Qualifications (NVQ) scheme in detail. It suggests the view that competences can become a national currency by which people can be more valued at work. It goes on to suggest a process by which a company can convert individual competences into *corporate* capability.

Chapter 4, 'The learning portfolio goes public' suggests ways in which a company can identify learning resources it never knew it had. It explores the implications of separating outcomes (competences) from inputs (resources needed to achieve them) and suggests this gives companies and trainers a much freer and more flexible approach to training and development. It suggests a number of ways in which companies can value, maybe for the first time, the learning resources that are available to them for investment.

Chapter 5, 'Management growth for all', focuses on the role of the manager in a changing world where positional power is no longer guaranteed. It explains what is behind the MCI (Management Charter Initiative) and suggests how companies can use the new MCI competences as a framework for exploring their *own* needs for management development.

Chapter 6, 'Evaluation – the hidden accumulator', brings together a wide range of material to help companies put a value on the learning process and its outcome in their own organizations. It draws on original research work I carried out into the nature of evaluation and demonstrates how various techniques of evaluation can be used to trigger off a process for putting value on the organization as a 'learning organization'.

Chapter 7, 'Corporate capability – putting a value on the learning organization', draws together many of the themes in the previous chapters. It explores the origins of the concept of a 'learning organization' and helps companies identify characteristics of their own organizations that match the requirements. Again, I draw on original work with companies helping them become learning organizations.

The final conclusion reached in Chapter 7 is that all the techniques and ideas explored in the previous chapters can lead to *potential* value for the organization as a whole; this is how I define 'corporate capability' – the capacity of the organization to add value to its human capital, i.e. its people. There is a final matrix which refers readers back to previous chapters and reveals how themes in each chapter can both improve current competence but, if taken further, can enhance future corporate capability.

In the final analysis, the success of the book will be measured by how many companies are able to make this transition – from individual competence to corporate capability.

References

1 Handy, C. (1989) *The Age of Unreason*, Hutchinson
2 TDLB (1992) *National Standards for Training and Development*, Employment Department, Moorfoot, Sheffield
3 Taylor, H. (1991) The systematic training model: Corn circles in search of a spaceship? *Management Education and Development*, **22**(4), Winter, 258–278
4 Mintzberg, H. (1989) 'Crafting strategy', in *Mintzberg on Mintzberg*, Free Press
5 Senge, P. (1990) *The Fifth Discipline: The Art and Practice of the Learning Organization*, Doubleday

2 Unlocking the national training bank

As the human capital intensity of products and services increases, the importance of human resource assessments (HRA) should become a greater part of the evaluation of corporate strengths and weaknesses.

Professor Robert Lindley[1]

Imagine the scene. You want a loan to develop your business. You approach your local bank. You are not asked for a Business Plan or a Marketing Plan or for financial statements. Instead you're asked to give evidence of just how you've used and developed your 'human capital' over the past five years and the kind of return you would expect to deliver if more human capital was released into your account. The bank you've come to is no ordinary bank. It deals in only one commodity – human potential and its use and misuse.

This could, of course, be a Video Arts 'bad dream' scenario were it not for the fact that it may not be so far away from the way companies of the 1990s will be viewed by their employees, their competitors, their customers and their shareholders. Evaluation would be as much against investment in people and the return obtained as on capital employed – because of the two it is likely that over the next decade it is people and people skills that will be the scarcer resource.[2]

But this isn't anything new. Over 25 years ago the Industrial Training Act was passed to offset the very same problem. What *is* new is the coming together of a range of conditions and prevailing attitudes which suggest we are on the threshold of a national paradigm shift towards integrating for the first time individual, company and national needs. The trouble is there have been so many initiatives proposed over recent years that the average employer could be forgiven for wanting to wait until conditions settled before taking account of any possible impact on his or her company.

The aim of this chapter is to try to help managers like you tip the balance of this paradigm shift *now* by enabling you literally to *capitalize* on just some of these initiatives in your own company. The chapter starts with a brief review of national initiatives and trends over the past 25 years which have led to the present focus on *investing in people*. It then considers the implications of the Government White Paper 'Employment for the Nineties' and how Training Enterprise Councils (TECs) – the main agents for delivering the changes proposed – could be used for topping up skills in much the same way your local bank safeguards the money supply. Attention is then focused on three specific initiatives which, if taken together, could create a framework for change within which companies could at the same time improve their corporate capability and their competitiveness.

2.1 The training see-saw since 1964

One thing is for sure, if the volume of training over the past decade was matched by the number of Government White Papers and National Reports on training, we would be in the top league. The Appendix to this chapter summarizes the critical legislation, influential reports and launch of national initiatives all of which have sought to address the problem of skill shortages and change the attitudes of a generation of managers. Only you can judge how effective any of it has been in changing *your* attitude.

ACTIVITY 2.1
- *Briefly review the initiatives in the Appendix and note which ones have had any impact on your company and/or yourself directly or indirectly.*

The events listed in the Appendix covering almost 30 years could be divided into three key periods:

- 1964–1981 The Industrial Training Board era
- 1981–1988 All change and transition
- 1988–   The TEC era – business back in charge

Summarizing the Industrial Training Board era in their excellent review of current training practice, *Training Interventions*, Kenny and Reid reflect on the fact that

This period began in an economic boom and with considerable optimism that the country's longstanding industrial training problems would be largely resolved by the radical 'carrot and stick' interventions to be provided by the Industrial Training Act. It ended in a severe economic depression with the dismantling of much of the ITB system and a return, for many employers to the status quo of *laissez-faire* practices.[3]

The 1980s provided a number of sharp shocks in the form of the reports 'Competence and Competition', 'Challenge to Complacency' and the two reports on the 'Making of Managers'. This had the effect of starting up a second order of initiatives (e.g. the Management Charter Initiative) while industry was still trying to absorb wide-ranging changes that had been at the heart of the New Training Initiative in 1981.

Now, in the 1990s, with the Manpower Services Commission (MSC) and the Training Agency no more, is it all back to square one with training once more dependent on the whim of individual employers with only a limited, short-term view and local networks who cannot take a national view? Or do the recommendations in 'Employment for the 1990s' match the mood of the times and the view that training is an integral part of management?

Traditionally, training in the UK has been craft-centred and/or focused on high status work. The survey *Training in Britain*,[4] carried out at the end of the 1980s, found that of those employers who did train (one in five did not), no more than 48% of the workforce were covered – which means that over half of the organization did not benefit from any training.

This attitude may have something to do with the division between what Becker calls 'general' and 'specific' skills. In the same year as the Industrial Training Act, Becker published *Human Capital; A Theoretical and Empirical Analysis, with special Reference to Education*.[5] In it he argued that there are two types of training a company might carry out: *general* training, which results in skills that are not only useful to the company but to its competitors in the labour market (e.g. word processor skills, management skills), and *specific* training, which results in skills that are of use only to the company (e.g. manufacture of products unique to the company). He further argued that a company would be prepared to invest in specific skills, because it would benefit from them directly, but not in general skills, unless individual employees paid for their training themselves.

Although the publication of Becker's ideas coincided with the passing of the Industrial Training Act, it is to be regretted that ITBs have not done more to encourage companies to invest in 'general' as well as in 'specific' skills.[6] If they had done so in the 1960s we might not have the skills shortages we have in the 1990s.

ITBs could also have done more to encourage companies to take a wider view when formulating training policies including such factors as:

- Learning from experience
- Job re-design
- Labour market skills
- Motives for training
- Recruitment
- Turnover costs
- Labour mobility
- Economic benefits

These issues were raised in a paper by Michael Oatey in 1970[6] but it is only *now*, I suggest, that the wide framework he envisaged is *potentially* available, albeit somewhat hidden under the range of schemes currently being marketed by the Government. We can get glimpses of some aspects of this framework from the proceedings of the 1990 NEDO Policy Seminar on Training, written up in *Training and Competitiveness*. In a paper called 'Corporate strategy and training', Chris Hendry – co-author of the report on 'Employers' Perspectives on Human Resources in the Training in Britain Survey' – outlines a general model of factors driving and stabilizing training. He argues that

> the 'necessary' condition for increasing company attention to training is likely to be environmental pressure and the business responses to this. But the 'sufficient' conditions involve the gathering together of a critical mass of positive or supporting factors. Training activities, moreover, are better sustainable when framed within broader HRD and HRM processes. . . . What distinguishes firms is the richness of the context for training and continuing development that key actors can mobilize.[7]

In examining some of the factors that contribute to 'the richness of the context', he is critical of the former Training Agency's emphasis on 'financial benefits' and argues that 'it would be on surer ground if it shifted the argument from company financial performance, which is too far removed, to measures of productive efficiency'.

Another factor he considers critical in the context of external pressures is customer requirements for quality: 'The significance of quality . . . is that it touches on a fundamental pillar of competitiveness and, like efficiency in production, generates criteria that Training can fix on'.[7]

The NEDO conference highlighted the need for training to be put in a wider context – much as Oatey had argued 20 years previously. It is well expressed by Sir John Cassels in his introduction to the papers:

> One may conclude that training – and human resource management generally – may be seen working on at least two levels. The first is reactive and short-term and concerned with avoiding the costs and set backs associated with *not* training. The second is at a deeper level and concerns developing *corporate capability* so as to enable the company both to perform well immediately and to develop in the future in such a way as to improve its market position . . . (emphasis added).[8]

An underlying theme of this book is that for too long 'training' has been somehow separated out from 'the business' for special attention. The Industrial Training Act started off the process for the best of reasons but, as the list of events chronicled in the Appendix shows, despite countless individual initiatives and warnings, our national stock of skills has only marginally improved. The signs are that the *volume* of training is improving – which is at least one consequence of the now defunct ITBs. A recent Labour Force survey carried out in the spring of 1990 showed that between

1984 and 1990 there had been a 84.9% increase in the proportion of people of all ages receiving work-related training.[9] But do not statistics of this kind only really measure the incidence of John Cassel's first type of training which is 'reactive and short term'?

Having worked for a national Training Board for 15 years (as well as dealing with another ITB from within industry), I have no illusions about the reality of having to balance the needs of the industry on the one hand while on the other having to introduce an ever increasing stream of initiatives emanating from Head Office in Sheffield. There was never time enough to embed in one initiative before another came along requiring 'marginal' adjustments. The problem has been that though there have been some very innovative initiatives – as a glance through the list in the Appendix will show – their impact has been lost within the sheer 'volume' of events. Added to this is the British characteristic of, as Handy puts it, letting things wither away and then replacing them. We are 'not a revolutionary people'.[10] I believe that really to effect the changes that are needed we need to be more revolutionary, at least in our *thinking* about the problems and opportunities we face.

The irony is we don't need any *more* initiatives, White Papers to tell us what we already know. Although they have been expressed in many ways, they are well summed up below in the TUC contribution to the NEDO conference on Training from Ron Todd the former General Secretary of the TGWU. Reiterating the underlying requirement for increasing skills Ron Todd identifies the following three challenges that face the British economy over the next decade:

> First – the challenge of demography, with the numbers of young people declining towards the middle of the decade; and with the associated increase in emphasis on the need for women workers (especially returners).
>
> Second – the challenge of competition, especially from continental Europe after the completion of the single European market by the end of 1992; but also from the rest of the world, in line with the intensification of competition over the past few years.
>
> Third – the challenge of quality, in services as much as in manufacturing, with the growing use of quality assurance measures such as BS5750 and Total Quality Management.[11]

His response to these challenges was to outline the need for national qualification targets (the Government subsequently set a target in relation to numbers of the workforce having NVQs – see Chapter 3) and a national skills framework. My response to these challenges is to move the debate away from *numbers per se* and to question what we *really* understand by the term at the centre of the debate – training itself.

Like most people involved in training, for many years now I have felt uncomfortable with the term 'training', with its association with achieving limited objectives, by definition, and above all with the assumption that training was about the running of 'off-the-job courses'. ITBs were criticized in their early days for putting too much emphasis on 'formal' training, such as courses (see Oatey[6]), but to be fair to ITBs, they themselves soon became more flexible about how training was to be delivered. The problem was that companies themselves preferred to think of training in terms of courses, plus it made it much easier when playing the numbers game. In my experience working for a Training Board, companies rarely explored with the ITB what was *possible*; in Handy's words, they preferred to accept 'the inevitable and make it their own'.[10]

My belief is that in attempting to intervene in what has been a traditional *laissez-faire* attitude to training and development in this country, trainers and successive governments over the past 25 years have between them managed to create a whole science and industry around training itself; in so doing, we have paid too much attention to the form the training takes and lost sight of what it is trying to achieve.

I have painful memories early in my ITB career of confronting pub managers with a systematic approach to training as devised by the Hotel and Catering Training Board and paying scant attention to how their new bar staff had managed to learn the job by themselves, with a little help from the manager. At that time (the early 1970s) our definition of what training was or was not was taken from the 1971 Department of Employment *Glossary of Training Terms* which defined Training as 'The *systematic* development of the attitude/knowledge/skill behaviour pattern required by an individual to perform adequately a given task of job (emphasis added)'.[12] If it wasn't systematic, it wasn't training.

But notice the difference of emphasis in the MSC's Glossary of Training Terms in 1981, where training is defined as:

> a planned process to modify attitude, knowledge or skill behaviour through learning experience to achieve effective performance in an activity or range of activities. Its purpose, in the work situation, is to develop the abilities of the individual and to satisfy the current and future manpower needs of the organization.[13]

Gone is the reference to 'systematic'; instead there is a reference to a 'planned process'; but most significant of all is acknowledgment of 'learning experience' as being central to the whole process. It also draws attention to the 'purpose' of training as being not just for the organization but for the benefit of the individual. The trouble with ITBs and their companies was they were too far locked into an ongoing debate about levy and how to become exempt from it that such niceties of distinction were largely overlooked.

Of course, there were significant developments in the 1970s and the 1980s which opened up the debate. There were, for example, reports from the

School of Management Learning at the University of Lancaster, which drew attention to limitations of a purely 'training' model when applied to management training, for example; to the need to become aware of the values and implicit 'learning theories' behind the design of management programmes.[14] Then the impetus of Open Tech focused on alternative ways of delivering training other than via instructor-run courses with all the limitations that imposed on the *learner*. Suddenly 'learning' became much more fashionable than 'training', which should not be limited to a time or a place or even to any one age, i.e. there should be continuous development for all. Trainers began to talk about their role as 'creating conditions within which others could learn' rather than 'running courses'.

But are these changes – which are still continuing and increasing – sufficient to bring about a real paradigm shift, i.e. a way of thinking about the world and how we relate to it which provides a basis for our *actions*?[15]

A current widely held paradigm is that for organizations to survive in a rapidly changing world there have to be radical new ways of thinking about their purpose and the relationship of their employees to that purpose. In the past five years there have been a number of books published promoting a new kind of thinking about the nature of work, of organizational behaviour and above all, of the need for organizations to be responsive to their customers. Notable examples include *Thriving on Chaos*, Tom Peters[16], *The Age of Unreason*, Charles Handy, [10] and *When Giants Learn to Dance*, Ros Moss Kanter.[17] We shall have cause to refer to them later in this book, but their significance at this stage is that they reflect a paradigm shift about organizational behaviour which urgently needs to be addressed by trainers and those who determine training policy.

In his book *The Future of Work* in 1984, Charles Handy first formulated some of the ideas for a new kind of society in which 'No longer will the question "What will I be?" be fully answered by "What job shall I have?" The job will not be the whole measure of one's identity, one's status, one's finances or one's purpose in life.'[18] In *The Age of Unreason* he argues for an 'Upside-Down Society' which can only come about by some 'upside-down thinking'. Here is one example of such thinking:

> Upside-down thinking suggests that we should stop talking and thinking of employees and employment . . . If work were defined as activity, some of which is paid for, then everyone is a worker, for nearly all their natural life. If everyone were treated as self-employed during their active years then by law and logic they could not be *un*employed.[10]

There is evidence of a real paradigm shift in the move away from specific jobs towards emphasis on generic and transferable competences (see Chapter 3). One way the Government is supporting this move, for example, is by the provision of individual training vouchers whereby an individual can purchase training *he/she* wants. A particular consequence of this is to give 'primacy to occupational labour markets [which] would place more emphasis on *fostering the individual's capacity to pursue an independent career* (whether planned or not . . .) (emphasis added)'.[1]

Underlying all the ideas above is a common trend towards greater flexibility, freedom and choice on the part of the individual and the need for organizations (and government) to respond accordingly. Will such freedom mean a dilution of national standards (a criticism levelled against NVQs, for example)? Handy thinks the reverse will be the case:

> A freer and more anarchic market will put more pressure on the individual consumer to decide what he or she wants and to check the product lives up to its specification. This is an invitation for more literature of the *Which?* variety, more standard setting institutions on the model of the British standards . . .[10]

Lindley makes a similar point with regard to the provision of 'good local employer' type guides: 'records of achievement of employers, publication of VET results, annual human resource reports written for and available to the wider community beyond the dominant shareholder or producer (i.e. employer and trade union) interest'.[1]

In this section I have painted an overall picture of some of the current issues that have an implication for training policy; we can now examine four specific schemes in the light of these issues and assess to what extent they can contribute towards a real paradigm shift. The test of such a shift is how it can inform and direct specific action. In this case I hope the action can be taken by *you*.

We briefly review each scheme and then subject it to some of Handy's 'upside-down thinking' before posing some questions, actions for you to take up in your own organizations.

2.2 'Employment for the 1990s' and the role of the TECs

> As we move into the 1990s the greatest need is to modernize and develop our training systems. We are now experiencing the first stages of the major demographic changes which over the next five years will cause a significant slowing down in the growth of the labour force and a dramatic fall in the number of young people entering the labour market. That means that most of the people on whom our economy will rely in the 1990s are already at work. Many of them have had little or no training since the initial training they received in their first job. Most of them left school at the minimum age and have not acquired any qualifications since then.
>
> The implications are clear. Employers large and small must undertake a massive training effort over the year ahead and this must be directed primarily at the people they already employ. Employers as

both providers and consumers of training have the primary responsibility for ensuring that our labour force has the skills to support our expanding economy.

These words are from the concluding paragraphs of a Government White Paper the aim of which was to shape training strategy for the next decade, 'Employment for the 1990s'.[19] Its theme is people and jobs and, as the extract above indicates, it focuses particularly on the responsibilities of individual employers in reskilling Britain. For its part the Government set five priorities to support these initiatives:

1 To invite local employers to set up Training and Enterprise Councils (TECs) to plan, deliver and promote training that met local needs. This is the key element of the framework being proposed.
2 The setting up of a National Training Task Force to coordinate the efforts of TECs and introduce/advise on national initiatives.
3 To launch through the Training Agency the Business Growth through Training (BGT) programmes to help companies develop training to meet their own business needs.
4 To begin the process of enabling existing Industry Training Boards to become independent, non-statutory bodies.
5 To begin the process of privatizing the Skills Training Agency.

As we have already seen, the current *intention* is to move from nationally prescribed policy to local determination of needs. Underlying the White Paper are a number of principles which have far-reaching implications (emphasis added below):[20]

● Training and vocational education, including management training and counselling for small firms, *must be designed to contribute to business success and economic growth.*
● *Employers and individuals need to accept a greater share of responsibility for training and its costs,* while Government have a role in setting a framework and in funding the training of unemployed people.
● *There must be recognized standards of competence, relevant to employment,* drawn up by industry-led organizations covering every sector and every occupational group, and validated nationally.
● *Responsibility for delivery of training and enterprise must, as far as possible, be devolved to local areas where people work and are trained.* It is there that we need to bring together private and public investment to meet the skill needs of business and individuals.
● The training must provide *young people and adults with the opportunity to secure qualifications in these recognized standards.*
● Enterprises, individuals and local communities *must be able to shape arrangements, programmes and opportunities to their changing needs and circumstances.*

TECs will be the means of realizing these principles in practice. There are 82 TECs covering all areas in England and Wales and 22 LECs (Local Enterprise Companies) in Scotland. Each TEC/LEC will be required to agree a contract with Government based on a strategy that meets both national aims and targets set by the Department of Employment and local needs identified by the TECs/LECs themselves. Each TEC/LEC is required to produce a Business Plan with details of this strategy.

A key part of the Government's strategy is that TECs should be run primarily by senior managers of local businesses. Thus at least two-thirds of each TEC Board must be private sector employers who are chairmen, chief executives or top operational managers of local major companies. There will typically be from nine to 15 directors who will manage an annual budget of something like £20 million. Funding from the Government is divided into

---

I'm a small employer in your area. I employ 30 staff. Most staff receive basic training in-house but I've come to the conclusion that we're too inward looking; if we are to grow we must be part of a wider market.

On the other hand I haven't the funds to take on more staff at the moment. I've therefore come to you as I might come to my local bank. I want to hand over to you all my staff – and myself – for you to decide how best these assets can be invested in the local market.

Specifically I want to know:

1 *Is such an idea feasible?*
2 *What information, collateral will you need from me?*
3 *Where and how do we start?*
4 *What is it going to cost me?*

Example response:

Certainly such an idea is feasible; although they don't go as far as you're proposing, the principles behind the TECs depend on just such a relationship between local companies and their TEC.

The first thing I need to know is more detail about your assets. I'd want a statement of your current account, i.e. existing skills, qualifications, experience, aspirations of all your staff and yourself. I will then be in a position to compare what you have to offer with our current and future needs. For example, I note that all of your secretaries are qualified to operate at least two word-processor packages. Perhaps we could arrange for some of our underemployed local assets to be temporarily lodged with you and for one of your secretaries to bring them up to her standard. This will at the same time increase the value of your secretary and provide you with additional resources.

We could also arrange for your buyer who you say lacks experience of the retail trade to spend some time with Millers & Sons who are starting to expand and I'm sure would be prepared to take her on board for a limited period. This will give you some idea how we could work together to increase your overall human assets. But I'd need to make a detailed analysis of your accounts after which we can agree a plan for every member of staff. As to overall costs to you there will, of course, be some contribution to TEC funds but overall the costs and benefits are likely to balance themselves out. You've already made the greatest step forward in regarding all of your staff as assets which can increase in value rather than simply costs to be incurred.

Figure 2.1 *Upside-down thinking and TECs*

five separate blocks, the first three of which are for supporting national initiatives: Employment Training (aimed at the unemployed); Youth Training; Business Growth and Enterprise; local initiatives; a management budget.

As has been made clear in criticisms of the TEC system, TECs will not be able to achieve their objectives on government funding only and will need to top up revenue from local initiatives. As in most things, it is the source of revenue that will largely determine the policies. Is there likely to be a conflict between meeting the national needs on the one hand (for which government funds have been allocated) and meeting local needs and the needs of existing businesses – businesses like yours?

Clearly you need to ask such questions of your own TEC (see Activity 2.2), but, I suggest, they have to be in the context of some upside-down thinking, such as is reproduced in Figure 2.1. It is this sort of thinking in which, I suggest, companies and TECs will need to engage if they are literally to capatalize on the opportunities the TECs can offer. But it will not come automatically by merely going through the motions of nominally support-ing the various initiatives in the compartmentalized form in which they have been handed down to TECs to administer: e.g. training for young people; ET; Business Growth etc. Both companies and TECs must take an overall strategic view of how together they can top up the skills of *all* the local workforce whether employed or not, at whatever age and however qualified they are. It is an opportunity to wipe the slate clean and build up a new account.

To conclude this section here are some suggestions for action and questions to ask of your local TEC.

ACTIVITY 2.2
- *Find out where your local TEC is located.*

- *Arrange an appointment and find out:*
  - *What are the local needs in your area.*
  - *Where are there skill shortages.*
- *How do local needs/skill shortages impact on your business plan?*

- *How can you 'invest' in some of the skills in the local bank (i.e. top up skills by taking on trainees)?*

2.3 Quality

One of the three key changes to affect industry in the 1990s which Ron Todd identified (see p. 9) was the increasing importance of quality. There are at least three ways in which this influence is being brought to bear: in the first place companies are coming under more pressure from ever more demanding customers; reduced spending power means that the value of goods and services are at a premium as never before. Second, ever since *In Search of Excellence* came out in 1982[21] popular pundits and management gurus like Tom Peters have been persuasively arguing that a company's survival above all else depends on being responsive to customer needs. Finally, British Standards Institution (BSI) has published a British standard, BS5750, which is increasingly being used by companies as a means of signalling to suppliers and customers alike that their product or service is the outcome of a *quality system*.

BS5750 was first published in 1976 as a quality assurance system which ensured that products or services met the customer's requirements. Companies could register with BSI and have their procedures independently assessed against a checklist which covered areas like management responsibility, inspection and testing, corrective action etc. Though the language of BS5750 is more appropriate to manufacturing, recently more and more services have realized the commercial consequences of conforming to BS5750 standards. Recognizing this development, BSI have introduced guidelines for services to help them focus on the criteria in a more complex and less standardized world than is common in manufacturing.[22]

The focus of any quality system must be the customer. Quality assurance is about ensuring procedures are in place which will guarantee that the customer's needs are met in relation to the delivery of a specific product or service. Where it revolves around a product, e.g. manufacture of a 'widget' to a client's specification, procedures can be precisely applied and measured. Where the customer is receiving a service there needs to be a different focus for applying criteria. It is this focus which I believe has important implications for decisions about investing in people.

> In most cases the control of service and service delivery characteristics can only be achieved by controlling the *process* that delivers the service. Process performance measurement and control are therefore essential to achieve and maintain the required service quality. While remedial action is sometimes possible during service delivery it is usually not possible to use final inspection to influence service quality at the customer interface where customer assessment of any non-conformity is often immediate (emphasis added).[22]

The guidelines recognize that important though 'quality managers' and 'inspectors' are, they do not *create* quality. That is the function of every single person within the organization and in particular members of staff who are in daily direct contact with customers. If a service organization is going for BS5750 it therefore seems to me that the *way* it involves every single person in what Peters calls 'obsession with the customer' is just as important as the volumes of documentation which standardize procedures for interactions with customers that can be specified. In personal service, for every customer transaction that *can* be specified there will be an infinite number that can't.

It is a similar issue which Giles and Williams address[23] in making a distinction between quality management and quality assurance. They regard quality management as being much more than quality assurance: 'It is a long term and holistic approach to people and systems which links quality into the whole business strategy.' They point to national quality awards instituted in the United States in 1987 for which winners have to provide evidence of achievement against seven criteria: leadership; information and analysis; strategic quality planning; human resource utilization; quality assurance of products and services; quality results; customer satisfaction. As they point out, BS5750 procedures only account for one of the seven categories. Quality Management, as they suggest, contains some fundamental assumptions and underlying values:

> It means turning the organization chart on its head so that managers coach and support rather than control and force. It relies on teamwork, feedback and a non-threatening environment where people work together to debate openly and solve problems. It requires carefully controlled systems and excellent management information, resulting in rule by data rather than rule by hunch or hierarchical position. Such a culture revolution for many western organizations requires consultancy skills of a high order to facilitate the change.[23]

It was just such a culture revolution which Tom Peters outlined in his book *Thriving on Chaos*. He suggests numerous prescriptions for bringing about what he calls a 'customer revolution'.

How do these kinds of activities and the cultural changes outlined by Giles and Williams square up with the specific procedures of BS5750? I believe there need be no conflict between the kind of creative process activities suggested above and the more bureaucratic procedures that have so far characterized BS5750 – as long as the procedures themselves *evolve directly from the process*. This means indulging in some more upside-down thinking.

Upside-down thinking and BS5750
● *Instead of a standards manual for a company being produced by and delivered from a central 'Standards' Department, why should it not be put together by a cross-section of staff who come up with their own recommendations based on their experience of meeting customer needs? Certainly they are more likely to take ownership for its upkeep and amendment if they were directly involved in its production.*
● *Do standards necessarily have to be written down? If they do, is their status fixed in stone? It is perhaps a UK characteristic to put faith in systems but the last thing we do is use the system as a way of reaching our own goals and meeting our own agendas.*

● *Consider to what extent all the documentation surrounding quality control 'reduces variety' and yet, certainly in a service organization, it is the variety of response to a multitude of customers' needs that differentiates one company from another as offering quality service. A feature of systems theory is a concept called 'requisite variety' which suggests that the internal regulatory mechanisms of a system must be as diverse as the environment with which it is trying to deal. How does your organization match the complexity of environment and range of customers with which it has to deal?*

ACTIVITY 2.3
● *In the same way as you approached the local TEC to test out the system, contact BSI Quality Assurance (PO Box 375, Milton Keynes) and explore how by meeting the requirements of BS5750 you can meet your own agenda for quality service*

2.4 Competences and the National Council for Vocational Qualifications (NCVQ)

The whole issue of competences and its implications for investing in people is the subject of the next chapter. It is introduced here because it takes its place alongside TECs and BS5750 as one of the four current initiatives I believe can help companies make a paradigm shift in their thinking about their staff. But, like the other two initiatives so far introduced, it will mean some upside-down thinking for companies to derive real benefits from them.

In 1986 the Government established the National Council for Vocational Qualifications (NCVQ) in a bid to ensure that *all* industries set **standards of competence** which were required in their respective sectors of employment. Industry Lead Bodies were set up to spearhead the analysis of all jobs within their scope. Currently there are well over 100 such bodies covering every conceivable craft and industry. Just a selection are summarized in Figure 2.2. The Government has set a deadline that by the end of 1992 there will be standards of competence set for every industry in this country.

So just what is so special about 'competence'? Its definition and potential *range* of application, I believe, are very important.

The concept of competence . . . is defined as the ability to perform the activities within an occupation or function to the standards expected in employment. *Competence is a wide concept which embodies the ability to transfer skills and knowledge to new situations within the occupational area.* It encompasses organisation and planning of work, innovation and coping with non-routine activities. *It includes those qualities of personal*

Refractories, Clay Pipes and Allied Industries Training Council c/o University of Sheffield Elmfield Northumberland Road Sheffield SE10 2TZ	Cleaning Industry Lead Body Hill House Skinners Lane Wroxham Norwich N12 8SJ
Insurance Industry Training Council 271A High Street Orpington Kent BR6 0NW	Hotel and Catering Training Company International House High Street Ealing W5 5DB
Confederation of British Wool Textiles 60 Toller Lane Bradford BD8 9BZ	Training and Development Lead Body TDLB Secretariat c/o NCITO 5 George Lane Royston Herts SG8 9AR

Figure 2.2 *Examples of industry-specific Lead Bodies*

effectiveness that are required in the workplace to deal with co-workers, managers and customers (emphasis added).[24]

As we shall see in Chapter 3, although the concept is wide and challenging, in seeking to set up systems to administer it we have done the British thing of creating bureaucracies that obscure its prime value. That is why we will need to indulge in some upside-down thinking. But first consider what this initiative should mean to you as a manager. I believe there are at least four benefits that could directly affect the way you invest in people:

1 It enables you to specify your employment needs precisely when recruiting a new member of staff. Furthermore it will help in selecting the very applicants in whom you will want to invest.
2 It enables you to recognize what people can do and achieve in the job. By the same token it enables your staff to get recognition for the skills they can perform. What makes the NVQ scheme significantly different from schemes in the past (like Task Analysis – see Chapter 3) is that there is a mechanism whereby staff can get professional accreditation if they can demonstrate that they can achieve the necessary standards laid down.
3 It also provides a way of giving credit for what people have done in the past; rather than just relying on qualifications, staff can use their experience and achievements from the past as evidence for accreditation. This process is know as Accreditation of Prior Learning (APL) and will have implications for staff who want to get professional recognition but lack the pre-qualifications which have hitherto been necessary.

4 It provides a route for development and career progression; by specifying competences for every level of job in your organization (including your own!) you are making it clear what needs to be achieved at a higher level. This has implications for your entire training and development policy, as we shall see later.

In a word, the concept of competence and the *explicit* way it makes clear what has to be achieved, are the equivalents of investing human capital on the stock exchange. Beforehand, there were job descriptions which companies generally kept to themselves locked up in the Personnel Department; but now every job can be defined not just in company terms but in competences which have *national value in the market place*. This enables individuals and companies alike to put a *precise value* on their human assets.

Figure 2.3 illustrates an example of how competences are being defined; this is taken from the Training Development Lead Body's published competences which apply to all trainers. Competences are broken down into what are called 'elements' which describes 'an action, behaviour or outcome which a person should be able to demonstrate'. In Figure 2.3 the element chosen is 'presenting information to groups of trainees'. For each element there will be a set of **performance criteria** which are the 'critical indicators that someone is performing competently'. There will also be what are called **range statements** which indicate the range of applications the element has.

Element C212 Present information to learners

Performance criteria

(a) Information is clear and accurate and presented in a tone, manner, pace and style appropriate to the needs and capabilities of learners
(b) Visual support materials are legible, accurate and used in a manner which enhances the clarity of the information presented
(c) Trainees are encouraged to ask questions, seek clarification and make comments at identified and appropriate stages in the presentation
(d) Clear and accurate supplementary and summary information is provided on request and where appropriate to reinforce key learning points
(e) Visual aid equipment is regularly maintained in full operating condition

Range statements

Type of information:	principles/theories, factual information (quantitative and qualitative); analysis/evaluation
Types of group:	One to small group with potential interaction, one to large group with limited interaction
Visual aid equipment:	projection systems, display systems

Figure 2.3 *Example of an element of competence and associated performance criteria and range indicators from the Training and Development Lead Body's National Standards for Training and Development (published March 1992)*[25]

This is very important because if you go back to the definition of competence on p. 18 it focuses on the importance of 'transferability' of skill.

Thus, if you wanted to assess the competence of one of your company trainers in this particular element (ability to present information to groups of trainees), it would not be sufficient to test their ability to present to a large group where there was little opportunity for interaction. You would also want to know that the trainer was competent at handling small groups where there would be questions and potential discussion, debate with the participants. Hence both of these conditions are specified in the 'Range statements'.

In Chapter 3 we will indulge in some upside-down thinking about competences which I hope will help you explore the underlying philosophy and how it can contribute to your organizational strategy. But in the meantime, here is an activity to carry out:

ACTIVITY 2.4
● *Find out the Lead Body that covers your industry and obtain a copy of the competences that have been specified.*

2.5 The 'Investors in People' scheme

The whole concept of 'investing in people' seems like an idea whose time has finally come, as the TEC scheme entitled 'Investors in People' will testify. Although – as I explained in the introductory chapter – the title of this book is derived from a programme I ran for MBA students in 1990 and not from the TEC initiative launched in 1991, the focus away from training as something done *to* people to investment *in* people may be the first signs of a national paradigm shift in thinking. As this extract from an introductory briefing pack produced by TECs to introduce the initiative proclaims:

> *Investors in People* is not just one more training programme scheme or initiative. Nor is it simply about persuading companies to spend more on training.
>
> It's about helping companies to realise the value of their most potent investment – their own people.[26]

This is a powerful statement and one which I hope the TECs will have firmly in mind when they come to assess companies against defined criteria (see below). While wholly supporting the aim described above, I have fears that the old British 'system' will take over, and that it could end up as just another scheme to reward companies for carrying out training. This is why we need to indulge in some radical upside-down thinking.

The scheme originated from the National Training Task Force – another of the outcomes of the 1988 'Employment for the 1990s' White Paper – which was established to raise employer commitment to training. The NTTF spent a year listening to businesses throughout the country and examining what were the *people* factors that made one company more successful than another. They found that successful companies had already asked themselves the following kind of questions in order to discover:

- How to manage and use people in a way that will directly contribute to improved performance.
- How to plan and organize the development of people so that they are able to contribute fully to the success of the business.
- How to develop and use people so they can become a real and flexible source of competitive advantage.

The Investors in People programme was launched to help all companies ask and answer questions like these for themselves. The aim is to enable

---

An Investor in People makes a public commitment from the top to develop all employees to achieve its business objectives

- Every employer should have a written but flexible plan which sets out business goals and targets, considers how employees will contribute to achieving the plan and specifies how development needs in particular will be assessed and met
- Management should develop and communicate to all employees a vision of where the organization is going and the contribution employees will make to its success, involving employee representatives as appropriate

An Investor in People regularly reviews the training and development needs of all employees

- The resources for training and developing employees should be clearly identified in the business plan
- Managers should be responsible for regularly agreeing training and development needs with each employee in the context of business objectives, setting targets and standards linked, where appropriate, to the achievement of National Vocational Qualifications (or relevant units) and, in Scotland, Scottish Vocational Qualifications

An Investor in People takes action to train and develop individuals on recruitment and throughout their employment

- Action should focus on the training needs of all new recruits and continually developing and improving the skills of existing employees
- All employees should be encouraged to contribute to identifying and meeting their own job-related development needs

An Investor in People evaluates the investment in training and development to assess achievement and improve future effectiveness

- The investment, the competence and commitment of employers and the use made of skills learned should be reviewed at all levels against business goals and targets
- The effectiveness of training and development should be reviewed at the top level and lead to renewed commitment and target setting

---

Figure 2.4 *National standards for effective investment in people*

companies to demonstrate practical evidence that they are meeting four key criteria. These are outlined in Figure 2.4. If they can satisfy the criteria they are awarded a logo which they can use for PR purposes (in the same way as, for example, BS5750 or the National Training Award, is used by companies on their letterheads and publicity material).

On the face of it the criteria outlined in Figure 2.4 provide a framework within which any company can shape its development policy for the 1990s. Thinking back to my early days in a Training Board, the provision of such a charter would have considerably simplified the whole process of assessing companies' training plans. It is an improvement on ITB policy in two major respects.

First, it provides a *focus* for such assessment which the early emphasis on systematic training (see Chapter 3) lacked. The focus is the *business plan*. In this way training is not seen as separate from the business – which in my experience was a big problem in the early days of the ITBs – but an integral *part* of the business's overall strategy. Implicit in this is that one cannot succeed without the other. As we shall see later in the book, this is a critical underlying assumption when we look in detail at evaluation.

Second – and in my opinion most crucially – it implies that the needs of *every* employee must be taken into account. What will be interesting to see, of course, is exactly how TECs will satisfy themselves on this criterion. By definition a systematic approach to training *should* take into account the needs of everyone in a company but, as I can testify from my own experience, this tended to be covered in a 'sheep-dip' manner. Thus, the fact that a company had made provision for 'bar staff training' was tacitly accepted as proof enough that it had taken into account the needs of the majority of its workforce. We made the token visits to sample evidence but, as everyone acknowledged, it was very much a paper exercise. It is critical, in my view, that assessment of this criterion in the Investors in People scheme is *not* a paper exercise.

Indeed, it seems to me that this could be a danger for each of the four criteria. Below we review each of the four Investors in People criteria in the context of the old ITB four-stage approach to systematic training. But we also identify what could be significant indicators for change and the kind of evidence TECs are encouraging companies to keep.

Thinking back to how ITBs assessed companies against systematic training, I remember the importance we gave in the early days to a company having a Training Policy signed by the Chief Executive. This was proof, as the first Investors in People criterion suggests, of 'public commitment from the top to achieve its business objectives'. The reality was that very often the policy was put under the nose of the CEO for him or her to sign by the Personnel Director and then hastily sent to the ITB as proof of the company's good intentions. This is not to say that many companies did not take this stage very seriously and maybe for the first time they started to focus on the kinds of issues that the first Investors in People criterion flags up. In fact I often felt that if we had spent much more time at this first, strategic stage embedding a training philosophy into the culture of the company we would have achieved much more than the subsequent paper chase for names on a training plan.

So, I hope that TECs will spend a great deal of time on this first stage. There is a hint of breakthrough in the second sub-criterion which states that 'Management should develop and *communicate to all employees a vision of where the organisation is going and the contribution employees will make to its success*' (emphasis added). But how do you measure a 'vision'?

TECs provide companies with a pack[27] which enables them to ask themselves the kind of questions assessors from TEC will ask of companies which are seeking recognition under the Investors in People programme. It suggests companies ask themselves questions like these to check out 'if employees at all levels are aware of the broad aims or vision of the organization':[28]

- What is the vision?
- Have senior management been involved directly in communicating the vision?
- Do employees understand the commitment?
- Do they believe it?

Typical evidence they would be required to present could include:[28]

- Mission/vision statement, expressed in a way that everyone can understand
- Employee survey
- Employee representatives' statement
- Employee briefing arrangements that work well (as shown by feedback)

Each company, of course, will express its vision in its own way. What TECs must avoid is the prescriptive approach that tended to underlie the ITBs' assessment of systematic training. What they lost sight of was the peculiar *context* within which systematic training could succeed in each company. What was needed (and what should characterize the TECs' approach to Investors in People) was an approach that recognized 'the notion of strategy as a *craft*' (emphasis added).[29] This implies

> first getting an intuitive feel through experience for phenomena rather than exactly measuring and manipulating them, and second, as a result a highly individually distinctive and loosely structured approach rather than 'one best way' following predetermined steps.[29]

Criterion two comes very close to the old 'identify training needs' stage in the systematic training cycle, even to the extent of the kind of evidence a company might provide to prove 'a review of employees' training needs at all levels' had been carried out. Thus documents are called for giving indications of employees involved and examples of training needs identified.

But the guidelines to employers also seek to encompass two of the national initiatives we have already covered – NVQs and BS5750.

> Where appropriate, training targets are linked to achieving external standards, and particularly to National Vocational Qualifications (or Scottish Vocational Qualifications in Scotland) and units.

Evidence of achievement in meeting such a criterion is 'BS5750 accreditation *throughout* the organization'. While not insisting on such evidence, it does encourage companies to take the same strategic view I have been advocating throughout this chapter.

But there is little indication of helping facilitate *personal* development and goals; where it does occur it is company focused rather than individual focused, i.e. it 'focuses on individual needs – *in the context of business objectives*' (emphasis added).[28]

Criterion three combines the systematic training stages of Training Plan and Implementation. The diagnostic pack also contains advice on Induction Training and the importance of keeping training records, not unlike the guidelines offered by the ITBs. The significant new factor, though, is the explicit recognition that 'All employees should be encouraged to identify and meet their own job-related development needs'. But there is little guidance on how such information might be collected (via learning contracts, portfolios of achievement linked to NVQs for example).

The final criterion, like the final stage of the systematic training cycle, focuses on evaluation, on evidence that training has actually made some difference. Unlike systematic training, however, where this final stage was usually an afterthought, the whole focus of an Investment in People strategy is that there should be some tangible return on the investment. This last criterion, I would suggest, is therefore the most critical of all. The danger is, of course, that companies will take an easy way out by providing merely the kind of 'simple record keeping' the guidelines suggest.

I well remember asking a company which had painstakingly put together volumes of information proving that training had been carried out what was the *value* they put on the *total* training effort as a result of reviewing its results. They could not see any value beyond the paperwork they had already prepared which documented past events only.

To be fair to the guidelines,[28] they do not see evaluation as wholly a review of historical data and individual records

> Evaluation should not be confined to the impact on individuals. Where appropriate, it should also cover the impact on team-working and on the way in which the organization works as a whole (e.g. in terms of Total Quality).

They also explore less quantifiable areas:

> Does the organization assess commitment and enthusiasm?
>
> Where training claims to change attitudes, how does the organization assess whether this has been achieved?

It is to be regretted, I feel, that the guidelines do not contain more of these radical kind of questions which help the company *go beyond* the familiarity of what they have done in the past to confront the issues of the future. This is a theme we will develop when we examine a model of evaluation in a later chapter. This emerged from research I carried out in the early 1980s into the nature of evaluation. One of the conclusions I arrived at was that evaluation is a dynamic process which by definition *changes whatever is evaluated*. Evaluation, as we shall see later, is a paradox:

> The developing man continually transcends his condition and in so doing renders inapposite the criteria for evaluating him.[30]

We could equally substitute 'the developing company' in Charles Hampden-Turner's description of the paradox. The practical consequence of this is that TECs should be looking for evidence of some kind of synthesis of value which goes beyond the paperwork. But the National Training Taskforce which is ultimately responsible for the interpretation of the standard through local TECs (and their equivalents in Scotland), will no doubt want more tangible evidence of a cost/benefit nature.[31]

While welcoming the company-wide and strategic approach of the Investors in People initiative, the test will be the extent to which there is evidence of a real paradigm shift in the way companies view their employees and measure their contribution. As we have found, there are elements of the scheme which can be used as a basis for real change and are, potentially, superior to the old ITB method of assessing training. But, the danger to be avoided is that of using a step-by-step and systematic approach rather than taking a holistic and systemic view which looks for transformation and not just improvement. (These are the conditions of the learning organization which we will be examining in the final chapter.)

In coming to assess companies using the guidelines provided, TECs may well come to the same conclusions. An initial survey carried out by Coopers and Lybrand Deloitte into 17 companies reckoned to be good trainers, resulted in only two meeting the Investors in People criteria. Commenting on these results Jane Pickard comes to this conclusion:

> It is evident from talking to companies which have taken part in the development of Investors in People that it is not uniformity of approach which matters but evidence of having arrived at the same destination – having become a 'learning organization' in which training is embedded, applies to all employees, is linked to business needs and is regularly evaluated.[31]

The concept of a learning organization is one in which *every* member of the company is involved in learning, the consequences of which *directly have an effect on the organization as a whole*. This is the model against which, I suggest, Investors in People should be evaluated. As Jane Pickard says, there is no uniform set of steps to get there but (as with the concept of quality, with which Investors in People has often been compared as the BS5750 for people) 'you'll know it when you see it'.

Having said there are no uniform steps to get there, there are some key steps which any company can take to start the process off. As with evaluation, I believe Investors in People is about a process, an attitude of mind, a way of perceiving staff *as the organization*. This is where, it seems to me, Investors in People has missed an opportunity: to redraw the boundary of the organization around its people and not focus wholly on the business plan. This is not to say the business plan is not important but only in so far as it reflects just *one* dimension, that of the view of the employer. For Investors in People to really make a breakthrough there needs to be a parallel attempt to find out the employees' view of the organization's 'vision' and then to evaluate the employer's with the employees' view. From such a comparison would emerge a picture of an organization which genuinely reflects an investment in people.

To some extent the second edition of the diagnostic pack provided by TECs to help companies assess themselves against Investors in People criteria provides the means for this feedback. An Employee Survey in the pack allows managers to check staff's answers to some of the questions posed with management's perception. An extract from the Analysis Sheet provided to make comparisons between manager and employee views is shown in Figure 2.5.[32] The managers were required to respond to each

Manager survey statement	Response code (A, B, C, D)	Corresponding employee survey question(s)	% Yes	Next steps
Our most senior managers are committed to developing people Their commitment has been made known to all our employees		Has your top management told you about their commitment to training and developing employees?		
Employees at all levels are aware of the broad aims or visions of the organization		Could you explain to someone who does not work here what the organization is trying to achieve?		

Figure 2.5 *Extract from analysis sheet for manager/employee survey comparison*

statement with A, B, C or D according to the extent to which the evidence in question was demonstrated. By contrast, employees were asked to reply with a Yes/No to the questions put to them (which represented only a sample from the range presented to managers). Unfortunately there is no requirement that companies seeking recognition have to collect such information from their employees – it is optional. It seems to me that such feedback and – most importantly – how the organization *responds* to such feedback is the essence of the Investors in People initiative. In Figure 2.6 I have outlined a series of questions to be put to both managers and staff which provide an opportunity for *everyone* in the organization to influence and share in the company's development strategy.

Use the checklist in Figure 2.6 to respond to the following activities, which will also involve some upside-down thinking.

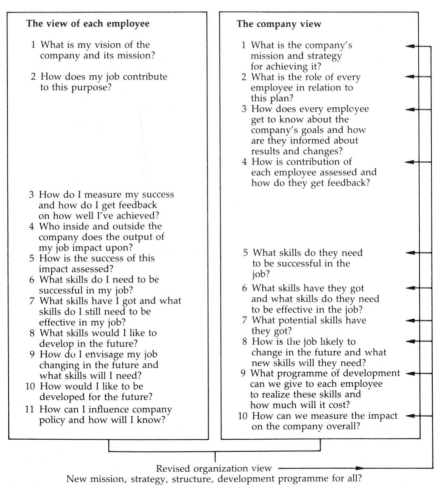

The view of each employee

1 What is my vision of the company and its mission?

2 How does my job contribute to this purpose?

3 How do I measure my success and how do I get feedback on how well I've achieved?
4 Who inside and outside the company does the output of my job impact upon?
5 How is the success of this impact assessed?
6 What skills do I need to be successful in my job?
7 What skills have I got and what skills do I still need to be effective in my job?
8 What skills would I like to develop in the future?
9 How do I envisage my job changing in the future and what skills will I need?
10 How would I like to be developed for the future?
11 How can I influence company policy and how will I know?

The company view

1 What is the company's mission and strategy for achieving it?
2 What is the role of every employee in relation to this plan?
3 How does every employee get to know about the company's goals and how are they informed about results and changes?
4 How is contribution of each employee assessed and how do they get feedback?

5 What skills do they need to be successful in the job?
6 What skills have they got and what skills do they need to be effective in the job?
7 What potential skills have they got?
8 How is the job likely to change in the future and what new skills will they need?
9 What programme of development can we give to each employee to realize these skills and how much will it cost?
10 How can we measure the impact on the company overall?

Revised organization view
New mission, strategy, structure, development programme for all?

Figure 2.6 *An organization view of investing in people*

ACTIVITY 2.5

- *Try to ask each and every member of your staff to respond to the questions listed under Employee View in Figure 2.6. In effect, each response will reflect a different organization; for example, from their responses to question 4 you can map a different organization structure which is likely to reflect very different functional relationships from the ones on your organization chart. From their responses to question 3 you will be able to build up a rich data bank of parameters for measuring effectiveness which are likely to go far beyond the normal top-down criteria that emerge from the board room; their responses to 8 and 9 will indicate skills you never before realized the organization possessed and their aspirations will surprise you. Finally, and most importantly, their responses to 1 and 11 will be more valuable to you than any market research consultant you might employ from outside. Had you ever thought about your own staff as your market, as defining the business you're in or, just as important, the business you ought to be in?[33]*
- *Depending on the size of your operation, of course, getting this kind of response from every person could prove costly. But then isn't this just what the Investors in People scheme is supposed to be all about? Finding out what people think does incur a cost. Look at those questions under Employee View again in Figure 2.6 and figure out the cost of not finding out this information.*

- -

- *If I was in the position of a TEC assessing you against the kind of criteria I've listed in Figure 2.6, my main interest would not be in whether you've answered every question and there is proof in a bundle of papers that every employee has responded. It would be rather in how you've gone about the task, in the processes you've had to develop to collect such information, whether it be by questionnaires, attitude surveys, briefing groups, one-to-one counselling sessions between boss and subordinate. But the more important issues would be just how you are going to continue the process and ensure you receive a regular up-date on how your employees see their organization and their place within it.*
- *Turning now to the questions in the 'The Company View' box in Figure 2.6, these are more in line with the four criteria we've examined in the Investors in People published standards (see Figure 2.4). Again, my emphasis would not be so much on how you answer each question but what is the overall conclusion you arrive at. Again, it is not an inexpensive exercise. It does involve you in carrying out a skills audit of your entire operation. But shouldn't you spend at least as much effort on an annual audit of your staff as you give to the annual accounts or to stocks or to maintenance of machinery? Without it you will not be in a position to capitalise on the service from your local training banks, the TECs. As to*

> *how you go about it, and what you do with the results, other chapters in this book will help you address these issues.*
>
> ● *Having built up a perception of your organization as your employees see it and how you see it, all that remains is to compare the two pictures or rather project them on to an imaginary screen and develop a new and revised organization. By definition this will mean reviewing your answers to the ten questions you answered previously. But the outcome will more than repay your initial investment. If I was in a TEC position it would be this revised organization development plan that would be the basis for my assessment as to whether you deserved the Investors in People award. It would tell me if you had made the first step to becoming a genuine learning organization.*
>
> ● *All that remains is to contact your local TEC and ask for a copy of their Diagnostic Pack to assess yourself against its criteria . . . Once again, test the system.*

2.6 Concluding overview

The aim of this chapter has been to provide an overview of some of the current initiatives which I believe when taken *together* could have a profound influence on the way companies employ their staff and the way in which those employees are trained and developed. The problem, as with most initiatives emanating from government, is that they have reached the market place in a piece-meal manner, each one seeming to add just another system, set of forms to be completed, new set of jargon to be absorbed. Even more unfortunate, they have emerged at a time of recession when companies tend to become even more insular and are preoccupied with the all important equation of costs versus profits. The notion of *investment* itself, let alone investment in *people*, is unlikely to be anywhere near the top of the board room agenda.

And yet the irony is that it is at just these kinds of time that companies do have an opportunity to take stock of where they are and the direction they need to take in the future. Above all it is a time to revalue current assets, especially human assets. I have suggested that each of the four initiatives we have explored in this chapter can be used *positively* to add value to your human assets. But this value does not accrue to you automatically by simply working through the procedures, conforming to the requirements of each scheme. However systematic the route it will not *of itself* lead to value (see Chapter 6 on evaluation). This requires the kind of upside-down thinking we have taken from Handy which puts *you* at the centre of the system to use it for *your* benefit.

In doing so you are likely to see your organization and the staff employed in a much more holistic way. Indeed, the boundaries between you and the market place will seem less fixed. It seems to me this is a critical prerequisite if TECs are going to succeed. A learning organization becomes part of a learning community; your staff (and you) belong to both so that organization boundaries become less important, organization charts less hierarchical, jobs less prescribed and staff rolls less critical. We have introduced the idea of TECs as exchange mechanisms in the local market place to bring about an equilibrium of skill utilization across the whole community.

The currency at the heart of the system is *people*. The national framework of competences as valued by the NCVQ enables you to prepare a statement of your current account. This can go into the red, as when people leave or new opportunities open up for increased development requiring investment in new skills. To balance the account you will need either to add value yourself, through training and development, or borrow from the market place (recruitment). But these assets will never become fixed; by definition they are on loan to you and on what you do with them will depend your future credit-worthiness in the market place (i.e kind of recruits you can attract).

The other kind of people at the heart of the enterprise are the customers; how you treat them affects even more directly your credit rating in the labour market. Despite its preoccupation with documentation, BS5750 does, I have argued, offer a process for examining just how much value you put on meeting customer requirements.

But it is only when all these initiatives are put together, it seems to me, that you can get the benefit of a synergy which should be at the heart of the new Investors in People initiative. This chapter has set the scenario for a different kind of relationship between employer, staff and community which I believe is a prerequisite if companies are going to get a proper return on their investment in people. Despite all the hype about the need for more training I believe the issue is more about adding value to your existing and future human assets. The rest of this book suggests ways this can be achieved, starting with the concept of competence, which properly used could become the central unit of currency in which you do business in the markets of the future.

References

1 Lindley, R. (1991) Individuals, human resources and markets, Paper given at 1990 NEDO Policy Seminar on Training, in *Training and Competitiveness*, Kogan Page
2 Prospect Centre (1990) *Strategies and People – 1990*, The Prospect Centre, Kingston
3 Kenny, J. and Reid, M. (1989) *Training Interventions*, IPM
4 *Training in Britain: Employers' Perspectives on Human Resources* (1989) HMSO

5 Becker, G. S. (1964) *Human Capital: A Theoretical and Empirical Analysis with Special Reference to Education*, Columbia University Press (2nd edn 1975, National Bureau of Economic Research, New York)
6 Oatey, M. (1970) The economics of training with respect to the firm, *British Journal of Industrial Relations*, **VIII**(1), 1–21
7 Hendry, C. (1991) Corporate strategy and training, in *Training and Competitiveness*, Kogan Page
8 Cassels, J. (1991) Introduction, in *Training and Competitiveness*, Kogan Page
9 Department of Employment, *Employment Gazette* April 1991
10 Handy, C. (1989) *The Age of Unreason*, Hutchinson
11 Todd, R. (1991) 'Skills towards 2000', *Training and Competitiveness*, Kogan Page
12 Department of Employment (1971) *Glossary of Training Terms*, HMSO
13 Manpower Services Commission (1981) *Glossary of Training Terms*. HMSO
14 Burgoyne, J. and Stuart, R. (1977) Implicit learning theories as determinants of the effect of management development programme', *Personnel Review*, **6**, No. 2, Spring
15 Kuhn, T. S. (1962) *The Structure of Scientific Revolutions*, Chicago University Press
16 Peters, T. (1987) *Thriving on Chaos*, A. A. Knopf
17 Kanter, R. M. (1989) *When Giants Learn to Dance*, Simon and Schuster
18 Handy, C. (1984) *The Future of Work*, Blackwells
19 Employment for the 1990s (1988) Government White Paper, HMSO
20 Training Agency (1989) *Training and Enterprise: Priorities for Action 1990–1991*. Employment Department, Moorfoot, Sheffield
21 Peters, T. and Waterman, R. (1982) *In Search of Excellence*, Harper and Row
22 BS1 (1991) BS5750 Quality Systems Part 8 – Guide to Quality Management and Quality Systems Elements for Services
23 Giles, E. and Williams, R. (1991) Can the Personnel Department Survive Quality Management?, *Personnel Management*, April
24 Training Agency (1989) *Development of Assessable Standards for National Certification* – Guidance Note 2. Employment Department, Moorfoot
25 TDLB (1992) *National Standards for Training and Development*, Employment Department, Moorfoot, Sheffield
26 Employment Department (1990) *Investors in People – The Framework*. Briefing Document 2, Employment Department Group, Moorfoot, Sheffield
27 Employment Department (1991) *Investors in People – The Route*. Employment Department, Moorfoot, Sheffield
28 Employment Department (1991) How will we gain recognition? Brochure 5 in *Investors in People – The Route*, Employment Department, Moorfoot, Sheffield

29 Taylor, H. (1991) The systematic training model: Corn circles in search of a spaceship? *Management Education and Development*, **22**(4), Winter, 258–278

30 Hampden-Turner, C. (1970) *Radical Man: The Process of Psycho-social Development*, Schenkman

31 Pickard, J. (1991) What does the 'Investors in People' Award really mean? *Personnel Management Plus*, **2**(3), March, 18–19

32 Employment Department (1991) How do we measure up? Brochure 3 in *Investors in People – The Route*, Employment Department, Moorfoot, Sheffield

33 Thomson, K. (1990) *The Employee Revolution – the Rise of Internal Corporate Marketing*, Pitman

Appendix
Key initiatives and influences on training strategy over the past 25 years

	Why it came about	What it proposed
1964 Industrial Training Act	• Shortage of skills • Inadequate training • Cost of training unequally shared	• Industry Training Boards (ITBs) to set standards and monitor for own industry (29 established between 1964 and 1970) • Statutory duty to collect levy out of which ITBs were funded and could award training grants
1973 Employment and Training Act	• No coordination of ITB activities • Range of levies imposed • ITBs did nothing for unemployed	• Manpower Services Commission (MSC) established, subdivided into the Employment Services Agency and Training Services Agency (which coordinated ITBs) • Levy limited to 1% from which company could be exempt if met ITB standards • ITBs' admin. costs funded by Treasury
1981 Employment and Training Act	• Downturn in economy; employers more reluctant to be bound by ITB bureaucracy • MSC carries out sector-by-sector review of industry to decide which ITBs should move to a 'voluntary' basis where training to be coordinated by employers	• 16 ITBs abolished • Admin. costs of remaining ITBs to be paid by employers (who therefore have critical powers in fixing levy and influencing policy of ITBs)

	Why it came about	**What it proposed**
1981 Government White Paper: 'A New Training Initiative – a programme for action'	• MSC propose strategic plan for 1980s covering: – developing skill training – equipping young people for work – widening opportunities for adults	• Three key objectives (each of which led to key initiatives in the 1980s) (i) to enable young people to 'acquire agreed standards of skill appropriate to the jobs available' (led to NCVQ in 1987) (ii) to enable young people under 18 not in full time education to benefit from 'planned work experience combined with work-related training and education' (led to YTS in 1983) (iii) to enable adults to 'increase or update their skills and knowledge during the course of their working lives' (led to development of open learning initially under Open Tech scheme and then Open College in 1987)

	Why it came about	**What it proposed**
1984 Competence and Competition (MSC and NEDO report)		Highlighted the strong cultural commitment to training in Germany and Japan
1985 Challenge to Complacency (MSC and NEDO report)		Highlighted that senior managers in UK were unaware of training activities of their competitors
1987 National Training Awards		Annual awards by Training Agency to those companies showing excellence in training linked with improved business performance
1987 Open College		To provide open access to training and reskilling to adults by means of open learning and the means of getting accreditation
1987 National Council for Vocational Qualifications (NCVQ)		To establish a national vocational qualification framework for all occupations in England, Wales and Northern Ireland
1987 The Making of Managers (Charles Handy NEDO report)		● Compared lack of basic management education and qualifications of managers in UK compared with US, W. Germany and France ● Proposed two part management qualification and need for a Development Charter to which companies would subscribe

	Why it came about	**What it proposed**
1987 The Making of British Managers (John Constable, Roger McCormick (BIM/CBI)		Makes similar recommendations for a basic Diploma in Business which all aspiring managers should take
1988 Management Charter Initiative (MCI) launched under auspices of the Council for Management Education and Development		● MCI offers opportunity for companies to subscribe to a charter pledging them to develop managers as central part of their business strategy ● Developing generic competences against which any manager can be assessed and get accreditation at certificate or diploma level
1988 Government White Paper 'Training for Employment'	To focus on the unemployed	● Recommended new Employment Training Scheme (ET) aimed primarily at those unemployed for over 6 months aged 18–24 ● Provides individual assessment leading to up to 12 month training programme
1988 Tripartite MSC abolished and rights transferred directly to 'The Training Agency' which reports to Department of Employment		

	Why it came about	What it proposed
1988 'Employment for the Nineties' Government White Paper	Strategy for training in the 1990s	● Proposes local employer-led training system through Training Enterprise Councils (TECs) which will identify and devise a strategy to meet local needs ● National policies determined through a National Training Task Force (NTTF) ● Remaining ITBs to be phased out to become non-statutory independent bodies
1989 CBI report 'Towards a Skills Revolution'	In response to concerns from employers about skill shortages	National system for ensuring all young people attain minimum NVQ level (NVQ level 2)
1989/90 'Training in Britain' Training Agency	Survey of training in London and five other areas taking account of employers' and individuals' attitudes	Some of the findings: – one in five employers provide no training at all – of those that did training, 48% of workforce covered – one third of individuals said they had received training in past 3 years (public sector employees get more than in private sector)

	Why it came about	**What it proposed**
1991 'Education and Training for the 21st Century' Government White Paper	To ensure better transition from school, through FE and HE to training at work	Some of the proposals: – wider use of NVQs (including school and college) – academic and vocational qualifications of same standard to have equal esteem/ recognition – training credits (£1000) to give buying power to school-leavers – extend influence of employers on education – FE colleges and sixth form colleges to be independent to meet demands of students and employeees
1991 'Higher Education: a New Framework' Government White Paper	To establish a single framework for higher education	● Abolishes distinction between polytechnic and university ● Creates HE Funding Councils to distribute public funds for research and teaching ● Council for National Academic Awards (CNAA) abolished: each institution to offer degrees under own quality control arrangements

	Why it came about	**What it proposed**
1992 'People, Jobs and Opportunity' Government White Paper	To give employees *individual* rather than collective contracts of employment (including details of training policy) plus individual incentives for training for employed and unemployed	• 'Skill check' credit scheme to enable employees to purchase careers guidance and assessment services • credits to unemployed to purchase open learning materials and support • employers to be able to recoup costs of investing in training of employees who leave prematurely

3 Converting training needs into performance credit

> Let's start with a simple idea. From now on we are going to base qualifications on the ability to do a real live job. We are not going to be bound by what trainees have traditionally been taught. Nor by what teachers or even training officers might devise between themselves. Instead we are going to stick simply to what it needs to be competent in real employment.[1]

What could be simpler? Indeed, this 'simple idea' goes back ten years, to the MSC's 'A New Training Initiative' in 1981. This introduced the need for a new kind of standard – a 'standard of achievement' which would be based on training to 'agreed standards of skill'. The aim was to develop a more versatile, motivated and productive workforce. In 1986 the National Council for Vocational Qualifications (NCVQ) was set up by the Government to 'hallmark' qualifications that met the needs of employment and to locate them within a structure which everyone could use and understand – the NVQ (National Vocational Qualifications) framework.

The drive towards 'competence' was further confirmed in the White Paper 'Employment for the 1990s':[2] 'Our training system must be founded on standards and recognized qualifications based on competence – the performance required of individuals to do their work successfully and satisfactorily.' By the end of 1992 the aim is for NVQs to be in place covering 80% of the workforce.

Whatever your opinion of NVQs they are likely to play a key part in the formulation of training and development policy into the 1990s and beyond. The purpose of this chapter is to help you address some of the underlying issues and, with some more upside-down thinking, get hold of the system and make it work for you. The concept of competence was introduced in the previous chapter, but I believe the underlying principles and more particularly the process associated with the way competences are derived and assessed are important enough to merit a whole chapter devoted to the subject. What, then, is the link between training need and performance credit?

To answer this means going back to the way training needs have been traditionally identified from the 1960s to the 1990s. The model used – which still continues to be advocated – is called 'systematic training' and was the basis on which Industry Training Boards made judgements about companies' training effectiveness. The model entailed a detailed analysis of all jobs in a company by what was essentially a task analysis approach. It must be said that this was an improvement on the way training was assessed in the early days of the Training Boards prior to the Employment and Training Act of 1973 when the 'task analysis' approach was adopted by most of the Training Boards.

The underlying principle was that before any training was carried out there should be a clear specification of the nature of the training need. This was determined by the 'gap' between the knowledge and skills considered necessary for satisfactory performance in a given job (now, and in the future) and the knowledge and skills currently possessed by the job incumbent. Initially a lot of work was done in industry breaking tasks down into series of activities and against each activity specifying the knowledge, skill and often the appropriate attitude that was needed. This came to be known as the 'job specification'. The first step in the process was to assess each person against the job specification. The resulting gaps were then identified as training needs and became the basis for a Training Plan in which separate objectives were set for training to be carried out either off-job or on-the-job. The third stage was then actually to implement the plan (providing appropriate evidence) and finally to evaluate the results of training against the original needs identified; and so on. A simple version of the systematic training cycle, as it came to be called, is summarized in Figure 3.1.

The intentions were admirable. It did provide a systematic framework within which evidence of training carried out could be assessed and grants/ exemption from levy awarded as appropriate. But there were serious flaws which, I suggest, still bedevil the debate about training.

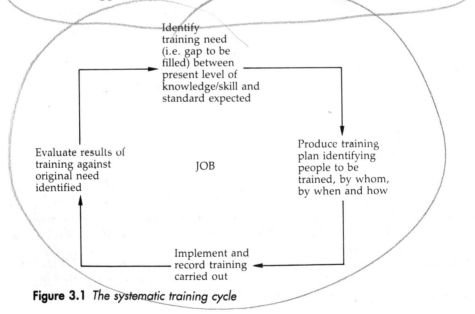

Figure 3.1 *The systematic training cycle*

In the first place, training revolved around a particular 'job'. A lot of useful analysis was often done leading to the generation of numerous manuals specifying requirements of each job. But by definition the training that followed was limited to that one job. There was little attempt to follow through the consequences of one job on another.

[handwritten margin note: limited to one job .]

Second, although the intention was to specify 'standards of performance' required in any job, very often the 'analysis' process took over and vast quantities of information were collected without a clear focus as to how useful this was in actually being effective. Again, this had implications for evaluation because without a clear standard there was nothing against which the training could be measured other than to say it had taken place.

Third, until comparatively recently, ITBs inclined to make judgements about training as being synonymous with 'planned events' like off-the-job courses. More attention was therefore paid to the design of 'the' training programmes (inputs) than was paid to assessing outcomes. It was just this inability to make clear connections between inputs and outputs that, I believe, was the greatest flaw of the systematic approach to training. It was designed to collect information about the status quo, about the job the person was doing at the time. It was not geared up to adapt to change.

Competence, on the other hand, is a much wider concept:

> The concept of competence ... is defined as the ability to perform the activities within an occupation or function to the standards expected in employment. *Competence is a wide concept which embodies the ability to transfer skills and knowledge to new situations within the occupational area.* It encompasses organization and planning of work, innovation and coping with non-routine activities. *It includes those qualities of personal effectiveness that are required in the workplace to deal with co-workers, managers and customers* (emphasis added).[3]

The concept of competence unlike the concept of task analysis – on which the 'systems' approach to training was based – embraces:

- The occupation
- The individual
- The organization

Furthermore, as we shall see, it provides a mechanism for giving credit to individuals on the basis of what they can *already* achieve. Thus, rather than focusing on training *need* as a gap to be filled, a competence based approach gives credit for what has been achieved as well as providing standards to be reached in the future.

In this chapter we will first examine the nature of the **standards** framework and then the process by which standards are derived (**functional analysis**). We will then identify 11 features of the process which can be used to help you enhance your investment in people – *regardless of whether you seek accreditation through the NVQ framework.* We then turn to a number of issues that are current in the debate about competences. We conclude with some upside-down thinking that compares three scenarios taking one fictional company and examining the implications of moving from the traditional 'systematic' approach of identifying and meeting its training needs, through introducing NVQs at selected levels and finally how it might 'transform' itself by allowing the processes discussed to shape the organization mission and structure of the future.

3.1 The standards model

In order to get the most out of the current initiatives now taking place through NVQs I believe it is important that you are fully aware of the design principles that *underlie* the overall model. To do this you must be familiar with the 'technical jargon' that abounds. As we have discovered in Chapter 2, any new initiative comes wrapped up in all kinds of systems packages and has layers of procedures to support it. But you are only going to benefit from it – which is after all why it was introduced – if you can unwrap all the outside layers and get to the prize that lies inside.

To begin with, it is important that you distinguish between three separate concepts:

● Occupational standards
● Assessment
● Accreditation

The key to the whole approach, which was first introduced in the MSC's New Training Initiative ten years ago, is the specification of standards. A standard is a specification of performance. It is used in a very precise way and it is important at the outset to be clear about what it *isn't* in order to fully understand the significance of the whole competence initiative:

> Occupational standards are not descriptions of the performance itself (specific activities or tasks), nor the means of achieving compctence (knowledge and skills learned through the training programme) nor the means of measuring quality or achievement (assessment) nor the process by which achievement is recognized publicly (qualification). Standards are *'benchmarks': descriptions of the expectations of employment against which the actual performance of individuals will be compared and assessed as competent, or not competent as appropriate* (emphasis added).[4]

One of the cornerstones of the whole approach is the separation of *outcome* from *input*. This has enormous implications for education and training. In colleges, for example, the message is only slowly dawning that the focus of attention should not be so much on the input (the course, how long it should take, where it should take place etc.) but on the *output* – on what *competences* the student will be able to demonstrate in employment.

In a sense trainers have been following this line for some time. By definition, as we have seen in Chapter 2, training is about the achievement of a very specific outcome. It follows, therefore, that unless this outcome is clearly defined at the outset, an appropriate method of training for achieving it cannot be determined nor can a judgement be made as to whether it has been achieved. This was, of course, the *raison d'être* of systematic training. The trouble was, as we have suggested above, that the 'system' got in the way and we lost sight of the principle underneath the layers of procedures designed to 'assist' the process! This is why it is important you are clear about what this new initiative is trying to achieve before coming to terms with the procedures that support it.

In the case of the initiative on competence the procedures do have a key role to play because of the underlying need to have a *common* framework of standards. This is where it goes beyond what was simply good training practice to set objectives. This was certainly an advance on programmes that had no objectives, so that students had no basis of making a judgement on what they should have learned and teachers had no basis on which to design cost-effective training methods. Having clear training objectives was (and is) a useful basis for choice between one programme and another but the focus of attention is still on the programme (the input) rather than the output. This would become even more apparent if the student were to change from one programme to another, in which case it is likely that what she or he had achieved already on the other programme would be less likely to influence future development than the need to conform to the new programme.

But if every provider of training is working within a common framework of standards – and a system is in place for recognizing which standards have already been achieved – we have a basis for giving credits for achievement in the past and a clearer focus for how to help the student achieve standards in the future. This is the prospect that you could look forward to, which all starts from the concept of common occupational standards:

> By adopting common structures (i.e. statements of outcomes) for different forms of education and training provision we have, for the first time, the possibility of relating different programmes, qualifications and forms of provision. The skills which are common between occupations can be recognized. The relevance of the skills and knowledge gained in schools to vocational and professional competence can be identified. This will make possible a much smoother transition from school or university to vocational and professional training.[5]

Exactly *how* you use the standards is up to you. Even if you do not choose to get them formally accredited (see section 3.2 on Assessment) the availability of standards 'offers the opportunity to develop a single, coherent and consistent specification of quality performance which can act as a resource document for many HRD functions'.[4] Thus they can be used for job descriptions, training systems, appraisal schemes etc.

But if there is to be a national framework of occupational standards they have to be specified in such a way that everyone is clear about exactly what is being described and measured. This is why a common format for describing occupational standards has been designed which incorporates three component parts:

- An element of competence
- Performance criteria
- Range statements/indicators

These terms were introduced briefly in Chapter 2 and an example of the format given in a unit taken from the Training and Development Lead Body's standards on training. But it is important to redefine them so you see exactly how they fit into the overall framework; as a result you will be in a better position to use them. The examples I have used below are largely taken from a chapter by Bob Mansfield in the Employment Department's publication *Development of Assessable Standards for National Certification.*[4]

Element of competence

An element of competence is a description of something which a person who works in a given occupational area should be able to do. It is a description of an action, behaviour or outcome which the person should be able to demonstrate (p. 13).[6]

As we shall see when we look at assessment and accreditation, it is the element of competence which is the focus of assessment.. The outcome can be tangible (i.e. the physical result of an activity) or intangible (i.e. the result of a cognitive or interactive process like a decision, advice or a sale). In Figure 3.2 there are two sets of elements, one reflecting tangible outcomes from the iron and steel industry and one demonstrating intangible outcomes from the financial services sector.

Performance criteria

Performance criteria are statements against which an assessor judges the evidence that an individual can perform the activity specified in an element.[6]

As we shall see when we look at assessment, performance criteria help to give an answer to the question: 'How would I know that a candidate is

A	B
Manufacture flat (steel) products by cold rolling	**Provide information and advice and promote service to customers**
Element 1 Process materials to remove iron oxide	Element 1 Inform customers about products and services on request
Element 2 Roll materials to specified thickness tolerances	Element 2 Advise customers about non-FSA inclusive products and services which meet their identified requirements
Element 3 Bright anneal steel to specified mechanical properties	Element 3 Promote the sale of additional products to existing customers
Element 4 Harden and temper steel strip to specified properties	Element 4 Promote the sale of products and services to potential customers
	Element 5 Ascertain customer details to determine eligibility for lending products

Figure 3.2 *Comparison of elements making up a unit of competence in the iron and steel industry (A) and the financial services sector (B)*

competent in a particular element?' Figure 3.3 reproduces the performance criteria appropriate to two of the elements illustrated in Figure 3.2. One element is taken from the iron and steel unit and the other from the financial services. What is assessed is the outcome, either the tangible outcome of rolled material in the case of the iron and steel example or the quality of information given to the customer of financial services. In both cases the performance criteria serve as a checklist to enable the assessor to focus on key aspects of the outcome on which evidence should be collected (see section 3.4 on Assessment).

Range statements

Range statements elaborate the statement of competence by making explicit the contexts to which the elements and performance criteria apply. Also they put limits on the specification to ensure a consistent interpretation. In particular they should be used to define the breadth of competence required, and may also act as a reminder of conditions under which competence is expected but not immediately obvious.[6]

In the first statements of competence that were produced, range statements were not included. A standard consisted simply of a statement of an element of competence and associated performance criteria. But it was soon found

---

Element 2 (Iron and steel): Roll materials to specified thickness tolerances

Performance criteria

(a) thickness measuring equipment is standardized/calibrated to produce the specified dimension
(b) materials are rolled to specified thickness and tolerance
(c) recoiling tension is compatible with materials' thickness and tolerance
(d) distortion during rolling is minimized
(e) production rate,shape and surface quality is optimized for individual rolling passes
(f) tracking devices are monitored and adjusted to minimize material damage
(g) protective oil is applied when specified

Element 4 (Financial services): Promote the sale of products and services to potential customers

Performance criteria

(a) appropriate and accurate information about the Society is offered
(b) potential customer needs and status are identified accurately and politely
(c) advantages and benefits of membership offered by the Society and relevant to potential customer needs/status, are described clearly and accurately
(d) options and alternatives are offered where specific products and services do not directly match potential customer needs
(e) customers are offered the opportunity to purchase
(f) potential customers are treated in a manner which promotes goodwill

---

Figure 3.3 *Performance criteria appropriate to two elements from Figure 3.2*

that there needed to be a statement about the context in which competence should be assessed to guard against it becoming too job-specific. A national occupational standard must be transferable from one job to another but different jobs may use different products, processes, expose the candidate to different customers. In addition, new technology will require an even wider scope for assessment. All of these variable aspects are summarized in the range statement. (NB: You will sometimes see the term 'range indicator' rather than 'statement'; this signifies that the criteria are still in the process of being finalized and should be regarded as 'indicative' until such times as they become finalized in an approved statement.) For example, for the element 'Promote products and services to potential customers' there would need to be specified under range statement the range of products and services a particular work role would offer. It would also need to specify the range of different customers likely to be encountered in normal practice.

I find that on first looking at the statement of an occupational standard in terms of element of competence, performance criteria and range statements, it is the range statements which give a very quick insight and clear picture of what needs to be covered. Have a look back to Figure 2.3 (p. 20). This is a typical statement of an occupational standard for trainers. It incorporates all three components – element, performance criteria and range statements.

But it is the range statements that give an insight into the breadth of knowledge required, the equipment that will be used and the different situations in which the competence needs to be delivered.

It is also the range statement – rather than the element and performance criteria – that will need to be updated as new technology is introduced, for example. Bob Mansfield[4] illustrates how reference to 'equipment range' for trainers might need to be updated over the years. Thus in the 1960s the list of equipment might have been: chalk boards, flip charts, 16 mm projector. In the 1980s the range would more likely have been rewritten as: flip charts, white boards, video recording and playback systems, overhead projectors and slides. In the 1990s we will need to add: interactive video systems, computer-based presentation packages, multi-media systems.

The implications for assessment and accreditation are that if a candidate is seeking to get an NVQ she or he would have to satisfy the assessor that they could demonstrate competence in all situations covered by the range statement. But, as we shall see later, it is up to the assessor what kind of evidence she or he needs to collect to cover all eventualities. But in some cases candidates may have to request a move to another department or another job before they are in a position to demonstrate competence in all aspects required. For example, if a candidate wanted to get accredited for being able to serve food in silver service, they would be unlikely to find an opportunity to demonstrate this competence in a fast-food operation. But consider this from another perspective. If you were the owner of a restaurant which offered silver service, you would be attractive to such a candidate because you could add value to their portfolio of skills.

So far we have established the basis for a national occupational standard framework within which the outcome of any job can be described, measured and accredited. It contains three components: an element of competence, performance criteria and range indicators/statements. We have suggested that this particular format could be useful even if you did not seek to get NVQ recognition. The CBI, in association with City and Guilds, has produced a very useful summary of different companies' experience of following a competence approach, *Business Success through Competence.*[7] In connection with the desirability of companies using national standards, they make this point:

> Where national standards can be most useful is as an indicator of the structure of company standards. If some aspects are included in the national standards, but not in company standards for the same jobs there may be a case for expanding company standards. It is certainly sensible for employers to be aware of best practice in their sector and adopt a common style where this is acceptable (p. 21).[7]

We will look later at specific examples of different industries they cite who have used a competence based approach. But before leaving this section on standards I want to focus on two other aspects of this national initiative which I believe have additional value in their own right as processes of analysis which you can use to build up the total picture of your human assets.

The first of these is called the *job competence model*. It was developed by Mansfield and Mathews[8] to help the Lead Bodies who were developing occupational standards to take account of factors that are wider than the tasks or tangible activities which characterize jobs and occupations. It identifies four types of skill which are present to a greater or lesser extent in *all* work roles. In fact the definition of competence itself (see p. 43) embraces all four of these characteristics. The four skills are as follows:

- *Task skills* – the routine and largely technical components that make up any job. For example, producing copies of documents, cleaning up desk/floor, shaping metals.
- *Contingency management skills* – the ability to recognize and deal with irregularities and variances in the immediate working environment. For example, dealing with a customer complaint, dealing with a breakdown in machinery.
- *Task management skills* – the skills to manage a group of tasks and prioritize between them. For example, serving a customer before loading a shelf, making sure there is enough paper before photocopying documents, allocating time to different tasks.
- *Job role environment skills* – the skills to work with others and cope with specific environmental factors. For example, interacting with customers, other colleagues on the shop floor, having to work in a laboratory environment. As Bob Mansfield says 'Modern economic systems have become more customer-oriented, and expect people to work in a variety of fast changing environments making job role environment skills increasingly relevant'.[4]

The idea is that as occupational standards are being developed these four skills are built into the elements, performance criteria and range statements as appropriate. Looking at Figure 3.3 you can see that most of the performance criteria relating to the iron and steel element reflect task skills but the range statements may say something about environmental skills, particularly as they affect health and safety. In the case of the financial service performance criteria we have a mixture as you would expect because this is less·of a routine job. By its very nature it involves a whole range of decisions. Thus performance criteria (a) and (c) could be described as task skills. Performance criterion (e) could be a task skill but it could be a task management skill if we consider that the assistant is making a decision about buying signals. Performance criteria (b) and (d) are really contingency management skills while criterion (f) is about environment skills.

I think you will agree that looked at in this way tasks that hitherto had been seen in only routine, technical terms suddenly take on a different dimension. Expressed another way, they have greater value. Consider the secretarial role, consider the range of task management and contingency skills she or he has to demonstrate every day. As we shall see later, this has interesting implications when it comes to selecting people for management positions. How many so-called management positions actually provide the opportunity for genuine task and contingency management skills? Could it be that these skills are being demonstrated every day at levels in the organization where we would never have looked before?

In the hotel industry the role of kitchen porter is one for which, despite unemployment levels, there are always vacancies. I have been working with a group of hotels to try to identify ways of enhancing the job, even changing its name to attract more applicants. We have produced a checklist, part of which is summarized in Figure 3.4, to interview existing kitchen porters to

---

1 What is the most important part of the job?
2 What other things do you have to do?
3 What do you like most about the job?
4 What do you dislike most about the job?
5 What contribution do you make to the success of the operation?
6 What other staff do you have regular contact with and how does what you do have an impact on what they do?
7 How do staff perceive your role?
8 What do they think makes a good kitchen porter?

Figure 3.4 *Profile of a kitchen porter: questions relating to the job itself*

find out how they see their role and the kind of contribution they consider they make to the business. As a result of a number of interviews we built up a picture of a job which through the eyes of the job incumbent was one in which you can 'use your own initiative' and have to 'anticipate the chef's requirements'. In other words, in a job which might seem mainly routine the job incumbent identified skills which involved task and contingency management and job role environment skills. It was very soon clear that the traditional title of 'kitchen porter' was an inadequate description for the range of skills that were actually employed. We came to the conclusion that 'kitchen technician' might more accurately describe the role.

Although we did not start out to apply the job competence model, it is apparent how it can provide a useful focus on what seems on paper (usually the existing job description) the most routine of jobs. When we come to look at accreditation below we will see that it plays an important role in terms of deciding on NVQ level of accreditation.

But we cannot leave a description of the national occupational standards framework without highlighting the process of analysis that gives rise to the standards in the first place; this is known as **functional analysis** and it is a critically important concept to understand. The key to it all is the starting point, which is the *purpose* of the particular occupational area that is being analysed. Functions are then identified which need to happen to achieve this particular purpose. Functional analysis is the process of continually asking the question 'What needs to happen for this purpose to be achieved?' until sub-divisions of functions are reached for which performance criteria can be set which will enable individual performance to be assessed. In effect, functional analysis proceeds to the point where elements of competence can be identified.

In my view, it is just this link between assessment of individual elements of competence and the overall purpose of the occupation itself which is of the utmost value. It contrasts sharply with the job and task analysis which was at the heart of systematic training. This process of analysis allows direct relationships to be drawn between training to achieve a particular element of competence and the overall purpose, mission of the occupation.

Furthermore the analysis of functions related to outcomes rather than tasks means that, as Jessup points out, 'These are more likely to endure as technology and work procedures change'.[3] But it is the fact that what any one person does, regardless of role, can now be linked to a central purpose that links together individual, organizational and national objectives. This has implications for any strategy for investment in people.

For example, the purpose of training and development has been defined as to 'develop human potential to assist organizations and individuals to achieve their objectives'. This means whether you are an instructor inducting a new entrant in the hazards of the workplace or a consultant brought in to introduce Total Quality Management, you both share the same purpose. If organizations paid more attention to this central purpose they might better be able to evaluate the contribution made by individual workers in individual roles. What functional analysis is doing is to ensure that individual contributions (as assessed against element criteria) in the majority of occupations in this country are directly linked to and capable of being evaluated against the key purpose of the respective occupation.

But to be manageable, elements and their associated performance criteria are grouped together to produce what are called *units* of competence. The elements that make up any one unit are determined by what would make sense to and would be valued by employers. Thus it is the *unit* which is certificated within NVQs but the elements which are separately assessed. Thus, in Figure 3.2, the unit 'Manufacture flat (steel) products by cold rolling' is made up of four elements, which represent the last state of a functional analysis that started with the purpose 'manufacture and supply a range of iron and steel goods, by processing raw materials to meet anticipated and actual market requirements' (see Figure 3.5).

Each of these elements needs to be assessed separately but the employee needs to satisfy the performance criteria of all four elements if he or she wants a unit credit.

Figure 3.5 illustrates the stages involved in an analysis of the steel

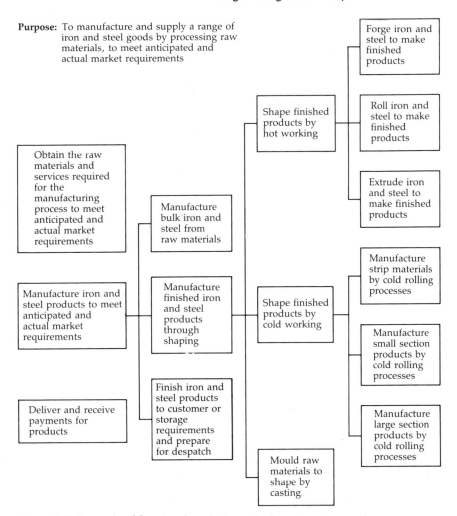

Purpose: To manufacture and supply a range of iron and steel goods by processing raw materials, to meet anticipated and actual market requirements

Forge iron and steel to make finished products

Roll iron and steel to make finished products

Shape finished products by hot working

Extrude iron and steel to make finished products

Obtain the raw materials and services required for the manufacturing process to meet anticipated and actual market requirements

Manufacture bulk iron and steel from raw materials

Manufacture iron and steel products to meet anticipated and actual market requirements

Manufacture finished iron and steel products through shaping

Shape finished products by cold working

Manufacture strip materials by cold rolling processes

Manufacture small section products by cold rolling processes

Deliver and receive payments for products

Finish iron and steel products to customer or storage requirements and prepare for despatch

Manufacture large section products by cold rolling processes

Mould raw materials to shape by casting

Figure 3.5 *Example of functional analysis applied to the steel manufacture sector*

manufacture function. All of the Lead Bodies have undertaken similar kinds of analysis to derive units of competence and elements for their respective sectors. The basic process would have involved a small group of occupational experts meeting with a consultant experienced in functional analysis. After agreeing the purpose of the occupation or sector they would then proceed to break statements down into smaller components using factors that are particularly appropriate to the sector in question.

Thus, in Figure 3.5 different factors are applied at four stages of the analysis. Initially, systems considerations as to input, process and output are used to break the main purpose down into three separate components. Just one function, that of process, is then taken further as an example. It is itself broken down into three sub-divisions of bulk, shaping and finishing. The shaping function can then be broken down yet further into three sub-divisions based on method of changing shape. Finally the cold-working and hot-working subdivisions are further broken down into separate subdivisions which are determined by different approaches – method in the case of hot-working and product in the case of cold-working. The final six statements are in effect units of competence, i.e. self-standing statements which can be accredited by NVQ and have a common value for all employers in this sector. But they will also need to be broken down further into their separate elements each with its own performance criteria. We have already examined one of these units in Figure 3.2.

In the preceding few pages we have tried to get inside the analysis process behind all of the national occupational standards currently available from the Industry Lead Bodies. The objective has not been to turn you into a functional analysis expert but to help you see the initiative in context. Later on we will draw out of the processes we have discussed some key benefits which I believe could be directly utilized in-company to further your investment in people. Next we turn our attention on to the process of *assessment*, whereby an employee is considered to be competent.

3.2 Assessment

> The basis of assessment is the generation of evidence by candidates to show that they can achieve the published standards. That evidence is collected by assessors who judge whether it is sufficient to merit accreditation. Their judgements are subject to a system of verification to confirm that they are accurate. Certificates are awarded to the candidates by the Awarding Body on the basis of the assessment.[9]

The description above summarizes the whole process by which a candidate can get NVQ accreditation. We examine the NVQ framework in the Section 3.3 below but the process of assessment plays a critical part and the framework that has been devised is, I suggest, of use to companies who wish to examine their skill base in competence terms regardless of whether they are seeking NVQ accreditation. The framework is summarized in Figure 3.6.

Basically there are four sources of evidence:

(1) Historical evidence: its most obvious form is a certificate testifying to a candidate's past 'performance', usually in a formal examination. But it could refer to *any* evidence, written, oral, visual, which supports a candidate's claim to particular achievement in the past – for example, a reference from a past boss cataloguing specific achievements in a secretarial role, or a report that gives an account of a successful project completed at work together with minutes from a subsequent management meeting that confirms the benefits accruing from the project. But this evidence could also be from

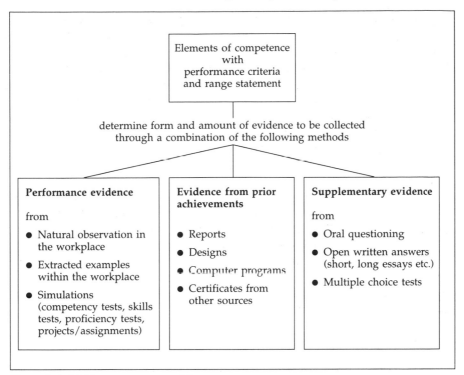

Figure 3.6 *NVQ assessment model*

outside work – for example, testimonials from neighbours as to a particular housewife's skills and care in looking after their children.

Increasingly the onus will be on the individual to maintain a portfolio of achievement which can be used in the future to get accreditation. As we shall see later, this process in itself constitutes a dramatic change in the way employees regard the workplace. Instead of seeing themselves as merely passive 'workers' who get paid for what they do, there is now the opportunity to use the workplace as a source of value which is independent of money. In this case value comes from accumulating evidence of their *own* achievement; they don't have to wait to be sent on a training course or to get promotion. But if employees can change their behaviour in this way, how should the employers respond? This is the question we will seek to answer in the latter half of the chapter.

(2) Performance at work: this is the preferred source of evidence of NCVQ and awarding bodies (see Section 3.3 on accreditation). It fulfils precisely the key condition of competence, i.e. 'the ability to perform the activities within an occupation or function to the standards expected in employment'. In this case the assessor is usually the candidate's immediate boss who, if the organization has been approved by the appropriate awarding body for assessment purposes, will have been trained and approved as an assessor.

Assessment is based on whether a candidate has 'provided evidence that they have met the performance criteria for each element of competence specified'.[4]

The advantage of the national occupational standards model we have already examined is that it provides a common and standardized framework within which assessment can be made. However, as numerous articles in the Employment Department's quarterly journal *Competence and Assessment* testify, it is one thing to have a system in place and quite another to have a national network of assessors all capable of interpreting the standards in the same way.

We come back again to the question we debated in the previous chapter: detailed information versus informed judgement. Assessment is made against the function described in the element of competence. The performance criteria lists the kind of evidence that is being sought but is only a guide to what is essentially a holistic judgement as to whether or not a candidate is considered competent in respect of a particular element. Indeed, more critical than ticking off each performance criterion is evidence that these criteria can be achieved in the different key circumstances identified in the range statement.

(3) Performance on specially set tasks: these could entail skills, proficiency, competency tests or projects/assignments. This is the more common way evidence has been collected at work or at training centres. It is of greater value in those situations where it is difficult or impossible to make a direct observation of performance (for example on a pilot's ability to make an emergency landing). In such cases simulation of the actual event is made as life-like as possible. A manager's ability to sort out an employee dispute, for example, could be reliably assessed in some form of role play situation. But this would presuppose both candidate and assessor having access to clear guidelines on what constitutes competence in this situation. As it happens, the Lead Body for agreeing management standards, the National Forum for Management Education and Development, has identified one such element of competence that would cover this eventuality: 'identify and minimize interpersonal conflict' (see Chapter 5).

More common pre-set tasks might be any assignment that allows employees to demonstrate evidence of competence at work. The great advantage of the national standards framework is that it makes available to *everyone* the kind of performance criteria that have to be satisfied and, more importantly, the range of circumstances in which competence has to be demonstrated. This gives the employee an incentive in actually *asking* his or her boss for particular assignments that can demonstrate this achievement.

(4) Questioning: this covers any situation or method in which a candidate could be asked a question the response to which would provide further

evidence of his or her competence. It could come about by oral question, e.g. by assessor asking the candidate to describe what they might do in a particular situation. It could be a written question, in the form of a questionnaire or examination. It could be a question generated by a computer, e.g. some form of diagnostic checklist which might be used in medicine or identifying a fault procedure of a particular machine.

Questions elicit evidence relating to the necessary knowledge and understanding that underpin all competences. But because by definition competence is about actual performance rather than simply knowing what to do, it is unlikely that this source of evidence would be sufficient on its own. This brings us to one of the key debates on competence – what part does knowledge play in the assessment of competence. This is even more relevant as NVQ turns its attentions to the professions where assessment is anything but routine and judgements have to be made about knowledge being applied to what will be largely unanticipated events.

The issue of 'knowledge', it seems to me, is at the very heart of the divide that still exists between the supporters of the more traditional and 'academic' school who really do believe in knowledge for knowledge's sake and equate it with courses and syllabuses of sufficient 'depth' and the new trend towards 'outcomes' rather than 'inputs'; in the case of the latter, value and accreditation is given to the demonstration of competence rather than, in the former case, to having a certificate which is a testimony of how much knowledge was remembered and reproduced on a particular occasion.

The debate about competence and its assessment has opened up a new perspective on the role 'knowledge' plays in this process. Lindsay Mitchell, one of the consultants advising NCVQ, addresses this issue:

> One of the realizations was that assessment of occupational competence was not an act of pure measurement. It was about gaining enough information on an individual's capabilities to make an informed judgement of his/her competence.
>
> In essence, we were talking about a legalistic notion of the judgement rather than a scientific one. The basis of the model is to build up sufficient evidence in order to allow sound judgements to be made, just as those in criminal courts do! It is the accumulation of evidence to a sufficient point to make confident predictions which is at the heart of the assessment process.[10]

What assessors therefore need, she argues, is guidance on the amount and type of evidence that is required to make just and accurate inferences about competence. It was thus that the importance of range statements was identified. Indeed it was the *context* of use rather than knowledge *per se* that was the clue. Although the range may not specify all the knowledge as such which is required,

The range would state the products, instruments, equipment, materials, clients, contexts, methods, medicaments, services, emergencies etc. for a particular element. These would serve to contextualize the standards and would reflect current view of acceptable, professional practice.[10]

In summing up, she concludes that they had not developed a 'knowledge' model but rather a 'further refinement of standards which happens to help us see where knowledge fits in'.

This approach to knowledge, I believe, has enormous implications, particularly for the professions which have for so long used knowledge as a defence against 'others' who would infringe their monopoly. I believe the arguments Lindsay Mitchell puts forward and the importance of identifying the 'context' of application of knowledge will lead to the development of a new 'mapping' of interlinked courses of study.

Donald Schon has also led an initiative on behalf of the 'reflective practitioner' which cuts through all the technical jargon associated with the professions and is helping them address the real underlying values – dare we say competences.[11] These themes are discussed in Chapter 5. But to end this section on the notion and complexities of assessment I include a final example of an element of competence developed by the National Working Party for Secretarial Standards. This includes the performance criteria and range statement. It is the degree of detail in the range statement which I would like you to focus on. Nowhere is knowledge mentioned, but I suggest that anyone devising a development programme to enable secretaries to be competent in this particular element has all the information they need in the statement outlined in Figure 3.7.

ACTIVITY 3.1
- *Have another look at Figure 3.7 and consider whether, regardless of whether you have been trained as an assessor or not, you can build up in your mind a very good picture of what competence in this element constitutes and just how you could test it.*
- *Secondly, consider any function in your own organization and what difference it would make if it was described in these kinds of terms.*

One thing is for sure, the very process of specifying competences and considering how they will be assessed keeps the function very much alive. You also begin to see applications and areas of importance you may not have identified before. For example, in relation to the example in Figure 3.7 you might consider that an additional area where competence needs to be demonstrated is in 'Facility required at accommodation' – for example fax, photocopier, sauna. But, as Lindsay Mitchell comments, 'The range of statements will only aid the process, they will not solve it completely as it is not possible to specify the absolute requirements for knowledge globally for

Element Arrange travel and accommodation

Performance criteria

(a) Travel, accommodation, entertainment and personal requirements are identified
(b) A clear and complete itinerary, containing all the arrangements made, is compiled well before the day of departure
(c) A proper balance is maintained between economy and the efficient use of time, in accordance with the organization's rules and procedures
(d) Selected bookings are correctly made and confirmed
(e) Travel documents are obtained and checked, and any discrepancies identified and rectified
(f) Credit transfers, currency and travellers' cheques are arranged correctly
(g) Medical packs are arranged for overseas emergency and high risk areas
(h) Safety/working practices are always followed and implemented
(i) Security and confidentiality procedures are always followed and implemented.

Range Statement

Competent performance must be demonstrated across a range of:

- Numbers and types of traveller – individual; small group; large party; own principal; more senior staff; clients or customers
- Modes of travel – road (inc. hire cars); rail; sea; air
- Destinations – UK; European; intercontinental
- Accommodation types and requirements – hotels; residential centres; overnight, meals only
- Health and insurance requirements – pre-travel; vaccinations and medicines during travel; personal accident; baggage and car insurance
- Travel documents – passport; visa; international driving licence
- Monetary requirements – foreign currency; traveller's cheques; letters of credit; valid credit and charge cards

Figure 3.7 *Element, performance criteria and range statement development by the National Working Party for Secretarial Standards*[9]

the population as a whole or for each and every individual'.[10] But what an improvement on the rigid and fixed task lists of yesterday.

3.3 Accreditation and the NVQ framework

In the previous two sections we have examined the framework of national occupational standards and the process of assessment against these standards which, I have suggested, are valuable as processes in their own right to help companies take a new look at their human assets. We will explore the usefulness of particular aspects of the various processes introduced later. But they were developed to be the basis of an NVQ framework within which every employee could be assessed and accredited against common and nationally agreed standards. We now need to examine the mechanism by which accreditation takes place. To use a metaphor we have used before, this enables you to convert local company value into a national currency. But, as you would expect, any investment incurs a cost and this is true of NVQ accreditation as it is for any investment. This section aims to help you assess the costs and the benefits of subscribing to the NVQ framework.

So where do you start? Let us assume you have decided to focus on one department, say the Accounts Department. You have a team of 12, comprising an Accounts Manager to whom report a Management Accountant, a Cost Controller and Payroll Supervisor. There are eight clerks. The first step is to find out if there is a Lead Body that has produced standards for this occupation. In this case there is such a body, part of the Association of Accounting Technicians. You find out that they have developed and published national standards and obtain a copy. This will break down functions in the format that should now be familiar to you, according to elements of competence, performance criteria and range statements. You are then in a position to collect evidence of achievement against such standards. But if you want to get accreditation, you need to find out more information.

Although the Industry Lead Body develops the standards it is not necessarily an Awarding Body. The function of an Awarding Body is to award certificates confirming competence. Examples include the City and Guilds, RSA and BTEC as well as professional bodies. It is the Awarding Body not the Industry Lead Body which can, if approved, issue an NVQ. Thus it has clearly been in the interests of Lead bodies to work with appropriate awarding bodies in the development and approval of the standards. The final hurdle is for the Awarding Body formally to apply to the NCVQ to get accreditation to award an NVQ certificate for a specified group of units of competence.

> An NVQ may be defined as a group of units which have relevance to employment and likely to make the holder of an NVQ employable. It is equivalent to the concept of an occupation, although in many areas and levels, NVQs are being created where occupations have not previously existed. An NVQ must cover a range of functions, represented by a range of units. This will frequently be broader than an employee's current job which might in some instances be limited to the equivalent of one or two units.[6]

It is for the Awarding Body to agree with the NCVQ the exact composition of the NVQ it is applying for. It is then obliged to issue two kinds of certificate: the NVQ certificate which testifies competence in all the units that make up the NVQ; and Certificates of Unit Credit which the candidate can accumulate until he or she has the others in the set to apply for the NVQ certificate.

One important piece of information the NVQ certificate will contain is the designated *level*, which NCVQ will decide in consultation with the Industry Lead and the Awarding Bodies. This is an important concept and one which will determine the level of qualifications in the future, from the most basic

Level 1 – competence in the performance of a range of varied work activities, most of which may be routine and predictable

Level 2 – competence in a significant range of varied work activities, performed in a variety of contexts. Some of the activities are complex or non-routine, and there is some individual responsibility or autonomy. Collaboration with others, perhaps through membership of a work group or team, may often be a requirement

Level 3 – competence in a broad range of varied work activities performed in a wide variety of contexts and most of which are complex and non-routine. There is considerable responsibility and autonomy, and control or guidance of others is often required

Level 4 – competence in a broad range of complex, technical or professional work activities performed in a wide variety of contexts and with a substantial degree of personal responsibility and autonomy. Responsibility for the work of others and the allocation of resources is often present

Level 5 – competence which involves the application of a significant range of fundamental principles and complex techniques across a wide and often unpredictable variety of contexts. Very substantial personal autonomy and often significant responsibility for the work of others and for the allocation of substantial resources feature strongly, as do personal accountabilities for analysis and diagnosis, design, planning, execution and evaluation

Figure 3.8 *Levels of NVQ*

to those representing the professions. There are five levels, which are summarized in Figure 3.8.

At the time of going to press the first occupational standards to be approved by NCVQ at level 5 are Management II standards developed by MCI (Management Charter Initiative) (see Chapter 5). Clearly level 5 is going to prove more problematic but if the whole framework is to have coherence it is essential *all* occupations are incorporated to enable a candidate to progress from one level to another. This is a key feature of the whole system. It also means that a candidate at any time might well get an NVQ at one level but also credit for units which can contribute to NVQs at *different* levels. Nevertheless, it does enable candidates to accumulate units which contribute to NVQs at a higher level so that when the time is appropriate they can capitalize on higher level skills. Once employees get hold of this idea I suggest this could well revolutionize the way employees view their jobs. But equally it provides employers with a more flexible framework within which to plan an organization's future.

It is tempting to allocate particular roles to each level – thus operators and clerical staff at level 1; craftsmen at level 2; technicians and some supervisors at level 3; supervisors/first line and middle managers at level 4; senior managers, directors and professional staff at level 5. On the other hand, it is also tempting to review the work your staff do against these levels and it may surprise you! Thus some clerical staff are in fact engaged in level 3 work while some managers have a primarily technician role. It is also interesting to speculate on the fact that while many management courses have indeed been delivering level 5 knowledge the students might not yet be in a position in industry to get accreditation at this level.

Returning to our hypothetical accounts department, how would you go about assessing and getting NVQ certification for your staff? The first issue is whether the Awarding Body has got approval from NCVQ for accreditation of respective groups of units. This involves a separate set of procedures which need not concern you except that you need to be aware of the overall process. NCVQ has to be satisfied that the Awarding Body has in place *verification* processes for monitoring assessment. The onus is on the Awarding Body to approve the assessors who will make the necessary judgements against the given elements of competence. In practice most Awarding Bodies license approved centres to carry out this assessment. This could be a company or college or training centre. A cost is involved in getting approval which will mean that for most small companies it may not be viable. Indeed the conditions for approval would also mean that a company was able to provide the range of situations within which staff could become competent and had the potential assessors to carry out the assessment.

Figure 3.9 summarizes the assessment and verification functions. The process of accreditation by NCVQ recommends there be both an internal verifier within the approved centre (e.g. a senior manager who would verify the assessment internally which could itself be coordinated by a second line assessor) and an external verifier, who is accountable to the Awarding Body and does not work in the same organization as the candidate seeking certification. So you can see there is a fairly elaborate process of verification which will involve cross-checking and sampling of assessments. This is to counteract a potential criticism of the NVQ model that it can lead to a dilution and variable assessment of standards. Given that a centre meets all these requirements, it will be approved by the Awarding Body.

In the case of our Accounting Department, unless it was part of a major company, it is likely that if it was seeking accreditation for staff who had achieved the necessary standards that equated to an NVQ it would look to a local approved centre. In fact, one of the Awarding Bodies approved by NVQ for certification of accounts functions, the Association of Accounting Technicians, is likely to approve local colleges who have expertise in the area. The evidence it recommends will be generated through candidates undertaking simulated exercises specially designed by the Awarding Body. One way of finding out who in your locality has been approved to assess which NVQs would be to contact your local TEC. Each TEC has an NVQ database on which you can identify which NVQs are available to you. They may also be able to advise you where and how they can be assessed.

The NVQ framework covers 11 major functional categories (e.g. Constructing, Transporting, Communicating and Entertaining, Providing busi-

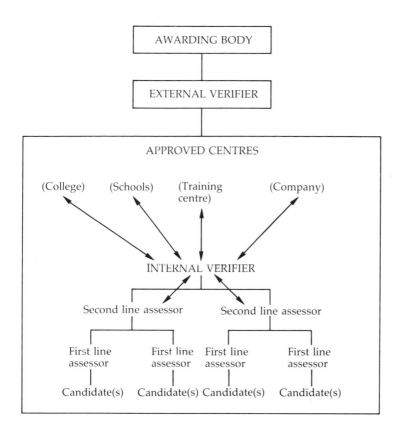

AWARDING BODY

EXTERNAL VERIFIER

APPROVED CENTRES

(College)   (Schools)   (Training   (Company)
                           centre)

INTERNAL VERIFIER

Second line assessor   Second line assessor

First line   First line   First line   First line
assessor   assessor   assessor   assessor

Candidate(s)   Candidate(s) Candidate(s)   Candidate(s)

Figure 3.9 *Assessment and verification model. (Source: NCVQ (1992)* National Standards for Assessment and Verification. *Report No. 13)*

ness services) broken down into some 58 sub-categories. The full list is summarized in the Appendix to this chapter.

A danger with such an enormous initiative as NVQ and the associated paperwork that accompanies it is that, as we have discussed before, the system can take over. But I believe underlying the initiative are some very powerful processes which, as I have tried to show, you can use in your own company without necessarily applying for certification or accreditation. What is important is that for the first time *everyone* can get recognition for their achievement. But this cannot be an automatic and unvalidated process. Therefore, by definition, evidence of achievement must be maintained. The benefit of collecting such evidence needs to start young and continue throughout one's working life.

To facilitate this process of collecting evidence NCVQ have developed and made available to all 16-year-old school leavers a National Record of

Achievement (NRA). This is a folder within which candidates can keep records, action plans, certificates that in later life they can trade in NVQ recognition. It is in this sense that I regard an NVQ and the units of competence it accredits as a unit of value that can be exchanged in the market place.

It was to test just such an idea that in 1989 NCVQ commissioned research from consultants which made a distinction between training that leads to 'high use value' (i.e. of direct benefit to a job) and training that leads to 'high exchange value' (i.e. increases promotion chances and/or status). In some ways this is the same distinction as that between specific and general skills which we explored in Chapter 2. The proposition was that NVQs will

> have high use (their relevance to actual tasks) and exchange value (in terms of progression and transfer) and so, according to our research findings should help motivate employers to train and make NVQs an attractive proposition to employers and employees alike.[12]

What the researchers found, apart from a low awareness of NVQs, was that NVQs could not achieve their high exchange value until employers found them credible and they would not find them credible until assessment procedures were seen to be more rigorous. So we have a Catch 22 situation: NVQs were meant to make access to assessment easier but it seems that employers will not accept NVQs until they have proved their worth by erecting more hurdles for the candidates to jump. And 'until a "critical mass" of NVQs embodying "new" standards with their attached NVQs are in place across all the primary occupational sectors of the economy, then there can be no entirely open access to assessment'.[13]

What, then, is the answer? 'The challenge ... is to create assessment regimes in the workplace compatible with work realities/cultures without compromising on the accuracy of assessment to national standards'.[13] David Bell then goes on to spell out the conditions in which this can happen:

> Enhanced access to assessment pre-supposes a clear market for such services, and ultimately local employers would be the primary client for TEC and LEC [Local Enterprise Companies: the TEC equivalent in Scotland] provision. This in turn *requires employers to operate more sophisticated systems of training needs analysis*. In the new system they would use national standards of competence in order to identify the required skills base, which would in turn set the agenda for internal skills audits involving the assessment of current levels of competence. The shortfall between the latter and the required levels of competence would form the basis of detailed learning needs analysis and negotiated training/learning programmes contracted to local providers or delivered in-house (with or without external assessment services) (emphasis added).[13]

This is a vision of not just a learning organization but a learning community at the centre of which is the TEC. My only reservation is with the words I have emphasized in the extract above. I wonder if the answer for the employer is not so much to engage in 'more sophisticated systems of training needs analysis' but to use the concept of functional analysis approach which is at the heart of 'the new system' to think afresh about their function as a business and the role of the people they employ. This is the theme we address in the next section which identifies 11 key factors derived from the developments we have so far been exploring. Each of these factors could be used, I suggest, in a creative way to open up new opportunities for investing in people.

3.4 Eleven ways of opening up competence and assessment in the workplace

Each of the 11 factors that follow is expressed as a dichotomy to reflect the scale of change that could take place.

(1) Outcomes *versus* Input

There can be few other subjects that are as capable of dividing the academic and training world as the distinction between 'outcomes' and 'input'. Of course trainers have accepted the need for outcomes ever since Mager's seminal work on *Preparing Instructional Objectives* was first published in 1962.[14] I remember very well being introduced to it in programmed instruction in the mid-1960s when it was considered the bible for describing what was called 'terminal behaviour', i.e. what the student would be expected to achieve after completing a given 'input' of instruction.

Once you got used to writing objectives in terms of an *action* word, a *standard* by which to measure the action and *conditions* in which the action should be carried out, it became a way of life. (Compare this approach to elements, performance criteria and range statements as applied to competences 30 years on.) The rationale justifying it all was Mager's oft quoted contention: 'If you're not sure where you're going you're liable to end up someplace else.'[14] But, of course, education was quite another matter. Education could not conceive how one could specify 'objectives' against which its voluminous input could be measured. I have recently had a discussion with a colleague at a college who could not conceive how one could possibly set outcomes for his particular subject, Marketing. Little has changed.

What *has* changed is that the competence framework has, at a stroke, severed forever the seemingly *inevitable* link between the outcome of a course of study and the means of achieving it. What both trainers and educators (especially educators) should realize is that this division sets them free.

This sense of freedom was vividly brought home to me some 20 years ago when I was introducing the concept of 'behavioural objectives' to a group of training managers. One very experienced trainer exclaimed: 'This means I could simply set objectives and make available my lecture notes and my students could learn by themselves to achieve these objectives and test themselves!' You could see the shackles from years of giving the same lecture week in and week out fall away in a second! But this *was* 20 years ago and training departments were not prepared to dispose of a lifetime's tradition for the sake of a new trend. Will competences go the same way?

The opportunity is the same as that instructor realized for himself 20 years ago. But this time there is an infrastructure which was lacking before and the opportunity can extend to every employee in the country. The words may have changed, the system become more elaborate, but the process is the same: the opportunity is there to help every employee identify the competences needed in their particular roles and then provide them with the appropriate descriptions relating to the element, performance criteria and range. This is the 'outcome'. Only *then* are we in a position to identify the most appropriate way to help that individual achieve that outcome. This is where the skill and the resources of the trainer and educator will be needed. But there will also be increasing emphasis on learning opportunities from *within* the workplace, as we shall see in the next chapter.

Most important of all:

> The new education and training model places the learner at the centre of the system. The learner is regarded as the client and the model is designed to provide him or her with more control over the process of learning and assessment (p. 115).[5]

This, I suspect, is at the heart of what worries some trainers and educators about the competence initiative. This is exactly what the division of *outcome* from *input* does and, I suggest, it is just this which provides you with a powerful tool of analysis.

ACTIVITY 3.2
- *Consider the implications of defining each employee's role in your organization in terms of competences (in the way we have described them in this chapter) and then draw up an action plan to help each person fully realize these competences. Question any input (training/instruction/ educational course) an employee receives in terms of just how appropriate it is to achieving this competence.*

What I have said above in no way precludes the individual employee being given development training and education that goes beyond the immediate competences identified. In my view a statement of competence can be as much a vehicle for starting a dialogue with an employee (client) about developments – laterally as well as vertically – for the future as for prescribing a present course of action. This is also where the competence approach is much wider based than Mager's instructional objectives. (For example, the range statement could play a very important part here.) They could become the basis for what Eisner calls 'directions for inquiry'[15] (a theme to which we will return in Chapter 6).

(2) Purpose *versus* job/task

We have already commented on the value of 'functional analysis' which is the basis on which all subsequent analysis and derivation of standards depends. Aside from its relationship with competence, I suggest it can be a valuable way of reviewing the contribution every role in the organization makes to the business's central mission or purpose. It is a salutary way of dividing up value within the organization!

I recently used a version of this approach in helping a leisure park to review the contribution of every job in the organization. We started with the organization's mission statement which was to ensure return customers by focusing on four aspects of service: safety; efficiency; courtesy; show. We then took each individual role and identified what each person needed to be able to do to demonstrate their contribution to each of these four aspects of service. We analysed their contributions vertically (i.e. impact on the boss and subsequently how the boss's behaviour affected his boss and so on) as well as laterally (i.e. how their behaviour affected colleagues who were, in fact, internal customers).

The outcome of such an analysis is that the organization structure might change but more likely is that each person's contribution to the business's goals is valued more.

(3) Competence *versus* Task

ACTIVITY 3.3
- *Whenever a statement of competence seems to be unrelated to anything else, ask yourself what was the original purpose that gave rise to it and then see if doesn't have enhanced value.*

Again we have spelt out the significance of the competence model (see page 50) and its incorporation of four key skills: technical skill; task management; contingency management; role environment.

It is salutary to consider what seems to be a straightforward technical task (see our example of kitchen porter, p. 51) and consider the implications of task and contingency management and the environment within which the task has to be performed. This is closely connected to the next factor.

(4) Context *versus* Content

If you look exclusively and in isolation at what a single individual does it might be hard to make sense of it. Indeed it could appear to be a series of incomplete tasks, and because of this high level of integration between different activities a realistic definition of competence might prove very difficult.

Put the individual into his or her context, however, and it all starts to make sense. When seen in relation to what other people are doing and the overall mission of the organization those incomplete and unrelated tasks now begin to have a purpose. We start to see the way one person's job and the standards which are required are shaped by the work of colleagues and, ultimately, by the goals and objectives of the organization.[1]

A useful way of illustrating this is by considering the 'role set' of any one employee. Put the employee in the centre of a page and then array around him or her colleagues on whom that person has a direct impact. Just like the exercise in 'competence versus task', above it can lead to some new insights about the value of staff you had seen only in isolation before.

While sharing very much Edward Fennell's view expressed above, I would want to add that by putting people in context in this way we see not only the way the employee is shaped by the organization but *potentially* how the organization can be shaped by the employee!

(5) Active *versus* Passive

We have hinted throughout this chapter at the potential power availability of competences gives the employee and what might happen if he or she realized this power and *demanded* the means of realizing particular competences and of being accredited for them. This is a theme Jessup picks up in his book *Outcomes*:

To achieve the learning society within industry we still need a cultural shift, not only in the way employers view training but also in the attitudes of employees. To achieve this, training and qualifications have yet to be valued by individuals. They must have meaning in terms of an employee's own aspirations and expectations (p. 98).[5]

Confirmation of how strongly an individual – in this case unemployed individuals – *can* identify with training *they* choose themselves comes from a report by Full Employment UK entitled *TECs and Individual Training Accounts*. It compares the views of unemployed, lower paid and higher wage groups regarding the introduction of 'Skillcard': this is a personalized learning credit card scheme whereby a sum of money is paid directly into a Training Account for an individual and he or she can draw on it as they choose. The unemployed group – far from reacting negatively to the proposal that they pay 2 per cent of their first year's earnings towards the cost of their training once they got a job – were adamant that if they contributed to it they would *own* it.

The authors of the report suggest that there is 'the belief that in undertaking training, individuals are mainly doing their employer a favour – and only secondly, benefiting themselves'. Skillcards, on the other hand, 'symbolize the proposition that training is, above all else, about individuals and *their* development'. They conclude with the following statement which, I suggest, could be a mission statement for the competence movement:

> Maybe the very essence of the new training culture should be a view of training as primarily being about individuals doing themselves a favour.[16]

(6) Open access *versus* Closed systems

We have already explored the significance and the implications of opening up access to accreditation for all. This is yet one further consequence of using *outcomes* to define training provision: 'if education or training is defined by its outcomes, it opens access to learning and assessment in ways which are not possible in traditional syllabus or programme based systems' (p. 89).[5] For example, it can take account of special needs, recognition of unpaid work, open learning and freedom from time and location.

(7) Assessment as Process *versus* Assessment as Terminal Condition

> We must not persist in viewing assessment as we have, often quite rightly in the past, as an unwanted addition to the process of learning which distorts the aim of the curriculum. In the new model assessment is a natural and integral part of the learning process (p. 101).[5]

The attitude towards the *process* of assessment is going to be crucial if the NVQ framework is to be firmly embedded as a national development process. Rather like the nature of outcomes – and for similar reasons – it arouses much emotion based, it seems to me, on an association with assessment as a negative force, linked with examination, failure, losing control etc. More than anything else, it seems to me, we need to adopt a different attitude towards assessment. In many ways the arguments we will develop when we look at evaluation apply to assessment.

Assessment is often viewed as something that is done *to* us over which we don't have a lot of control. In contrast, assessment against competences is very much within our control. Furthermore, the aim should be to carry it out in a culture in which assessment and support for achieving competences go hand in hand.

Building up a learning culture is at the heart of this issue. By definition, if every employee in a company is aiming to add value to her or himself they can only do that by getting value *from* someone else through the process of assessment. So far from it being a process with us as the victim, it is we who activate the system: 'ideally it should normally be the learner, when feeling competent in an aspect of the programme, who asks to be assessed' (p. 101).[5]

(8) The workplace as learning centre *versus* College

Strictly speaking this should not be a dichotomy, an either/or situation. In the new system of training and education we are exploring, both workplace and college should be seen as learning centres. Colleges are just beginning to explore ways they can begin to change their culture to make it more student based and provide a more flexible menu of options.

But organizations still have a long way to go to become learning organizations – this is the theme of our final chapter. What the competence initiative provides is a neutral framework within which, as we have already suggested, employees can explore a range of development opportunities within the work situation which is where they would be naturally assessed.

(9) Mentor *versus* Manager

In considering the implications of 'the new model for education and training' for schools, Jessup considers 'building into the curriculum a further attainment target concerned with facilitating the learning of other students'.[5] Thus, at a very young age, every individual would acquire the skills of supporting the development of another. In fact the practice is growing in sixth form colleges and colleges of further and higher education – though often for reasons of scarce resources rather than for any developmental purpose.

But the concept is also having an effect on the way managers are being developed. As we have seen in the previous chapter, the view of the manager as always being in control and directing others is changing to one where the manager is required to be a mentor, a supporter and resource to a team. This fits in very well with the assessment role each person will need to have in relation to his work group and the mentor and facilitator skills he or she will need to help individuals develop and acquire a wider range of competences.

(10) Mobility *versus* Static role

The NVQ framework has been constructed, as we have seen, to facilitate development not only upwards to different levels but also laterally and to embrace competences that may fall outside of an immediate job role. This has enormous implications in the workplace where individuals should be encouraged to extend their range of skills (see Figure 3.11).

This is particularly critical to prepare our workforce for the next recession, by which time they may have built up a repertoire of skills that can be transferred across a range of possible occupations. As we shall see, the structure of organizations in the future should allow individuals to progress sideways as well as vertically and should encourage such moves with appropriate accreditation.

(11) Accreditation of prior learning *versus* New experience

I have already drawn attention to the value of Accreditation of Prior Learning (APL) in helping individuals get credit within an NVQ type framework for past achievement. But, as I have also stressed, it will not happen automatically. The onus is on individuals to collect the evidence that can be used later. But organizations can also assist by providing the framework within which such evidence can be collected and using appraisals, for example, as opportunities to review with each employee the credits they have gained so far.

ACTIVITY 3.4
- *Consider each of the 11 factors and make a commitment to examine how they can be used to open up your own organization to recognize and accredit the value of the contribution each of your employees makes to the organization's goals.*

3.5 Companies, competences and some upside-down thinking

In this final section we look at how different companies have capitalized on competences and then finally indulge in some more upside-down thinking by comparing the approaches of three hypothetical companies and examining how an organization could be transformed by tapping into its corporate capability.

As an employer led, interconnecting system of standards and qualifications, based on the performance requirements of the workplace, NVQs are far closer to the needs of employers than previous qualifications. The ability to assess for competences to the national standards in the workplace not only gives tangible evidence that a job can be done, but can be less disruptive of working arrangements and avoid unnecessary and expensive over-training.[7]

This is how the CBI publication *Business Success through Competence* endorses the competence initiative. In fact the approach it adopts is very similar to the one I am advocating, that companies should engage in the same kind of analyses that led to the development of the national standards which we have been focusing on so far in this chapter. The CBI outlines a very practical set of steps for companies to follow which covers the following areas:

1 Take a strategic view of how people fit into the business: this requires a radical look forward into the future and the kind of skills people will need.
2 Decide on skill objectives. It advocates a kind of functional analysis approach resulting in 'profiles for each job' which contain skills written in outcome terms and using the format of element, performance criteria and range statements. It also advocates that companies consult national standards as a guide to developing their own standards.

> Where national standards can be most useful is as an indicator of the structure of company standards. If some aspects are included in the national standards but not in company standards for the same jobs there may be a case for expanding company standards.[7]

3 Audit existing skills against the standard and clearly show on a 'skills matrix' which skills have been achieved and what still needs to be achieved. (An example of a format for such a 'skills matrix' is given below in Figure 3.10.)
4 Produce action plans for individuals based on job/skill profiles.
5 Evaluate the outcome of such action plans against business objectives.

Given the steps summarized above, it is not surprising that the sub-title of the CBI publication is 'Investors in People'; indeed the steps are intended 'to help any organization maximize its investment in people', which is embraced in the Investors in People scheme we explored in Chapter 2.

The CBI guidelines illustrate how various companies have used this approach. One such company is Nissan. It began the process with its mission statement: 'To build profitably the highest quality car sold in Europe.' The senior directors were then asked to consider what the company required of the workforce to meet this goal (a kind of functional analysis). The directors came up with some 250 topics. This list was then circulated to individual job holders who expanded it to 1200 topics! These were then broken down into categories of skills:

1 Those skills everyone needed (core skills).
2 Skills that were specific to particular jobs.

For each skill Nissan identified levels of competence. Figure 3.10 gives an extract from a skills matrix which is used to illustrate vividly the level respective workers have reached, in this case in 'standard operation'.

Another company the CBI cites in which competences have been used to capitalize on investment in people is Glaxo. This is how Glaxo capitalized on its people:

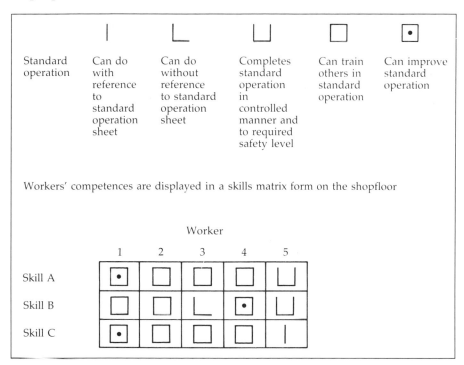

Figure 3.10 *The Nissan* |⌐ ⊔ *system. Each level of competence has a particular symbol assigned to it*

> Skilled craftsmen were taken away from some tasks requiring lower levels of skill to concentrate on higher level work, broadening the range of skills carried out by shopfloor workers. Quality control and assurance were devolved more directly to engineering staff, removing much of the 'policing' role of quality controllers.[7]

This process was facilitated by Glaxo working with the Association of British Pharmaceutical Industries and the Chemical Industries Association to integrate its own standards with the national standards for chemical and pharmaceutical manufacturing. They were able to widen their perception of people's potential skills by using such a framework. Figure 3.11 contains an example of how the company integrated its own skills within two functions it identified within the national NVQ framework thus providing an

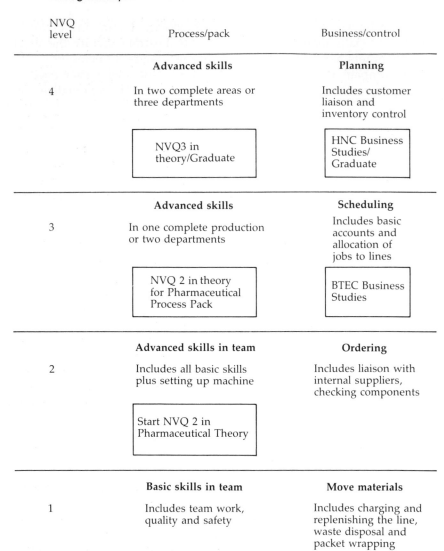

NVQ level	Process/pack	Business/control
	Advanced skills	**Planning**
4	In two complete areas or three departments	Includes customer liaison and inventory control
	NVQ3 in theory/Graduate	HNC Business Studies/ Graduate
	Advanced skills	**Scheduling**
3	In one complete production or two departments	Includes basic accounts and allocation of jobs to lines
	NVQ 2 in theory for Pharmaceutical Process Pack	BTEC Business Studies
	Advanced skills in team	**Ordering**
2	Includes all basic skills plus setting up machine	Includes liaison with internal suppliers, checking components
	Start NVQ 2 in Pharmaceutical Theory	
	Basic skills in team	**Move materials**
1	Includes team work, quality and safety	Includes charging and replenishing the line, waste disposal and packet wrapping

Figure 3.11 *Extract from Glaxo's General Skills Framework*

integration between the old (including existing qualifications) and the new. The framework in Figure 3.11 only illustrates the process. In fact there were five functions altogether and the company stipulated that before progressing from one level to another each employee was proficient across all five functional skills. Every employee would then be very clear what they were expected to do to achieve success in the company. Such an approach makes the whole process both visible and accessible to everyone.

As we shall now see, many companies may have in place development programmes such as Glaxo, operating at separate levels, but they do not have the framework within which to describe the total picture and thereby benefit from the resulting synergy. Both Nissan and Glaxo were able to use the NVQ framework to arrive at new insights about their staff and their contribution to the overall goals of the business. In their turn the staff found themselves doing more productive jobs and getting accreditation for what they were able to achieve. There are more case studies in the CBI publication which I would recommend to companies who want to find a way of starting out on the competence path.

To conclude, it is time to indulge in some more upside-down thinking, the objective of which is to help you extend your perception of the themes we have been discussing and visualize their application not only to capitalize on what you already have but to transform your view of the organization itself.

To do this I would like you to focus on three companies. We will not be giving them names or even functions. For our purposes it is enough that they remain organizational forms on which you can project your own views. These forms appear in Figure 3.12. We will call them organization A, B and C. In each case we will describe them from two perspectives, from outside looking in at the organization as a total entity and from the perspective of an employee from within.

The scenario of Organization A is one that we would designate as task based. It is best represented as the typical hierarchy where progression is seen as essentially vertical. It probably carries out training specifically targeted at each task level. So task level 1 get operator craft training; level 2 get supervisor training; level 3 get management training. The top person probably doesn't get any training at all but ensures everybody else does. It is likely that training needs are identified systematically and implemented efficiently; it is even possible that training is evaluated against the needs at each level. It is also quite possible this company has received a National Training Award.

Looked at from inside, each employee is likely to have a job description, a copy of the company's organization chart. So he or she knows the positions of power they can aspire to but they are probably not clear exactly how to attain them or even what goes on inside each position. After a while, once he or she has become proficient at their respective role they will look to either be promoted or leave to join a similar company but starting at a 'higher' level.

Organization B has the same number of people in the same number of positions but this time they are connected within an overall framework. You will recognize it as the kind of integrated model Glaxo used to show the connections between different positions in the company. Here progression is both lateral as well as vertical. The company is able to describe itself at any time in terms of integrated competences or functions.

Looked at from the individual employee's point of view, he or she will have a profile describing the competences required for their particular job and will agree an individual development plan drawing on a range of resources both inside and outside the company. But they will also have access to the profiles of any other

A Task based

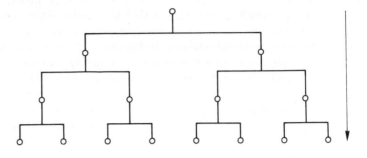

B Competence based

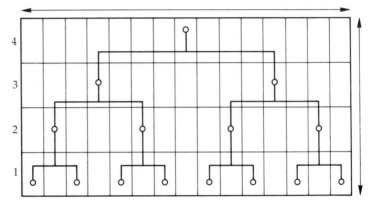

C Corporate capability

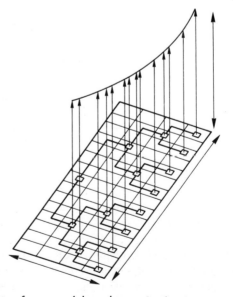

Figure 3.12 *Stages in moving from a task based organization to corporate capability*

employee in the company (including the person at the top) and access to whatever resources are recommended for achieving appropriate levels of competence. They can request to be assessed and accredited for demonstrating evidence of achievement in any competence (whether contained in their role or not). This will be done either through internal assessors and/or assessors outside in assessment centres, colleges etc. Each employee will be building up an individual portfolio of achievement and will be carrying out regular audits, using NVQ database at the local TEC, of accreditation for which they are eligible as well as planning to combine different skills for accreditation in the future. When they are unable to gain any more credits in the company they will join another company, using their portfolio as evidence of what they have achieved, and contract with the new company to develop specific skills which are both of value to the company and to the individual.

Organization C contains all the characteristics of Organization B. Thus the same people are represented within the overall framework. But this time there is a third dimension added which incorporates within itself at any one time the changing levels of competence of every member of staff and the consequences of these changes on every other member of staff. The third dimension represents what I would call corporate capability, which by definition is changing all the time and is therefore difficult to describe in a static picture.

The essential difference between organization B and C is that B's framework of competences is static. It represents the status quo. In a sense this is a potential criticism of competence assessment in that it is a kind of rubber stamping of what already exists. By contrast, the ultimate value, it seems to me, is open to those companies that are literally able to envisage the shape of their organizations changing as individuals realize and extend themselves beyond competence. But this is difficult to represent. What I have tried to depict in Figure 3.12C is the reality of individuals within the overall framework gaining different competences at different times that go beyond their particular role and which can have an impact on the organization as a whole.

In this scenario there is only the corporate view, there is no individual view; by definition corporate capability is not just the sum total of all the competences that are currently having an impact on the organization but also the potential capacity of each employee for the future. It is not just an extension of Figure 3.12B, it is a transformation of the structure itself. We will return to this 'transformation' theme when we turn our attention to the learning organization in the final chapter.

In operational terms there is a similarity with the model we developed in Figure 2.6 when we were discussing the Investors in People scheme in Chapter 2. There we were trying to build up an organization view of investing in people by comparing two pictures: the company view and the view of every single person in the organization as a result of which a third picture emerged (the third dimension) which was a composite picture of the two. We are trying to describe the same process in Figure 3.12 but this time using the competence grid as a common framework for describing *corporate* capability.

The CBI guidelines, for example, make a laudable case for carrying out a competence based analysis of the organization's needs. This entails basically two steps. Step one is to identify the organization's mission statement and the kind of skills needed to enable the organization to achieve it. Step two is to carry out an audit of everyone's competence at the moment. You take one from the other and you are left the key skills that need to be developed. (This is not unlike the Training Skills gap in systematic training except the competence analysis is related to purpose and outcome.) In my view this gives you a picture of *your* view, the company view of what you think people *can* do. It doesn't take account of what *they* think they *do*, *can* do and *could* do. To do this we have to engage in the same exercise as in Figure 2.6, i.e. compare the individual view with the company view.

Let's take a look at an instance based around one employee. Ada works as an accounts clerk. The competence she might be expected to achieve could be defined by referring to the AAT's national standards (see page 60). This could well be the company view based on a functional analysis starting with the company's mission. But what does Ada think she does in relation to her purpose in the company as she sees it? (In other words, from a perspective of her own functional analysis.)

Let us suppose we ask Ada what she does. Let us assume that what she tells us corresponds to much of the detail that relates to the technical tasks in the national standard. But what about other aspects of the competence model? Task Management? Contingency Management? Environmental Management? Has anybody ever given Ada an opportunity to reflect on these competences in relation to her own job? What kind of picture would then emerge from Ada? Let's imagine what might happen

'You've given us a list of the kind of duties you do every day, Ada. Can you think of some incident that's happened recently when you had to do more than what would normally be expected of you?'

'Well, there was this telephone call last Thursday. It was from Mr Francis asking about the weekly B33 figures. Normally my supervisor, Mrs Jones, would deal with it but she'd been called away. Anyway, I knew all about the figures and gave Mr Francis the information he wanted. He was a bit unsure of how they'd been calculated so I explained it to him. He said it was the first time he had understood what they were about!

So, without any prompting we have evidence of Contingency Management (deciding to give the information herself rather than wait for the supervisor); Task Management (she was able to explain the basis of the figures' calculation); and Environmental Management (she knew who Mr Francis was, presumably his status in the organization and what was the best way of communicating with him). On our competence grid in Figure 3.12 (Organization B model for example) Ada might have been placed at level 1 though it is clear that her *capability* is at a higher level. How then can we capitalize on Ada's skills?

This brings us to the Organization C model, which tries to adjust the state of the organization as each employee's competence is upgraded. In the case of Ada we might follow up these questions by getting Ada first to recognize that she can achieve competence at a higher level and then to reflect on how she *could* utilize these skills further, with organizational support. This does not necessarily mean making her a supervisor (which would be the first solution in the task based Organization A model), but may entail adjusting her role so that these capabilities can be utilized.

There's an Ada in every employee and model C is trying to describe how an organization continually adjusts to capitalize on its corporate capability. In the organization of the future it will matter

> less who your boss is (or how well the boss manages you), more how well you make the right connections with a supportive mentor or a sponsor to champion your ideas and contributions (p. 84).[17]

Ada also needs to know exactly how she can make these kinds of connections and the resources that are available for her to access. This leads us on to the next chapter where we move from outcomes – the subject of this chapter – to the *inputs* and *processes* of learning and development that can make them happen.

References

1 Fennell E. (1989) TAG Guidance Note Number 2: Developing standards by reference to functions. *Competence and Assessment*, Issue 8, Spring
2 Employment for the 1990s (1988) Government White Paper, HMSO 1988
3 Training Agency (1989) *Development of Assessable Standards for National Certification*, Employment Department, Moorfoot, Sheffield
4 Mansfield, B. (1991) Deriving standards of competence. In *Development of Assessable Standards for National Certification* (ed. Edward Fennell), Employment Department, HMSO
5 Jessup, G. (1991) *Outcomes: NVQs and the Emerging Model of Education and Training*, Falmer Press
6 Employment Department and NCVQ (1991) *Guide to National Vocational Qualifications*, Employment Department, Moorfoot, Sheffield
7 Confederation of British Industry (1991) *Business Success through Competence; Investors in People*, CBI
8 Mansfield, B. and Mathews, D. (1985) *Job Competence – A Description for use in Vocational Education and Training*, Further Education Staff College, Blagdon

9 Gealy, N., Johnson, C. and Mitchell, L. (1991) Designing Assessment Systems for National Certification. In *Development of Assessable Standards for National Certification* (ed. Edward Fennell), Employment Department, HMSO

10 Mitchell, L. (1989) The identification of knowledge, *Competence and Assessment*, Issue 7, Winter, 4–6

11 Schon, D. (1983) *The Reflective Practitioner*, Basic Books

12 Saunders, M., Fuller, A. and Lobley, D. (1990) *Emerging Issues in the Utilisation of NVQs*. NCVQ R & D Report No. 5, January 1990, NCVQ

13 Bell, D. (1990) Access with credibility. What needs to be done to increase access to assessments for NVQs and SVQs. *Competence & Assessment*, Issue 14, 9–10

14 Mager, R. (1962) *Preparing Instructional Objectives*, Fearon

15 Eisner, E. (1977) Establishing a direction. In *Beyond the Numbers Game* (ed. Hamilton, D., Jenkins, D., MacDonald, B. and Parlett, M.) Macmillan

16 Full Employment UK (May 1991) *TECs and Individual Training Accounts*, Full Employment UK

17 Naisbitt, J., Aburdene, P. (1986) *Re-inventing the Corporation*, Macdonald

Appendix

NVQ framework: classification by areas of competence

1 Tending animals, plants and land
1.1 Farming
1.2 Landscaping and gardening
1.3 Tending animals
1.4 Fishing

2 Extracting and providing natural resources
2.1 Mining
2.2 Quarrying
2.3 Locating and producing (gas and oil)
2.4 Providing energy and water

3 Constructing
3.1 Planning, designing and surveying
3.2 Building
3.3 Finishing
3.4 Installing and maintaining services

4 Engineering
4.1 Civil engineering
4.2 Mining engineering
4.3 Mechanical and automative engineering
4.4 Electronic and electrical engineering
4.5 Marine engineering
4.6 Aeronautical engineering
4.7 Process engineering

5 Manufacturing
5.1 Processing minerals
5.2 Processing organic matter
5.3 Manufacturing textiles and garments
5.4 Manufacturing consumables
5.5 Manufacturing metal products
5.6 Manufacturing chemical products
5.7 Manufacturing basic materials
5.8 Manufacturing electrical and electronic equipment

6 Transporting
6.1 Transporting by road
6.2 Transporting by air
6.3 Transporting by rail
6.4 Transporting by water

7 Providing goods and services
7.1 Purchasing and procuring goods
7.2 Wholesaling and handling goods
7.3 Retailing goods
7.4 Providing accommodation and catering services
7.5 Providing cleaning and repair services
7.6 Providing travel and tourism services
7.7 Providing hairdressing and beauty treatments
7.8 Providing leisure, sport and recreational services

8 Providing health, social care and protective services
8.1 Providing health care
8.2 Providing social care
8.3 Rehabilitating and resettling offenders
8.4 Maintaining a healthy and safe environment
8.5 Maintaining a secure environment

9 Providing business services
9.1 Providing business and administrative services
9.2 Providing banking, financial and insurance services
9.3 Providing accounting services
9.4 Providing legal services and administering the law
9.5 Providing information technology services
9.6 Providing property service

10 Communicating and entertaining
10.1 Publishing
10.2 Broadcasting
10.3 Performing
10.4 Interpreting and translating
10.5 Promoting and advertising services
10.6 Providing library and information services
10.7 Designing and exhibiting

11 Developing and extending knowledge and skill
11.1 Providing learning opportunities
11.2 Researching

4 The learning portfolio goes public

We were seeking to gain the vital commitment from managers at all levels and generally change attitudes to training away from: 'What has the training department got by way of courses?', or 'Can I go on a course, please?' (Training perk), to 'Training is a continuous all-year-round process for which I personally take a large share of the responsibility' and 'How can I improve my skills and/or knowledge because I know I need to get better at, say, accounting, as our department is about to become an autonomous profit unit?' or 'I don't seem to get the results I should like from my reports. Perhaps I could express my ideas better and achieve the desired outcome' (p. 110).[1]

This is a description of the ideal which I suspect most trainers have wished upon their organization at some time or another. But thanks to the kind of initiatives we have already explored in the previous two chapters, this could well become the norm rather than the exception in the future. Before introducing the key themes of this chapter, I'd like to start rightaway with some upside-down thinking and invite you to join John as he starts his first day of work at Jenkins Foods Ltd. The date is sometime in the future.

After the Personnel Manager had greeted him, she picked up a floppy disk and loaded it into a PC on her desk. John was surprised to see his name appear on the VDU followed by his qualifications and list of competences and skills. He remembered from his interview that he'd been asked a lot of questions about his past experience. John's last job had been with a small company and he felt he wasn't getting anywhere. What was interesting now was to see how what he'd told the Personnel Manager about his last job had been translated into a list of skills which he didn't realize he had!

The Personnel Manager then called up another file which revealed another set of skills which John recognized as his response to what were his goals for the future. But they were expressed again as skills. For example:

> Able to programme and operate the new model in the X561 series.
> Able to identify faults in the new machine and, where appropriate, remedy them himself or arrange for the necessary parts to be supplied.

There were also some skills which he didn't recognize, like:

> Able to operate the following machines safely (G671, B789 and X561).
> Able to instruct new staff in the operation and maintenance of the X561.

Then there was another section which was headed Other Areas of Influence. Again, John recognized them from what he had told the Personnel Manager about the kinds of role he would like to have and develop in the future:

> Would like to move into sales.
> Would like to develop project management skills.

There was also reference to another role which he didn't recognize:

> Member of quality control team working on operation Fat Reduction.

Although John was a little taken aback by all this personal information that was staring out at him from the VDU he couldn't help feeling a sense of confidence and pride about his new job. He'd never ever seen himself like this before. The Personnel Manager must have sensed his feelings: 'You must be wondering if you haven't joined the secret service rather than a food processing company! But in actual fact this kind of system is the very opposite of a secret service. This floppy disk is not our property but yours. Some of the details on it I'm sure you will recognize from what you told us at your interview – so there is nothing secret about it. But there are some new items which we've introduced where we believe you can make a particular contribution to the company both now and in the future. We believe they would enhance your skills as well as be of benefit to us. But normally these wouldn't be added to your DP – Development Profile, that's what this floppy disk is called – without your agreement in discussion with your boss. In fact I think this is a good time to bring in Giles who you will remember from your interview.'

With that the Personnel Manager brought in Giles Green, John's Team Leader and both of them explained how they saw John becoming an instructor to new staff on the X561. Instructional and coaching skills would also be important as John progressed towards being a Team Leader himself. At the same time they also felt his operational expertise would be a useful contribution to the monthly quality control interdepartmental group that was exploring how to reduce more fat from processed foods. Membership of this group would also bring John in contact with the sales team which was where they agreed he would be making a big contribution in the future. How did John feel about it?

John felt very good about it. For the first time in his life he had some clear goals at which to aim which were not being set by himself in isolation but were being *agreed by others who would, presumably, be instrumental in helping him achieve them. But this led him to wonder just how he was expected to acquire these skills. Again, the Personnel Manager was one step ahead of him. With the depression of another key the VDU flashed up a list under the heading Development Resources. (You can see these in Figure 4.1.) She continued: 'As you can see, in this company we have a vast range of resources which will help you acquire the kind of skills we've*

People skills you can draw upon
- Self
- Manager – your immediate manager
- Mentor – planned use of colleague other than your Manager
- Tutor – use of specific tutor skills
- COL leagues
- SUB ordinates
- CUS tomers
- P ersonnel Manager

Skills
- IN struction
- FE edback
- DE monstration
- QU estions

Support facilities
- B ooks
- A rticles
- MA nuals
- V ideos
- CC TV
- A udio tape
- O verhead transparencies
- S lides (35 mm)
- C omputer based training software
- D atabase
- L anguage laboratory
- OP erational technology (i.e. machinery)
- CA se studies
- OP en learning
- ST ructured learning exercises
- PR ojects
- RO le play

Learning context
- F ormalized instruction
- W orkshop
- WO rkplace
- SE condments
- CO nference
- EX ternal visits
- PRO blem solving group
- F M eetings (formal and planned)
- I M eetings (informal and unplanned)
- COLL ege

Figure 4.1 *Development resources*

been discussing. You can get more information about each one and where it will be available by keying in the code letter beside each resource. So if we press V you will get an update about the technical and training videos the company possesses, where they are held and how to make arrangements to see them.'

John was very impressed but one thing puzzled him. He couldn't see any reference to any courses. Even at his previous employers they had a catalogue promoting technical courses which occasionally John glanced through in the personnel office but there was never an opportunity to actually attend them. John remarked about the absence of course and the Personnel Manager smiled – as one who had to respond in this way not for the first time: 'It's not that there aren't "courses" going on all the time – I'll show you what I mean in a minute – but we don't describe them as such. You see a "course" is only a convenient label to cover a complex range of resources and skills which are made available at a particular time and place. What this list of development resources does is to break down all the resources, facilities and skills the company possesses which can be used by every member of staff to develop themselves. Every member of staff has their own Development Profile in the form of a floppy disk, just like this. It is then YOUR responsibility, not the company's, to choose the combination of resources that best suits you to achieve your objectives.

'Of course, in making the choice you can use two of the resources that are present in this room – your boss and myself. Every time you use a resource you are asked to record the fact by updating your DP. You do that by keying in the letter again – in this case you are using two resources so you would key in both codes, M and P and depress function key F4 which is the update function. What appears then is a template in which you record the date and time used. It may sound terribly bureaucratic but you'll be surprised how quickly you get used to it. What it provides you with is a permanent record of a development plan and resources you've chosen to use. This enables us to know how the resources have been used, to what effect and at what cost. One of my tasks is to look at the weekly pattern of use of resources and projected forecasts – I'm a kind of Personnel Accountant.

'This Development Profile is literally a data BANK in which we want you to invest. All you have to invest is the time but it's our time too. In fact Giles here will not only be encouraging you to invest your time in using these resources he will be expecting you to do so. You see Giles's own performance is judged as much on how he has helped you invest in these resources as it is on meeting criteria like gross profit, reduction in waste etc. Of course we believe there is no difference between these criteria – we can only maintain high standards if every member of staff is continually updating and developing themselves.

'So if you stop a colleague from what he's doing to ask a question, you're using a key resource; the time that person takes to answer your question and maybe go on to demonstrate a particular skill, is not "down time" – it's accounted for as an investment in the Company Development Bank. Let me show you. I am at this very moment taking time out to introduce you to the Development Profile system. Just as you would be expected to record your time in using me, I would be expected to record my time in investing in you. To do this I key in Y and then the function key

F3. *You will see this brings up another template in which I record what resources I've used and the overall time taken. So, we have a kind of 'double-entry-book' system which balances debit (your time using resources) with credit (my time in investing in you). Of course it never does actually balance but it gives us an overall picture of demand versus supply.*

'Just as each person is expected to make use of the development resources so are they expected to invest in them too. You will be surprised to learn that we expect you to be a resource as from now! You see the fact that you are new to us makes you a very important resource. You will find colleagues will be drawing on your experience as both a potential new internal customer as well as someone who has valuable experience of outside competitors. So, you see, we don't waste any resource.

'Giles will agree with you some guidelines on what kind of use we would expect you to make of resources as well as what input we would expect from you over the next month. But first let's explore what kind of combination of resources you may want to use to acquire the kind of skills you will need.

'It is vital that right from the outset you have the choice as to what resources to use. We believe you will then have complete responsibility and ownership for achieving the goals you are set. Let's take two very different functions: Safety and Fault finding in the X561.

'As you will appreciate, Safety is a critical factor in so far as it affects all our staff and customers alike. I notice you attended a one-day course on safety at your last job, covering similar machines to the ones you will work on here. But there is no record of your having been assessed on the outcome. Here we insist that you be assessed as "competent" in all safety aspects in the workplace. In fact until you are, you will not be able to operate the machinery so it is number one priority you get assessed as competent as soon as possible. You will not be surprised to learn that successful outcomes from any form of development are recorded in another file on your DP. After using any resource (and recording in the way I've described) you use function F2 to update the Competence File. This is the file we started with, which so far records what you've achieved in your career to date. As you become competent in other skills you automatically move a skill from your DP-Goal File to your Competence File.

'If we call up the DP-Goal File you will recall it contains four competences each having a priority code:

C1 Able to operate the following machines safely (G671, B789 and X561)	P1
C2 Able to programme and operate the new model in the X561 series	P2
C3 Able to identify faults in the new machine and, where appropriate, remedy them himself or arrange for the necessary parts to be supplied	P3
C4 Able to instruct new staff in the operation and maintenance of the X561	P4

Clearly it is number one priority you get assessed as competent in safety before you go on to becoming familiar with a new machine which you will need to do before being able to carry out a faults analysis; only then will you be able to proceed to development as an instructor.

'But how you become competent in all these functions is up to you using a mixture of the resources that are yours to explore. What is fixed is the assessment you will be expected to take when you are ready. You can get details of what criteria will be used to assess you by keying in the competence number and then F2. So, if we key in C1 this gives you the details as follows:

Element to be assessed:	To be able to operate all the machines on the shopfloor safely
Performance criteria:	Safety guard in operation at all times Speeds always kept within limits No waste impeding operation Immediate space kept free of obstructions
Range indicators:	To apply on following machines: G671, B789 and X561; speed appropriate to each machine
Approved assessors:	Giles Makin; Joyce French

You will see it not only tells you against what criteria you will be assessed but also whom in the company is eligible to assess you. All you need to decide is what information/support you need to meet all these criteria.'

John thought he was already competent but then he wasn't sure about speed limits; perhaps they were different here from his last company. So he'd need to have this information but apart from that he was confident he could get himself assessed as competent at safety rightaway. Looking down the list of resources he thought he would try a mix of the following: (1) Get access to the respective operating manuals and speed limits; (2) Ask a colleague to check him out. The Personnel Manager was pleased at the way John had begun to think about using the resources for himself. Then she let him into a secret. 'In fact we've already isolated for you a mix of resources that might be appropriate. You can tap into these yourself by depressing F5 against a particular competence. So in the case of safety of these machines it comes up with the following list:

	Location
● Manuals G671, B789, X561	Store cupboard 45 (see map)
● All staff in room E	
● Video on 'Safety First at Jenkins'	Contact Jane Thompson x456
● Report 'Safety record of the G, B and X series'	Library
● Tutor – Safety Officer	Don Gibson x879

'Now let me come back to your comment about courses. Once upon a time Don Gibson used to run regular one-day safety courses but it was impossible to predict demand. Now by concentrating on the outcome rather than the input everyone has the responsibility of organizing their own development. But by the same token if a resource is identified then it must be made available. So, although Don Gibson isn't running a regular course he is, as you can see, a key resource and it is expected that a proportion of his time is going to be taken up with staff like yourself asking for his help.

'You will notice he appears as "tutor". This means that he is able to run an instructional programme if the demand warrants it. Any member of staff who has been assessed as competent in instructional technique in a specific subject is called a "tutor". You can use this code to find out the name of company tutors for particular competences; you will also get details of the particular resources these tutors employ and how they're organized. Let's take another one of your competences to be developed in the future: "Able to instruct new staff in the operation and maintenance of the X561." If you key in T (for Tutor) and F5 you will see it identifies a particular tutor who will enable you to achieve this competence. But not only that, it reveals particular resources she will be using and how these are organised.

'In this case there is a regular demand for this skill so Joan Durham runs a regular session, every Monday morning. But this doesn't mean we necessarily expect staff to attend all the morning – this is where it differs from a conventional course. You can see how the morning is structured and you may therefore opt to attend for those sessions from which you get the maximum benefit.

Competence:	Able to instruct staff in operation and maintenance of the X561
Tutor:	Joan Durham – available every Monday morning 0900–1200 in seminar room 3
Resources used:	Informational input (Code ref. F) 0900–1000 Video (code V) 1000–1030 Structured exercise (ST) 1030–1100 Demonstration by tutor (DE/T) 1100–1130 Demonstration by learner (DE/S) and feedback from colleagues and tutor (FE/COL/T) 1130–1200

'So, for example, you may choose to sit in for the theory session and for the video and structured exercise and demonstration by tutor but feel you need to do some reading and checking with colleagues before you're ready to do a mini-session of your own. Having done this you come back on a subsequent week and join the session at the point where you can try out a session yourself. As a result of this and the feedback you get you're advised to get some more practice. The way you do this is to practise on a colleague in front of fixed CCTV set up in room 101. You then go back again

to another Joan Durham session and this time you get assessed as competent by Joan. She will then update your Competence File. In the meantime this is how you might have recorded use of the resources over the two or three weeks you were getting ready for the final assessment

Date	Resources used	Approx. time
2 Feb	F/T	1 hr
	V	0.5 hr
	ST	0.5 hr
	DE/T	0.25
3 Feb	MA	0.5
4 Feb	DE/SELF	0.25 hr
	FE/COL	0.25
9 Feb	DE/SELF	0.25
	FE/COL/T	0.25
11 Feb	DE/SELF/CC	0.25
	FE/COL	0.25
16 Feb	DE/SELF	0.25
	FE/COL/T	0.25

This might be a good time to step outside of this scenario and reflect on its implications. The introduction of such a 'Brave New World' scenario was deliberate in order to paint a picture of what is possible. But even so I can imagine the kind of reaction you might have:

> This kind of organization seems more like a totalitarian state with everyone having to 'log on' and 'log off'.

> With all this time 'learning and developing' when does anybody get to do anything productive to earn the money to keep the company going?

The use of computer technology is entirely optional. It is just a convenient way of recording development as it happens. In Chapter 6 suggestions are made as to how it could have a dramatic impact on the way training and development is evaluated. But the use of personal 'learning logs' would do just as well; these could simply be notebooks which individuals use to record any learning and development in which they have been involved.

As to the second reaction – this reflects the company culture and mission statement and the extent to which it is prepared to change to adapt to a changing world. We have already explored this theme in Chapter 2 and we will return to it when we consider the nature of what constitutes a learning organization.

The scenario was necessarily extreme to reflect the need I feel for a radical re-evaluation of what is meant by terms like 'training', 'development', 'courses', 'learning' in the context of the organization. It is not by chance that this chapter follows hard on the heels of the previous chapter on 'Outcomes' because more than anything else the separation of 'outputs' or competences from the 'inputs' or resources needed to achieve them is making trainers and lecturers think again about just what 'a' training course *means*. The shift is away from the trainer as provider and sole determinator of what shape the course will take to the learner as being in sole charge of choosing what methods suit him/her best to achieve a particular outcome:

> The new education and training model places the learner at the centre of the system. The learner is regarded as the client and the model is designed to provide him or her with more control over the process of learning and assessment (p. 115).[2]

In particular, as the quote that opened this chapter testifies, learning is not limited to what happens on courses; as we shall see in the last chapter a learning organization is *not* necessarily one in which a lot of training goes on; it is one which consciously facilitates the learning of every member of staff in the way Jenkins Foods was seeking to do. In this chapter I want to provide you with a framework for examining the kinds of resources that are available in your organization to help achieve the types of competences we were exploring in the previous chapter.

Look again at Figure 4.1 which illustrates the kind of resources that might be found in any organization. It is true that not every organization will have or need a language laboratory, for example, but every organization employs people who are capable of giving demonstrations and feedback to their colleagues.But they are rarely aware they have these skills and even less are they encouraged to use them.

Every organization has a wealth of information stored away in umpteen reports, memoranda and manuals; but it is rarely valued as a learning resource which could be shared more widely. For example, when the MD calls for a report from the Production Manager it is likely that no one else except himself and possibly board members will see it. But there might be ideas, sources of information which if made available more widely could be of benefit to other departments, or individuals (supervisors doing a NEBSS course, for example). This is what is meant by the title of this chapter, 'The learning portfolio goes public'.

I believe that not only should the resources themselves be made more widely available, but that staff who are themselves following a programme of development should make their development process more public. Perhaps this is why one of the practices recommended for evaluation in the 'Investors in People' initiative is that 'training success and major achievements will be publicized as a matter of course – because they are seen as important'.[3]

The trick is to see *every* member of staff as a potential tutor to another, every scrap of information that is generated as a potential learning guide and every meeting as a training course. This is not by any means to lessen the impact of the official role of the trainer in this process but to recognize the *unique* skills he or she can bring to bear once an organization frees them from the classroom. In the new world of learning and development *anywhere* inside/outside the organization can become a potential classroom.

I first mulled over these notions more than ten years ago when I began to explore the nature of evaluation as applied to training programmes. What struck me was how evaluation techniques seemed to be applied to programmes as being somehow indivisible products in their own right,

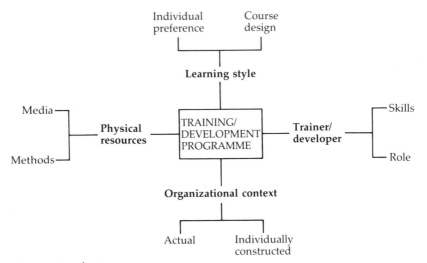

Figure 4.2 *The Learning Mix*

whereas it seemed to me a programme was simply a convenient way of labelling a very complex range of resources. I categorized these into four groups (see Figure 4.2) and called it the 'Training Mix'. Now I would prefer to call it the *Learning Mix*.

ACTIVITY 4.1
- *As we explore each of the four groups of resources below, consider to what extent they are present, identifiable and publicly acknowledged in your own organization.*

Learning style

In Chapter 2 we touched on the nature of learning. It is only comparatively recently that learning has been embraced by practitioners and as a result has ceased to be the monopoly of psychologists. A major influence on this transition has been the concept of 'experiential learning' which was promulgated by David Kolb[4] in the US in the late 1960s:

> It can be conceived of as a four stage cycle: (1) concrete experience is followed by (2) observation and reflection, which lead to (3) the formation of abstract concepts and generalizations, which lead to (4) hypotheses to be tested in future action, which in turn lead to new experiences.

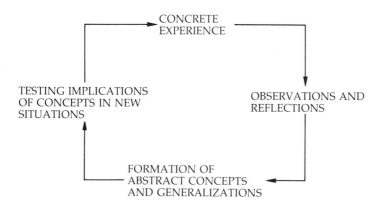

The argument was that in learning anything we all go through the same cycle. But some of us have a natural preference for one or more stages. Kolb went on to devise a test whereby by choosing one of four adjectives a person indicated the kind of preference they had. This could then have practical consequences as far as choosing, for example, one type of course rather than another which suited their particular style.

In the UK Honey and Mumford have built on what has become known as 'the Kolb Cycle' and developed a Learning Style Questionnaire comprising some 80 statements to which the learner has to give a tick or cross according to whether they agree with it or not (e.g. 'I tend to solve problems using a step-by-step approach'). As a result they identify four basic styles of learner according to the stage of their own four-stage cycle on which they place greater emphasis.[5]

Thus, what they call an 'Activist' would 'involve themselves fully and without bias in new experiences'. They would tend to place most emphasis on Stage 1. 'Reflectors' 'like to stand back to ponder and observe from many different perspectives'. They are more focused at Stage 2. 'Theorists' 'adapt and integrate observations into complex but logically sound theories'. They are operating at Stage 3. Finally, 'Pragmatists' 'are keen on trying out ideas, theories and techniques to see if they work in practice' (Stage 4).

So, what use is all this to you? Well, if you knew the learning style preference of each of your staff you could help them make the best use of

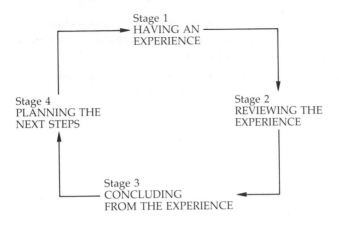

Stage 1
HAVING AN
EXPERIENCE

Stage 4
PLANNING THE
NEXT STEPS

Stage 2
REVIEWING THE
EXPERIENCE

Stage 3
CONCLUDING
FROM THE EXPERIENCE

different resources because different styles prefer different activities. Let's illustrate by reference back to the Jenkins Foods company.

If John were an 'activist' he would prefer to be involved in some kind of practical experience, e.g. role play or business game if learning took place on a course or perhaps having to cope with a challenging new project or secondment. If John were a 'reflector' he would prefer to have time to think things out for himself, perhaps having access to reports and books he could 'read up'. If John were a 'theorist' he would want to question what makes something tick; he would be happiest in the company of colleagues or tutors who would stretch him intellectually. If John were a 'Pragmatist' he would prefer being shown what to do by someone who could coach him and give him tips and techniques on how to apply it in his job.

Honey and Mumford have also produced a 'Learning Diagnostic Questionnaire' and supporting manual[6] which enables anyone to identify their own capabilities for learning from experiences and what learning opportunities they can draw on in their immediate environment. It is quite conceivable that our fictional company in the future would use such diagnostic techniques to enable people like John to identify his learning style and help him choose appropriate resources that match his style. The results, of course, would all be logged on to his learning portfolio disk.

So far we have considered the usefulness of 'learning style' in the Learning Mix model from an individual point of view only. But Kolb went on to characterize entire organizations and occupations according to what was the dominant learning style. I have used it to build teams. By becoming aware of each others' learning styles it is possible to put together a productive team representing all four styles who can support each other. Equally, learning style can underline the way a training programme is designed and delivered (though it will rarely be identified as such).

In the past, the 'course' has been such a uniform, static entity that participants would be unlikely to question the designers or the tutors on what underlying philosophy of learning it was based. But in the future I suggest that this is exactly what participants should do as well as be free to choose which 'parts' of the course to attend to maximize their own learning. In short, to do what John did at Jenkins Foods.

By separating 'output' from 'input' it allows us to pay much more attention to the appropriateness of the 'learning processes' chosen to achieve the given objectives. There is evidence of this approach in many of the elements of competence in the National Standards for Training and Development (as produced by the Training and Development Lead Body). For example:

B22   Design learning programmes which meet learning needs.
C22   Prepare and provide opportunities for individuals and groups to learn by collaboration.
C23   Prepare and provide opportunities for individuals and groups to manage their own learning.

There is also greater scope for using diagnostic techniques to generate evidence that trainers are really attempting to adapt their own style to meet the learning needs of their students. Tom Boydell has devised a diagnostic questionnaire to measure the extent to which a course was 'learner centred' or 'tutor centred.[8] Participants had to rate 48 statements describing a course they had attended. For example:

- The teaching-learning process involved the learner discovering things for himself [Scored high on learner-centred dimension]
- The course was based on a pre-planned content or syllabus [Scored high on tutor-centred dimension]

In evaluating courses in the past more emphasis has been placed on the outcome (which is right and proper), but the process of learning by which the outcome was achieved has received far less attention. But it has value in its own right and furthermore *adds* value to the course itself.

By the same token – as the National Training and Development Standards testify – the skills of the person/s providing the training have to embrace a wider repertoire to take into account the recognized differences between the way people learn. We therefore now look at the role of the trainer/developer.

4.2 The trainer/developer

Skills

The philosophy of Jenkins Foods was that everyone was a resource to everyone else but there were some staff designated as 'tutors' which meant they had developed particular skills to 'facilitate' the development of others.

It is interesting to note that the competences laid down for training and development have moved away from the traditional concept of the 'trainer' as instructor. While recognizing this is a key skill there is an emphasis on the trainer of the future being able to select and share appropriate resources to achieve specific purposes.

But this does not mean that basic instructional skills should be undervalued. On the contrary what it means is that they should be valued by more not less people. In fact there is a lot to be said for *every* member of staff acquiring basic instructional skills which would do much to take away the 'mystery' of the trainer and release innovative energy where it is needed in the workplace.

ACTIVITY 4.2
● *Look at the checklist of basic instructional skills in Figure 4.3 and identify which of your staff could meet these requirements in instructing another member of staff in a task of your choice.*

In Figure 4.3 the key words underlined are just some of the key skills which are likely to be covered in any course on one-to-one training or coaching. But by definition the style being adopted is prescriptive and 'tutor-centred'. In many circumstances this style would be very appropriate, for example in instruction in most skills and procedures where the learner first needs a demonstration of what has to be done and then step-by-step

---

1 **Getting learner's attention**
1.1 *Explain* clearly what has to be done
1.2 *Give reason* for completing task
1.2 Make task *interesting*

2 **Introducing task**
2.1 *Demonstrate* complete task
2.2 *Explain* what has to be done and why

3 **Breakdown of task**
3.1 Break down task *step-by-step* to suit task and learner's ability
3.2 *Check understanding* at each stage and *give feedback* as necessary
3.3 *Give positive feedback and encouragement* at each stage

4 **Consolidation**
4.1 *Summarize* at end and *check understanding*

5 **Check**
5.1 Get each trainee to *complete whole task* at end
5.2 *Give feedback* on how well learner has performed
5.3 Point out *faults* and give *coaching* as appropriate

Figure 4.3 *Checklist for good instructional practice*

instruction and feedback. On the other hand, there may be other resources available – open learning for example – which enable the learner to get some insight into the process by himself, which is then supplemented by tutor feedback. The Jenkins Foods scenario illustrated how right from the outset a new employee had to work out for himself – but with guidance – the best way to achieve particular objectives.

The skills listed in Figure 4.3 tend to apply to one-to-one instruction, e.g. a boss explaining to a subordinate the functioning of a particular machine. When it comes to a group undergoing training/development, a much wider repertoire of skills is needed on the part of the trainer/developer. All too often the concept of a course is a pre-determined programme using pre-determined resources without regard to the learners. But, as competence B22 of the National Training Standards confirms (see above), in the future trainers are going to be assessed as much on how they have adapted their training methods to meet the needs of the learner as on whether they have met the training objectives. Below is an extract of the kind of dialogue that should be going on in a tutor's mind as he or she is confronted by 'the present state' of a group of delegates and considers what approaches can be used to bring them up to 'the desired state':[9]

Present state	*Desired state*
Interest in topic generally low	To have discovered that topic is relevant to job
Some hostility towards trainers and course	Positively friendly towards trainers
Low energy, only willing to do minimum work to get by	Motivated to do further work after course

Internal debate: 'Tough! Going to have to work hard with this group. No good telling them how important topic is. Long formal inputs will be out. I need to create an exciting discovery process right at the beginning. Role play? No! Probably an inter-group task of some sort with an element of conflict built in ... I'll also need to do something about the hostility ... like join in the process rather than be highly directive.'

Do you or your trainers engage in this kind of debate? This requires skills that go beyond the basic face-to-face instructional kind illustrated in Figure 4.3. They relate more to the style of the trainer and developer of the 1990s as a 'facilitator' rather than a trainer. Below are six different kinds of 'behaviour' which John Heron identified[10] after working with doctors and therapists. They are equally valid descriptions of the kind of skills the developer as facilitator will need to *help* the learner achieve their objective or reflect on experience:

Nature of skill

Prescriptive	Gives advice to, recommends behaviour to the client
Informative	Gives new knowledge and information to, interprets behaviour to the client
Confronting	Challenges the restrictive attitudes, beliefs, behaviours of the client
Cathartic	Releases tensions in the client; elicits laughter, sobbing, trembling, storming
Catalytic	Elicits information and opinion from, self-directed problem-solving in, self-discovery in, the client
Supportive	Affirms the worth and value of, enhances the self-image of the client

So, the 'developer' of human potential of the future has got to have both kinds of skills, those of the instructor (listed in Figure 4.3) and those of the facilitator listed above. These skills, I suggest, are valuable in themselves once they have been *recognized* by both the provider (the developer) and the receiver (the learner). In the past they tend to have been subsumed under the general title of 'trainer', but once we break down what skills the trainer/ developer brings to their role we can better appreciate their value. But it is not an automatic process.

I once used the above six skills broken down into more specific behaviours as a checklist and asked members of a particular course after a given input from a tutor to tick which of the behaviours they were aware of and to what extent they were helpful. As the course proceeded they became aware of a greater number of skills and were able to value them accordingly.

It has always seemed to me that organizations employing training personnel full time undervalue such skills by assuming that the role of the trainer is to stand in front of a class and give out information. The kind of skills listed above could be as useful if not more so if deployed in the board room. Why is it that trainers have rarely had the opportunity to use their skills facilitating *anywhere* in an organization where these skills could be useful (i.e. not just in the lecture room); this could involve simply attending management meetings as an observer and using their skills to summarize, reflect on, draw out ideas at critical times during the meeting.

This issue takes us into the second dimension of a trainer/developer in Figure 4.2, that of his or her *role*.

The trainer/developer role

I once asked a group of training managers in a national brewery company to identify what role they considered they played in their organization by placing themselves on a scale that lay between two dimensions

Mainly an instructor _____	Mainly a change agent and consultant

I then asked them to identify on the scale the role that they thought they *ought* to be performing. Without exception they all considered that their company saw them as mainly instructors, whereas they saw the role of change agent as making the greatest contribution to their organization.

In 1978 the then Training Services Division (TSD) published its recommendations for *The Training of Trainers*. These recommendations included four 'role elements' which in one combination or another are present in any training manager or training officer type of post.

1 *Direct training element*: In this element the training specialist is involved in preparing for and carrying out direct tuition.
2 *Planning and organising element*: In this element training specialists carry out tasks to provide a framework for the training activities of an organization.
3 *Determining or management element*: This element is characterized by the exercise of effective structural power at a policy influencing level. It would normally involve an organization or division-wide control of training activities and close contact with operational and manpower issues and developments.
4 *Consulting and advisory element*: In it the training specialist provides an advisory and/or consultancy service to managers and others at any level. He or she achieves results through expertise and ability rather than through formal authority. The extent of competences required will vary considerably with the level and scope of the job.

Similar roles can be found within the three 'levels' of qualifications proposed by the National Training Standards.[7] The levels relate to NVQ levels 3, 4 and 5:

Level 3: Deliver training specified and designed by others, assess the outcomes of that training and, from identified learning needs, design training which facilitates learning and meets objectives at operational level.
Level 4: Design, deliver, manage delivery and evaluate training and development programmes and learning experiences to meet individual and organizational objectives.
Level 5:* Contribute to the formulation of strategic objectives and the identification of future capability requirements; design and implement HRD systems to meet these objectives and design and operate procedures for the evaluation of outcomes.

* At the time of going to press the TDLB has only developed standards approved at levels 3 and 4.

What the TSD called 'Direct Training' relates to NVQ level 3; while 'Planning and Organizing' and 'Determining or Managing' bear a close similarity to level 4. 'Consulting and Advising' correspond to some of the competences needed at level 5, which relate to a strategic role within the organization as a whole.

If the components for a more flexible approach to the role of the training instructor/officer were present in 1978, why is it that the recommendations of the TSD have had little impact on the way the role of the training officer is traditionally viewed in most organizations? Will the same fate befall the TDLB National Training Standards?

Both the TSD recommendations and the National Training Standards sought and seek to open up the role of the trainer, to make public the skills or she can have, needs to have, if they are to make a valuable contribution to the organization. But, up to now, organizations have chosen to view 'the trainer' as having a uniform kind of role and that is 'to deliver training' whether it is to craft trainees or senior management. The hope is – as we have explored in the previous chapter – that a competence approach to training (as to any other function in the organization) will reveal aspects of management in that role which can be released and have a direct value to the organization in their own right.

There is also another factor which may hopefully play a greater part in the 1990s than it has done hitherto – the recognition that training and development is not an isolated activity which only takes place in a course or lecture room. Remember the overriding purpose of training and development from which the National Training Standards were derived:

> To develop human potential to assist organizations and individuals to achieve their objectives.

If the organization of the future is to be a learning organization in order to survive, the 'trainers' and 'developers' will be the front line not the rearguard troops. To be successful they must have a pervasive influence which crosses boundaries and functions.

This was a powerful message that came out of a research study carried out in 1977 by Reason and Pettigrew.[12] They analysed the different roles performed by 39 training officers in the chemical industry and identified five types of role in terms of the kind of influence the respective training officer was perceived to have. Reason and Pettigrew identified the missing factor that made the difference between being effective and ineffective within the organization – 'boundary management'. Trainers, of course, need to have trainer skills, however

> Such training skills . . . have to cross many boundaries to be used and therein lies the problem for the training officer. Without awareness of and skills in the personal management of their role, including boundary management and influencing skills, many training officers

do find their role and their achievements more limited than they desire
(p. 27)[12]

It is interesting that most training officer and 'Train the Trainer' courses
pay more attention to the technical skills of the trainer than the social and
political skills necessary to embed those skills within the organizational
culture. Some of the National Training Standards go some way to
recognizing the kind of influential skills that are necessary to ensure training
skills are translated into the best value for the organization:

A111   Agree and obtain support for the contribution of training and
          development to organizational strategy.
B114   Negotiate and agree allocation of resources.
C111, 112 Obtain and allocate resources to meet the requirements of
          training and development plans.

Reason and Pettigrew concluded that the key factor in determining the
effectiveness of a Training officer was the way he or she managed the
interface between their role and their local organizational context. The
organizational context is the last component of the Learning Mix we explore,
but before we do so we need to consider the various physical resources, the
methods and media that the trainer/developer (or anyone else for that
matter) can use in that context.

4.3 Methods and media

A key theme underlying this chapter has been the importance of divorcing
'outcome' from 'input' in such a way that learning resources within an
organization can be released; in so doing, I suggest, we are better able to
assign a value to individual components of what I have called the Learning
Mix (see Figure 4.2). So far we have examined the importance of 'learning
style' (both for the learner and the designer of learning events). So often in
the past little attention has been paid to the way people learn and courses
have been designed on the assumption that everybody learns in the same
way. Then, in the previous section, we examined the role of the 'trainer/
developer' in an organization and the increased value such a person could
have to the organization if his or her key skills were appreciated and put to
use outside as well as inside the classroom. In this section we examine the
methods and media the trainer/developer might use to assist him or her in
achieving their objectives. In doing so we pose the same question: What is
the intrinsic value of these media and methods separated out from the prime
user (i.e. the trainer) and the context of the classroom?

The kind of media and equipment available to the trainer in the classroom
has changed dramatically over the past 30 years. This has been illustrated

already in Chapter 3 (p. 49) in considering how the 'range statement' might need to be updated in relation to the equipment a trainer needs to be competent to use. Thus in the 1950s the main medium was 'talk and chalk'. Then in the 1960s the trainer would have had additional access to 'flip charts' and maybe 16 mm projectors. In the 1970s the OHP (overhead projector) would have transformed the trainer's life. In the 1980s white boards and video recording and playback systems arrived to help augment 'talk and chalk'.

In the 1990s and beyond media are likely to be dominated by computer-mediated systems applied to other systems, for example video (interactive video) and communications (electronic mail); the use of computer based training (CBT) is also likely to become more commonplace. The other revolution will be in the use of satellite TV for the purposes of tele conferencing: groups of people throughout the world can thus be linked up for the purposes of hearing the same presentation, for example, and then have opportunity to discuss and give feedback to each other.

Before we become overawed by the sheer scale of technological possibilities, we need to be clear as to exactly *how* a particular medium or piece of equipment can help us achieve a particular objective. In other words, we need to assess its potential value. A methodology for carrying out such an analysis was devised by Oatey in the 1970s as part of his PhD thesis on the cost effectiveness of different media of instruction. Oatey makes a distinction between 'media' and what he calls 'method factors'.

> Media are the physical sources of stimuli presented to the learners, which include the instructor as well as videotape, film, paper and the blackboard etc.[13]

On the other hand, method factors

> are concerned with the nature and timing of stimuli presented to learners and the nature and timing of learner responses and activities (p. 55).[14]

Examples of method factors would include visual motion, aural responses, multiple-choice responses etc. Method factors are

> defined by the organization of stimuli (presented by media) and learner responses. Method factors are operational, media independent, instructional variables (p. 73).[14]

For Oatey 'methods not media determine instructional effectiveness' (p. 57).[14] Thus, if the requirement was for the instructor to present something visual but motion was not needed – OHP transparencies might suffice; if visual definition was critical he or she would probably need 35 mm slides. Video would only be warranted where visual motion was required. In the context of the technology available today if the instructor required visual motion and constructed responses, interactive video might be indicated.

The benefit of such an approach again lies in the fact that it *separates out* the key criteria on which value of media is based and makes them *explicit* so that anyone can use them and make informed judgements. When Oatey devised this methodology he mainly saw its use for practising instructors. But it also puts in the hands of every learner a framework within which to make decisions about the kind of media that are most appropriate to them. Thus in the Jenkins Foods scenario John was able to choose the most appropriate media for him. This would partly be determined by his learning style.

I once tried to match up individuals' learning styles with the kind of media they might prefer. In addition to finding out what tutor styles a particular group found valuable, I also sought to know which media used by the tutor (e.g. slides, video, practical exercises) they found most useful. The hypothesis was that individuals who tended to be more reflective and liked to review data would prefer visual media (films, models). Those who wanted evidence would prefer access to facts and figures, case studies, while the 'activists' would recognize the practical exercises. There was some evidence for these kinds of choice.

My argument was that if one could help individuals recognize elements in the course programme that were particularly valuable to them one could extend the process and suggest how they could continue to use these resources outside the classroom. This has been a theme that has been close to my heart for the past 25 years. I remember as a training development officer in BEA in the early 1970s discussing with colleagues the viability of disposing with the traditional syllabus of courses and making available a 24 hour 'learning resources' room which would contain self-instructional aids, films, books and would be manned by tutors on a shift basis. The idea was to shift the focus from the trainer and the media that were tutor-directed and make media freely available together with a tutor who would guide the learner through material appropriate to his or her individual needs. This seemed a pipe dream in 1970; 20 years on it has become very much a reality in many organizations. The reason for the change has been the impact of so-called *Open Learning*.

The most popular definition that still characterizes Open Learning is that it is a process whereby a student:

Learns *what* he/she wants
Learns *when* he/she wants
Learns *where* he/she wants
Learns *how* he/she wants
Learns *at the pace* he/she wants

In other words, the learner, rather than the tutor or trainer, *chooses* what and how they will learn independent of *place* (e.g. course or campus) and *time* (e.g. only in academic term time or between 0900 and 1700). The concept has been around for some time. In 1969 Carl Rogers published *Freedom to Learn* in which he put forward the basic philosophy which in 1952 he had first articulated to an astonished group of educationalists. The role of the teacher, he maintained, was the 'facilitation of learning rather than the function of teaching'; under such circumstances

> he organizes his time and efforts very differently than the conventional teacher. Instead of spending great blocks of time organizing lesson plans and lectures, he concentrates on providing all kinds of resources which will give his students experiential learning relevant to their needs (p. 131).[15]

Thus were the principles of Open Learning established. In fact Britain leads the world in the preparation and pioneering of Open Learning techniques. It started in 1971 with the Open University (OU) and the view that higher education should be open to all. Using a combination of very attractive and highly professionally produced text material and TV and offering tutor support, the OU put Open Learning on the map. In addition, 'correspondence' type courses had always been used mainly by students 'cramming up' to take a particular exam. These provided 'distance learning materials' (i.e. materials that could be worked through independent of a central location) and a tutor who marked assignments sent in by the learner and returned them with feedback.

But it was not until 1983 when the Government launched Open Tech that Open Learning really got under way. The main motive behind this move was the perennial concern about skill shortages in industry and the need to improve knowledge and level of qualifications in industry. The proposal was that in addition to the traditional route of providing access to colleges and further education, government would pump prime industry to produce 'Open learning' material in all areas to help staff develop new skills and get professional accreditation. The programme lasted three years as a result of which hundreds of 'packages' were produced providing hundreds of thousands of student 'learning hours'.

But it should be remembered that Open Learning is not only for delivering 'knowledge', with which it tends to be traditionally associated. The media can deliver – if the method factors are appropriate – a variety of experiences. Students

> can gain access to first hand accounts, which can be far more compelling than a tutor's second hand account. For example, one of the most effective teaching items I have observed in use is a tape-recording of one woman's problems – and her emotional reactions – arising from caring for her elderly mother suffering from senile dementia. No class teacher's description could have the impact of this harrowing story as told by the person who experienced it (p. 41).[16]

In this case media such as audiotape had intrinsic properties which could change attitudes as well as give information:

It was not only that it was a first-hand account, but the spoken word had the ability to communicate feelings and emotions and gain sympathy and a sense of what the world looked like through one woman's eyes. (p. 42)[16]

Imaginative use of such media and an understanding of which method factors are critical (in the above case it is 'direct reporting of actual experience') opens up the use of all kinds of resources within the scope of any organization. Audio tape is a case in point. Without going to the cost of video (though the price of Camcorders is now very competitive) one can use audio to present a wide range of experiences. Supported by text it provides, in my opinion, the most cost effective and versatile of all instructional media.

Having been involved in the design of a number of Open Learning schemes I would suggest there are three key 'method factors' which Open Learning can make available and which can be delivered through a variety of media:

1 *Questions* which require student to respond to text or experience; in other words requires some kind of *response*.
2 *Examples* which illustrate the kind of response required.
3 *Feedback* which allows learner to compare his or her response with that of the programme.

It is in the last area, feedback, where the early packages produced under the government's Open Tech scheme were subject to most criticism. Initially Open Tech wanted material that was as far as possible self-contained, requiring no additional support. Very soon it was realized that Open Learning was not simply a function of well-written and well-presented material, it required a network of support and tutors who were available to give 'verbal assurance'. The key role of the 'tutor' as medium was not as instructor but guide and facilitator. We are much clearer about these issues now compared to the early days of the 1980s.

One model of Open Learning that has helped widen people's perception of the concept and hence its value in applicability across the organizational spectrum is that drawn up by Roger Lewis. Rather than a given product which is or is not representative of 'Open' Learning, Lewis introduces the 'Open–Closed' continuum which can be applied to any form of education or training. In this context we move from 'Open' to 'Openness' to learning. Figure 4.4 summarizes some of the questions he proposed (pp. 5–6)[17] to ask of your own systems of making learning resources available to your staff.

ACTIVITY 4.3
● *Take some time out to apply this framework to how training and development are organized in your own organization.*

Basic question	Aspects	
	Closed ——————————————————————— Open	
Who?	Scheme open to select groups only	Scheme open to all
Why?	Choice made by others, e.g. tutor, employer	Learner choice
What?	Entire syllabus set out in advance, e.g. by validating body; no choice possible within it	Learner formulates own objectives and syllabus
How?	Only one method/style provided for; little variation in learner activity	Choice of learning methods/ styles; varied activities
Where?	One place only (e.g. at work)	Learner chooses place (e.g. home, work, on train)
When?	Fixed starting date(s)	Start any time
How is learner doing?	Externally mixed method of assessment e.g. formal exam	Variety of assessment methods; learner choice of assessment methods; learner constructs method of assessment
Who can help learner?	No support outside course/ package	Variety of possible kinds of support (e.g. advice, guidance, counselling)
Where does it lead?	One destination	Various possible destinations

Figure 4.4 *The Open Learning continuum. (Based on the table which appears on pages 5–6 of* Open Learning for Adults. *Reproduced with kind permission of Longman Group UK)*

On the criteria in Figure 4.4 the Open University would not score marks on every dimension of the open scale. It will take a different kind of organization to fulfil all these requirements. If you apply the scale to the Jenkins Foods scenario it comes close to being totally open but this is because the environment and context within which learning takes place recognizes the kind of needs that require to be met. It is the *context* in which the media are used which gives added meaning and value to the use of the media and resources themselves. This is a lesson which still has not been learned.

In her book *In the Age of the Smart Machine*[18] Shoshana Zuboff examines the effect of introducing computers into a number of companies in the US. She analyses in depth what it is about what is presented through the medium of computers that can have such a dramatic effect on working relationships and above all on the potential power of the workers: the key power is *knowledge*, which is suddenly made available to workers who have what she calls 'the intellective skills' to recognize and use it.

> Knowledge freed from the temporal physical constraints of action . . . can be appropriated and carried beyond the moment (p. 180)

> When meaning is uncoupled from its action context and carried away in symbols, a new playfulness becomes possible. Events and the relationships among events can be illuminated and combined in new ways (p. 181).[18]

She vividly describes how workers faced with data unconnected with their immediate context strive to make sense of it, to give it meaning, in short to learn. But, this poses a threat to managers who introduced the computers simply to automate procedures. They had not bargained for the fact that workers would try to figure out what all this information meant! We will return to this theme and to Zuboff's research later on.

I see a parallel here in the way Open Learning has been introduced into many companies. The motive has often been to introduce a more cost effective method of instruction (which is a valid reason) but management had not taken account of the needs of employees to make sense of all this new found knowledge which went beyond the boundaries of a particular package. This required a greater awareness of the *context* in which the learning had not only to be delivered but also supported. This is the subject of our final section.

4.4 The organizational context

In reviewing the literature on evaluation of training in the late 1970s, I was struck by the amount of time taken up with the traditional problem of 'transfer' of learning from a course to the reality of the work-based organization. Researchers were searching for the definitive organizational variables that either helped, or impeded learning transfer.

It would have been surprising if such variables as 'job autonomy', 'relations with subordinates', 'relevance of training to job' were not found to be influential.[19] It seemed to me that by creating a separate black box and labelling it 'course' and separating it out from any supporting environment the problem of 'transfer' was largely a problem of trainers' and evaluators' own making.

Once we cease to regard a 'course' or programme of training as having a fixed boundary, we enable it to utilize directly the rich vein of resources to be found in any organization and indeed outside. Even in the late 1970s there were some commentators who recognized the worth of the informal resources, the value of which organizations rarely acknowledged. Bell, for example, describes how a large manufacturing company realized the value of the restaurant over the road as being the place where all levels of staff discussed and communicated with each other, so much so that

> When the lounge went out of business ... it resulted in such a breakdown in interunit communication amongst managers that the company seriously considered underwriting the reopening of the business.[20]

This syndrome will be familiar to any trainer who appreciates that the most significant learning on a course takes place not in the classroom but in the bar! Or indeed anywhere where people feel relaxed enough to share significant thoughts, feelings with each other. I once ran a training session for managers in a training room half of which had the traditional U-shape table, OHP and screen at the end and in the other half of which were three very large sofas – enough to accommodate all the course delegates. For most of the course we found ourselves sitting on these sofas informally sharing experiences which a member of the group might write up on a portable flip chart. The quality of the experiences shared on these sofas was far superior to the feedback that took place in the more formal half of the room.

Bell comes to the following conclusion:

> The increasing complexity of work in Western society requires new ways of meeting the ever changing learning needs of employees. The popularity of commuter train courses, universities without walls, external degree programmes, college courses in newspapers and on home television, indicates that our society is finding novel methods for delivering needed growth to the populace. Organizations can maximize the moment at minimal cost by fostering a learning society within their walls.[20]

About the same time Knowles came to a similar conclusion in an article entitled 'Gearing up for the eighties':

> We may be coming to the realization that the quality of human growth and development that takes place in a corporation or agency is a function of the educative value of the total environment of the workplace. If this is so then the role of the training specialists will become essentially one of environmental engineering.[21]

This theme is one which we will come back to in the final chapter but to put it into its historical perspective it is one which did, in fact, become increasingly popular (at least in concept if not in practice) during the 1980s as the idea of first the 'learning community' and then the 'learning organization' became established. Pedler[22] conceived the 'learning community' as resting on two major principles:

1 That each individual takes prime responsibility for identifying and meeting their own learning needs.
2 That each person is responsible for helping others identify their needs and for offering themselves as a flexible resource in the community.

It seems an eminently desirable goal at which to aim. The first goal is becoming increasingly more viable – aided by the kinds of development we have been discussing in the previous two chapters. The second goal will take much longer, requiring a radical shift in thinking about what organizations are about and above all in how they need to be managed (see Chapter 6).

What we are trying to provide in this chapter is a framework within which existing organizations can review the kind of resources they can make available *now*; this does not need a radical review at this stage, simply a recognition of potential value in the resources available and then *communication* of just what these resources are. What I have described so far are the kind of 'natural' resources *any* organization – with or without a training department – can preview. Figure 4.1 describes some of these resources. In *Informal and Incidental Learning in the Workplace*,[23] Marsick and Watkins describe a range of ways in which trainers and managers can help staff get the most out of the resources available.

But it is undeniably true that at the end of the day the organizational context within which learning will be realized will be as much a *construction* of the learner as it is fixed by the kind of resources illustrated in Figure 4.1. The core of the argument is that as life becomes more uncertain and the data that we have to process less structured, there is a need to impose our own structure, our own reality, in short to *create* our own learning environment. Zuboff describes this as an 'informating process':

> The informating process takes learning as its pivotal experience. Its objective is to achieve the value that can be added from learning in the situation. Informating assumes that making the organization more transparent will evoke valuable communal insight. From this perspective learning is never complete, as new data, new events or new contexts create opportunities for additional insight, improvement and innovation (p. 305).[18]

If an organization *recognizes* the power of such processes it can use them effectively to *re*-create the organization. Eden et al.[24] advocate use of computer-mediated systems for generating data whereby individuals can 'reflect on' decisions that could have a potential impact on the organization. Rather than seeing learning as 'organization centred', they saw an effective organization in terms of a negotiated reality as it can be produced by individual members of the organization; and thus seeing person-centred learning as the essential ingredient for continuous negotiation between different realities (p. 6).[24]

Peter Senge draws on a similar theme with what he calls 'microworlds' describing them as the 'technology of the learning organization'.[25]

To what extent do your tutors, your facilitators help make 'the organization more transparent' by using resources, technology to reveal its nature to your staff? Or are they so busy running scheduled courses they haven't got the time?

ACTIVITY 4.4
- *Try this experiment: Identify two members of staff who have management potential. Each should have a very basic appreciation of finance. Arrange for one to attend a typical 'Finance for the Non-Financial Manager' course while the other is encouraged to develop such skills for himself/herself using such resources as:*

  Management accountant
  Access to reports and accounts
  Tutor skills as defined above

  Arrange to give each the same test at the end. Compare which one is not just best able to handle the technical side but more importantly the social and authority levels. Also compare whether you haven't got an improved accounting system into the bargain.

In the age of the 'learning organization' learning not only reinforces the existing system but *transforms* it because each member of staff is not just a passive recipient of knowledge but should be challenging organizational resources as part of the process:

> Whereas the student within an educational institution has lecture notes, text books and a library to form the core of learning resources, the independent learner within an organization must develop his own information and references and negotiate with other persons for them also to develop and disseminate information that he requires (p. 86).[26]

Honey and Mumford[5] and Marsick and Watkins[23] provide guidance to help 'opportunist learners' (as Honey and Mumford call them) derive maximum learning *from* the organization. But to become a learning *organization*, the organization has got to be directly affected by this process. Unlike a course, it is not happening in a vacuum. This is discussed in detail in the final chapter.

4.5 Conclusion

There have been two underlying themes in this chapter:

1 In order for an organization to value its learning resources, it must first break them down and value their intrinsic worth as well as their unique value when combined together in various combinations. We have looked at a Learning Mix comprising four kinds of resources which an organization often takes for granted:

   - Learning style (of individuals and the effect on course design).
   - The range of skills and roles trainers/developers can make available to an organization (not necessarily in the classroom).
   - Media and methods that abound in the organization and extent to which an organization makes these available in a closed/open way.
   - Recognizing the importance of the organizational context within which learning takes place and how individuals can create their own learning environment.
2 The second theme relates to what Zuboff calls 'visibility' when applied to knowledge and learning. The more it becomes explicit the more it can be used and so influence the organization itself, generating further resources.

I suggest that the discovery and release of resources for learning in the organization produces the same shock to the corporate system as Zuboff found from the 'informating' consequences of information technology. Knowledge can no longer be packaged separately whether it is in an Open Learning package or in a course. It is available and visible for all to use.

This has enormous consequences for the organization structure and, most significantly, for the way this is managed, as we shall see in the next chapter.

References

1 Durrell, J. (1991) Learning Resource Centres. In *Self-Development in Organizations* (ed. Mike Pedler, John Burgoyne, Tom Boydell and Gloria Welshman), McGraw Hill
2 Jessup, G. (1991) *Outcomes: NVQs and the Emerging Model of Education and Training*, Falmer Press
3 Employment Departments (1991) How will we gain recognition? Brochure 5 in *Investors in People – The Route*, Employment Department, Moorfoot, Sheffield
4 Kolb, D. A. and Fry, R. (1975) Toward an applied theory of experiential learning. In *Theories of Group Processes*. (ed. C. Cooper), Wiley

5 Honey, P. and Mumford, A. (1992) *The Manual of Learning Styles*, Honey, Maidenhead
6 Honey, P. and Mumford, A. (1989) *The Manual of Learning Opportunities*, Honey, Maidenhead
7 Training and Development Lead Body (1992) *National Standards for Training and Development*, Employment Department, Moorfoot, Sheffield
8 Boydell, T. (1976) *Experiential Learning*, Manchester Monograph 5, University of Manchester
9 Binstead, D. (1978) A framework for the design of Management Learning Events. *Journal of European and Industrial Training*, **2**(5), 25–28
10 Heron, J. (1977) *Behaviour Analysis in Education and Training*, University of Surrey
11 Training Services Division (1978) *Training of Trainers*, Training Services Division, Sheffield
12 Pettigrew, A. M. and Reason, P. (1977) Alternative interpretations of the Training Officer role: A research study in the chemical industry. Research report from the Chemical and Pharmaceutical ITB
13 Oatey, M. (1972) Effectiveness and costs of instructional media. Research report for Air Transport and Travel ITB
14 Oatey, M. (1976) Cost effectiveness of different media of instruction with special reference to Industrial Training. Unpublished PhD thesis, London School of Economics.
15 Rogers, C. (1969) *Freedom to Learn*, CE Merrill
16 Rogers, W. S. (1987) Adapting materials for alternative use. In *Open Learning for Adults* (eds Mary Thorpe and David Grugeon), Longman
17 Thorpe, M. and Grugeon, D. (1987) Moving into Open Learning. In *Open Learning for Adults* (eds Mary Thorpe and David Grugeon), Longman
18 Zuboff, S. (1988) *In the Age of the Smart Machine*, Heinemann
19 Vandenput, M. A. E. (1973) The transfer of training: some organizational variables. *Journal of European Training*, **2**(3), 251–262
20 Bell, C. R. (1977) Informal learning in organisations. *Personnel Journal*, June, 280–313
21 Knowles, M. (1978) Gearing up for the eighties. *Training and Development Journal*, July, 12–14
22 Pedler, M. J. (1981) Developing the learning community. In *Management Self-development* (eds T. Boydell and M. Pedler) Gower
23 Marsick, V. J. and Watkins, K. E. (1990) *Informal and Incidental Learning in the Workplace*, Routledge
24 Eden, C., Jones, S. and Dims, D. (1979) *Thinking in Organizations*, Macmillan
25 Senge, P. (1990) *The Fifth Discipline: The Art and Practice of the Learning Organization*, Doubleday
26 Walker, R. (1976) Independent learning in relation to organization development. Unpublished MEd thesis, University of Aberystwyth

5 Management growth for all

The traditional system of imperative control, which was designed to maximize the relationship between commands and obedience, depended upon restricted hierarchical access to knowledge and nurtured the belief that those who were excluded from the organization's explicit knowledge base were intrinsically less capable of learning what it had to offer. In contrast, an informated organization is structured to promote the possibility of useful learning among all members and thus presupposes relations of equality (p. 394).

This does not imply that differentials of knowledge, responsibility, and power no longer exist; rather, they can no longer be assumed. Instead, they shift and flow and develop their character in relation to the situation, the task, and the actors at hand. Managing intricacy calls for a new level of action-centred skill, as dialogue and inquiry place a high premium on the intuitive and imaginative sources of understanding that temper and hone the talents related to *acting-with*. The dictates of a learning environment, rather than those of imperative control, now shape the development of such interpersonal know-how (p. 402).[1]

We begin this chapter where we left off in the previous one, with Zuboff's vision of the role of management in the informated organizations of the future. The two extracts above contrast very well the old and the new. At the beginning of Chapter 4 we explored my own attempt to describe the 'learning organization' of the future in which a new employee is offered not a job description and a copy of the organization chart, but is given a map to help him navigate his way through a series of learning opportunities. Where everyone is managing themselves in this way, what should be the role of 'the' manager and how can it be developed?

This is the question this chapter seeks to answer in the light of current developments and initiatives. Most notable of these initiatives is the Management Charter Initiative (MCI) which was the speedy response to two reports published in 1987 critical of Britain's inability to train and develop its managers. Constable and McCormick in *The Making of British Managers*[2] argued for a basic Diploma which all aspiring managers should take. Charles Handy in *The Making of Managers*[3] compared practice in the United States, France and West Germany and also advocated the introduction of a two-part Management Qualification for 'a new breed of young managers ... who would be both business literate and have behind them a formal period of planned self development in their early years'. He also recommended the establishment of a Development Charter to which companies would subscribe.

Just one year after these reports were published, the Management Charter Initiative (MCI) was started under the auspices of the then Council for Management Education and Development (CMED) which published a Charter of ten criteria of good practice to which companies were encouraged to subscribe. These are reproduced in Figure 5.1.

---

1 To improve leadership and management skills throughout the organization
2 To encourage and support our managers in continuously developing management skills and leadership qualities in themselves and in those with whom they work
3 To back this by providing a coherent framework for self-development – within the context of our corporate goals – which is understood by those concerned and in which they plan an active part
4 To ensure that the development of managerial expertise is a continuous process and will be integrated with the work flow of the organization
5 To provide ready access to the relevant learning and development opportunities – internal and external – with requisite support and time released appropriate to our organization
6 To encourage and help managers to acquire recognized qualifications relevant both to their personal development and to our corporate goals
7 To participate actively in the appropriate networks of the Management Charter Initiative and thereby share information, ideas, experience, expertise and resources that will prove mutually beneficial to the participants and help us to further the aims of this code
8 Directly and through networks, to strengthen our links with sources of management education to ensure that the training offered best complements our management development programmes, matching our corporate needs and future requirements
9 To contribute to closer links with local educational establishments to promote a clear understanding of the role of management, its challenge as a career and the excellent opportunities for young people to develop professionalism in its practice
10 To appoint a Director or equivalent to oversee the fulfilment of these undertakings; to review our progress annually and, after evaluating the contribution to our performance, set new targets for both individuals and the organization; and to publicize highlights from the review and the new targets

---

Figure 5.1 *The Management Charter – a code of practice*

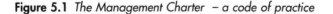

ACTIVITY 5.1
● *How far does your organization match up to the criteria in Figure 5.1? If you would like to know more about activities and the network of MCI in your area you can contact the MCI at Russell Square House, 10–12 Russell Square, London WC1B 5BZ, Telephone 071 872 9000*

In addition to setting up the Charter, initiatives were put in motion to introduce the kind of standard management qualification both reports were advocating. What was the CMED has now become the National Forum for Management Education and Development which has become the Industry Lead Body for developing management and supervision standards within the competence framework we discussed in Chapter 3. Later on in this chapter we will examine the framework that has been designed to assess management competence and the arguments for and against.

In just four years there has been an unprecedented drive to 'systematize' the way managers are trained and developed at the same time as management gurus like Ros Moss Kanter and Tom Peters have been drawing our attention to the need for organizations to free themselves from management hierarchies. If managers have not got a clear role in a management hierarchy, how can they manage? (I should also make it clear from the outset that I have not differentiated out 'supervisors' for special attention. The reader should read 'manager' as covering all roles involving responsibility for achieving results through others which, clearly, includes roles designated by the title 'supervisor'.)

In trying to answer these kinds of questions we begin by looking at just what *is* management and at significant theories of management that have had an influence during this century. We then look at trends over the past 15 years in management development. Then we explore the current preoccupation with competences and finally look at current trends and draw a scenario of the organization of the future and just how managers might operate and be developed.

5.1 The manager and management

Garratt[4] traces the origin of 'manager' to the sixteenth century Italian word *maneggiore* which meant the 'breaking in of horses'! He then moves to France in the eighteenth century when the word *ménager* came closer to our concept of 'manager'; it meant 'good housekeeping', in particular good housekeeping in respect of the domestic running of the kitchen. (This should give comfort to countless numbers who have always believed that managing the affairs of a household was every bit as demanding and responsible a job as their partner's! In fact, they may now be able to get accreditation for these 'household' management competences.)

A definition of 'manager' which has stuck, attributed to Mary Parker Follet, is the 'art of getting things done through other people'. The use of the word 'art' is an interesting one – as we shall see later. But it is more as a science than an art that management has been studied since the early part of this century, when Henri Fayol and Frederick Taylor laid the foundations for a systematic and scientific analysis of the management function.

Fayol[5] concluded that a manager is responsible for eight basic functions, regardless of the nature or size of the organization:

1 Determining and deciding objectives
2 Forecasting
3 Planning
4 Organizing
5 Directing
6 Co-ordinating
7 Controlling
8 Communicating

He depicted these functions as a wheel with 'communicating' at the hub. By and large these functions are still at the core of most management training programmes and are taught in the context of the traditional divisions of an organization into its marketing, financial, production and personnel departments.

The 'dividing up' of management into discrete areas of control was the basic principle of 'scientific management' which Frederick Taylor introduced in 1911.[6] Underlying the principles he outlined was a basic philosophy which it is important to understand because it still influences attitudes towards management. Taylor believed that there were those people who 'managed' and then there were the rest who 'worked' for managers. *But* he did believe that both managers and workers wanted the same thing, economic reward. The only way to secure that reward, he argued, was to organize a company's affairs around a strict *control* of functions – which was the manager's responsibility – in order that the worker could perform his or her tasks more efficiently. *Efficiency* drove his approach to work and the worker, whose main reward in life was 'a fair day's pay for a fair day's work'.

There were five principles that directed his approach to management:

1 Shift all responsibility for the organization of work from the worker to the manager.
2 Use scientific methods to determine the most efficient way of doing work.
3 Select the best person to perform the job thus designed.
4 Train the worker to do the job efficiently.
5 Monitor worker performance against laid down procedures.

With the exception of the first principle, the others remain a model of good management practice today. But ironically it was the very division of 'management' from 'worker' that prevented an organization really getting the value from the workforce it was painstakingly organizing and training – which in many organizations is the case today.

The significance of the 'worker's' own motivation (beyond seeking economic reward) and the essentially social nature of work came to light in the 1940s and 1950s following the research of Elton Mayo and his colleagues at Western Electric's Hawthorne Plant near Chicago.[7] The results came to be known as the 'Hawthorne' effect and led to what has become known as the 'Human Relations' School of Management. Significant contributions were to be made in this school by people like McGregor,[8] Maslow[9] and Herzberg.[10]

The Taylor approach and the Human Relations School of Management have become the opposite poles of a management continuum that favours either 'the task' or 'people'. Blake and Mouton[11] used these principles to develop a Managerial Grid which enables managers to position themselves on two scales 1–9 according to how far along the respective scale they rate their concern for people and/or production. Thus a 9.1 style is highly task-orientated with little concern for people. A 9.9 style is that of the 'team manager' who has an equal concern for the task and for his employees.

These were the kinds of theories about management that predominated in the 1960s and 1970s. Unfortunately they tend to be seen only as theories and not what Schon calls 'knowledge-in-action',[12] i.e. they are not born out of practical experience. They have their place in the management programme (usually under the subject of 'Organizational Behaviour') but have not made a radical difference to the way management is practised.

One other management commentator who had a major influence during the same period was Peter Drucker, who, in 1954[13] emphasized that success in business was not determined by production but by the consumer. Though it is now fashionable to place emphasis on the customer, hitherto it had been largely Taylor's principles of efficiency that had driven business. Drucker it was who stressed 'effectiveness', i.e. not just doing things right but doing the right things. He also introduced what became known as 'Management by Objectives'. The emphasis was on results which the manager had a responsibility to deliver not only for the business but, Drucker argued, for society of which 'business is the wealth-creating and wealth-producing organ'.

Drucker's message was that 'Management was not an end in itself' – it has continually to justify its existence through results in the market place. But his message had to wait until Peters exhorted American companies to look at themselves from the customer's point of view in the 1980s. There was a significantly new approach to management in the 1970s, however, which started with Henry Mintzberg[14] challenging the popular notion that what managers did was plan, control, direct etc. He observed the behaviour of five executives over the period of a week to find out how they spent their time. The data he collected were supplemented by studies of managers in the United States and abroad. He discovered that all the managers' activities could be divided into three main *roles* which could be further subdivided into ten sub-roles. These are summarized in Figure 5.2, together with

Interpersonal role

1 Figurehead: these are classed as 'ceremonial' duties, like taking a client to lunch, attending social functions of employees
2 Leader: where manager directly or indirectly influences employees' views, motivates them, directs them
3 Liaison: where manager builds and maintains a network of contacts both within and outside his department

Informational role

4 Monitor: where manager collects and processes information received from contacts and employees
5 Disseminator: where manager passes on information to subordinates and colleagues
6 Spokesman: where manager informs and influences people outside his unit

Decision role

7 Entrepreneur: where manager looks for ways of improving his business and his employees' performance in the light of external/internal changes
8 Disturbance handler: where manager reacts to pressures and unexpected events
9 Resource allocator: how manager allocates resources like staff, money and his own time and decides between one project and another
10 Negotiator: how manager uses his position, resources to negotiate with and influence boss, subordinates and colleagues

Figure 5.2 *The manager's roles*

examples. Regardless of whether you would agree that a manager should spend his or her time in this way, what Mintzberg's study did was to provide a framework within which managers could inspect and review their own performance. This was something that the various 'theories' of management had never done.

The 1970s threw up a number of such approaches which looked at what effective managers actually *did* based on research with practising managers. One such study led Rosemary Stewart to propose a model of management based on interpersonal activities.[15] She found that managers have a degree of *choice* in their jobs which enables them to chart a path between the *demands* of the job (the accountabilities for which they are held responsible) and the *constraints* (resources, organizational culture, attitudes) which limit what they can do. Again it provides a framework within which an individual manager can assess his or her position and maybe identify factors of which they were unaware which could be *managed* differently. Managers might then realize they have more choice than they imagined.

Another research study led to an influential book on management development, *A Manager's Guide to Self-Development*, which we shall return to in the next section. Burgoyne and Stuart identified a number of qualities which they found were possessed by successful managers and not by unsuccessful managers.[16] They finally define 11 qualities[17] which they divide into three groups. These are listed in Figure 5.3.

Basic knowledge and information

1 Command of basic facts
2 Relevant professional understanding

Skills and attributes

3 Continuing sensitivity to events
4 Analytical, problem solving, decision/judgement making skills
5 Social skills and abilities
6 Emotional resilience
7 Proactivity – inclination to respond purposefully to events

Meta qualities

8 Creativity
9 Mental agility
10 Balanced learning habits and skills
11 Self-knowledge

Figure 5.3 *Qualities of a successful manager*

Contrast this list and Mintzberg's ten roles with the functional analysis of management that has been central to much of this country's management education in the past. Increasingly there is a shift of emphasis from content to process. This is reflected, as we shall see when we look at the MCI's work on competences, in the recognition that all managers at whatever level require to develop 'personal' competence.

In the same way as we have argued that separating 'outcomes' from specific training or educational inputs has freed the trainer to use a wider repertoire of skills and methods (see Chapter 4), the making 'explicit' of management skills opens up the whole area of management development in two important respects:

● First, it makes them available to all. They are no longer buried within exclusive courses for senior managers that take place in special centres.
● Second, if we can specify the kind of activities, competences that 'effective' managers display, we can develop programmes of development specifically designed to help managers achieve them.

5.2 Changing trends in management education and development

It is only comparatively recently that 'management' as a subject in its own right has become a popular commodity, with books like Blanchard and Johnson's *The One Minute Manager* becoming a best-seller after its publication in 1983.[18] Since then Tom Peters in the United States and more recently John Harvey Jones and Charles Handy in this country have done much to stimulate public debate about the role of the manager in the organization of the future.

This is in contrast to the kind of 'text' book I remember when doing by DMS in the early 1970s which was divided up into chapters on 'Management Control', 'Personnel', 'Marketing' and 'Finance'. This is not to say, of course, that there are not similar text books today but in addition there is a much wider repertoire to stimulate the student of management. Nevertheless, the kind of vision these books portray is very often peripheral rather than at the centre of the programmes and syllabi on management today.

The traditional functional divisions of management are testimony to what a good job Fayol and Taylor did to establish an essentially analytical approach to management. These divisions are reflected in the way both in-company and college courses have treated management over the past 25–30 years. Figure 5.4 depicts the kind of in-house management programmes a large company might offer its managers. At BEA, I remember, management training/development tended to be aimed at three levels. First there was supervisory training. This was covered in a separate brochure and was undertaken at a training centre. Then there was a separate series of courses aimed at middle managers (functional heads). These were all residential and were held at a separate staff college. There were also special programmes aimed at senior managers which were arranged as required.

Series 1: Short courses suitable for the first line manager

1.1 Principles of supervision	2 days
1.2 Communication skills	3 days
1.3 Managing people at work	3 days
1.4 Trainer skills	3 days
1.5 Employee relations	2 days
1.6 Controlling costs	3 days

Series 2: Courses suitable for heads of department

2.1 Financial management	5 days
2.2 Marketing	5 days
2.3 Human resource management	5 days
2.4 Strategic planning	5 days

Figure 5.4 *Mitchell Holdings Ltd: Management Development Programme*

I suspect this pattern of courses was not untypical of many large companies in the 1960s and 1970s. Managers went on courses that corresponded with their grade in the hierarchy. Content was largely knowledge-based and it was rare for there to be any measurable outcome. Upon being appointed to a certain position there was an appropriate course for which you were nominated.

Then, under the influence of the ITBs in the 1970s and 1980s, companies were required to be more systematic in how they selected staff for training.

Courses became more flexible and practical, particularly at the level of first line manager/supervisor. Hitherto it was likely that courses for middle managers would have lasted two to three weeks. How could you cover a subject like marketing, for example, in less time?

But emphasis shifted from input to output and it became apparent that by specifying 'outcomes' of courses it was possible to redesign course content so that it could be fitted into a shorter time span rather like the example suggested in Figure 5.4. Also, the sharp divisions between levels of management became more blurred and there dawned the possibility of actually developing from one level to another. But it still tended to be viewed as 'manager' training rather than 'management' development. Managers had a right to attend given courses to equip themselves for the position to which they had been appointed. The organization had no expectation that this individual training could somehow have an effect on the organization as a whole.

Individual training inside the company often went on in parallel with 'education' outside. Again it was accepted policy that at a certain level in the organization you were eligible to study at a local college for a DMS, for example. For many companies, of course, the syllabuses offered by the local college were not just education but also provided the training that could not be given in-company – at least not in management subjects. Colleges, for their part, have been slow to recognize this market although they are increasingly developing a 'short course' programme to run parallel with their traditional academic syllabuses.

The Constable and McCormick report revealed that most of the UK's 2.75 million managers lack formal education. Currently about 12,300 people in the UK are receiving formal education in management – at any level from Higher National Diploma to postgraduate degrees, but – so the McCormick report argues – this is a fraction of what is needed. Since the 1960s the two main postgraduate programmes offered by higher education have been the Diploma in Management Studies (DMS) and the Master in Business Administration (MBA).

The popularity of the DMS has waxed and waned as a middle management qualification while the MBA has – until quite recently – been taken up by the elite few. Over the past few years, however, there has been an MBA boom, as on the one hand companies see the support of an MBA as a way of creating a high track management route while on the other potential high fliers see the MBA as their passport to business promotion. But there is little evidence that companies are capitalizing on the skills an MBA should offer; it is the same story, the qualification goes with a job, with a role.

Perhaps there has been too much attention given to the postgraduate qualification with the result that a lot of the reforming work done by BTEC at lower levels has been forgotten. For many years now BTEC have sought to modularize and standardise courses in terms of outputs as well as inputs.

They also put particular emphasis on the need for the development of generic skills that are independent of a particular management function. It is sad that students who fail to get on a business degree course, for example, look upon the Higher National Diploma as being in some ways inferior. The irony is that they could be developing skills on an HND programme which are still being argued about at higher levels.

In the final analysis, however, it should not be government reports or trends in education policy that determine management development programmes – it should be company needs. There is evidence that more companies are beginning to realize that the standard fare offered by colleges and business schools is not meeting their needs.[19] Some companies have therefore decided to negotiate their own programmes of development; the competence movement – as we shall see in the next section – should help provide a national framework for such negotiation.

What is needed is a national programme that recognizes management skills in the context of their execution – what Schon calls 'knowledge-in-action'. The problem is that the company training centre or the college lecture room can only simulate this kind of learning. But what if the managers themselves came together and learned from each other's problems and experience? It is ironic that colleges and commerce alike are only now in a position to fully appreciate the significance of a paper published by the Mining Association of Great Britain in October 1945. Its author, Reg Revans, was making recommendations for how managers in the coal industry should be trained and developed. His conclusions – drawn from experiences in the Second World War when he saw the value derived by 'comrades in adversity' – was for the establishment of a rather special staff college:[19]

> Its clientele would ... tend to be drawn from among those in the higher executive and technical positions, and those would provide, in the large majority of cases, both the teachers and the taught, or the group leaders and the groups (pp. 30–31).[20]

Thus the seeds were sown for what was to be called Action Learning. Even at this early stage it sets out some powerful principles:

- There is no formal teacher, just a 'leader' whose role would be to help the others focus on problems from which they could all learn.
- Co-opting of formal academic staff 'for special purposes' is a possibility. (This is interesting considering Revans' later vehemence against 'academics'.)
- Problem solving sessions should have a flexible time span determined solely by the requirement to solve a problem.

Another key principle to emerge was that it was critical that members of the 'set', as it came to be called, should be engaged on *real* problems for which they were accountable. Revans argued that real learning came from reflection on the consequences of action for which managers were individually responsible. Thus any kind of role playing or discussion of hypothetical case studies would not be considered Action Learning.

On the other hand, he did not dismiss formal knowledge which was a necessary part of an equation he expressed as follows:

$$L \text{ (learning)} = P \text{ (programmed} + Q \text{ (questioning}$$
$$\text{knowledge)} \qquad \text{insight)}$$

But equally important was the need to question and probe.

It was not until the 1970s that business schools began to implement Revans's ideas. Why did it take so long? Ian Cunningham was involved at Anglian Regional Management Centre in developing a DMS based on Revans's thinking and now as Roffey Park Management Centre's Chief Executive he has developed an MBA based on Action Learning principles. He is the first to acknowledge that one reason Action Learning has been resisted so long is because academics fear that, if adopted, they would no longer have a role:[21]

The problem is that it's a threat, because you're saying that the trainer or academic has no role or maybe that role is only to get people together and help them to talk to each other, but certainly not to teach. Because maybe the teaching's what gets in the way and stops managers learning.

There is evidence, however, that colleges and academic staff are having to change the way they manage their *own* business. This is partly because of economics; having been set free to manage their own resources they are having to look for more effective ways to manage scarcer resources; this has meant reviewing the main method of delivery of their product to the consumer, the lecture. Is this the most cost-effective way to enable managers of the future to develop the knowledge and skills they will need? Alternative methods making greater use of Open Learning materials, seminars, tutorials and – yes – Action Learning sets are being investigated.

But changes would not happen if it was *only* a question of economics. There is a detectable shift in attitude which reflects some of the trends we discussed in the previous chapter. In particular there has been a shift from a teacher-led to a learner-led strategy. This has been partly forced on colleges by bodies like BTEC who have pioneered a more flexible and practical approach to classroom teaching. Also, of course, the move towards competence based assessment, as we shall see in the next section, is putting enormous pressure on colleges to adopt radically different policies towards both teaching and assessment.

But I suspect a change in attitude would have happened anyway without these external pressures. Indeed it is ironic that these external influences on policy come at a time when colleges are addressing related issues internally; the problem is that any institution can only take so much turmoil at any one time!

Donald Schon's book *The Reflective Practitioner*[12] and the subsequent *Educating the Reflective Practitioner'*[22] have focused the attention of academics as to how professional people really *learn* to become professional. Schon concludes that in practice professional people learn in real life in a very different way from how we try to teach them in college. Syllabuses are determined primarily by what he calls 'technical rationality'. As we have argued, Taylor's 'scientific' approach to management has been very influential not just in the board room but also in the college prospectus. In contrast, Schon believes true professionalism comes through intuition as to what 'feels' right and process is much nearer to 'artistry' than science. In *Educating the Reflective Practitioner* he examines how architects, musicians, psycho-analysts and counsellors learn their profession. The context in which they learn is more akin to a 'studio' than a classroom. It is also based on two key skills which are at the heart of how the professional (and manager) learns. He calls these skills 'knowing-in-action' and 'reflection-in-action':

> I shall use knowing-in-action to refer to the sorts of knowhow we reveal in our intelligent action – publicly observable, physical performances like riding a bicycle and private operations like instant analysis of a balance sheet. In both cases the knowing is *in* the action. We reveal it by our spontaneous and skilful execution of the performance; and we are characteristically unable to make it verbally explicit (p. 25).[22]

We are unable to explain what it is we are doing or why we are doing it *until* something happens to make us *question* what we are doing. This could be a surprise remark, action or error or somebody simply asking of us the question 'Why?' or 'What if?' This leads to what Schon calls reflection-in-action:

> In reflection-in-action the rethinking of some part of our knowing-in-action leads to on-the-spot experimentation and further thinking that affects what we do in the situation at hand and perhaps also in others we shall see as similar to it. (p. 29)[22]

If these processes, as Schon suggests, are at the core of how professionals learn, how should colleges respond? Schon's solution is for colleges to provide what he calls a 'Practium' which he describes as 'a setting designed for the task of learning a practice'. The key word is *setting* – it is less like a classroom and more like a studio where student and tutor reflect *together* on *outcomes* of a learning process which is never made explicit. But it is not just the tutor that is involved, but one's fellow students because

> A professional's knowing-in-action is embedded in the socially and institutionally structured context shared by a community of practi-

tioners. Knowing-in-*practice* is exercised in the institutional settings particular to the profession, organized in terms of its characteristic units of activity and its familiar types of practice situations and constrained or facilitated by its common body of professional knowledge and its appreciative system (p. 33).[22]

The language may be different, but do the notions described by Schon above – 'knowledge-in-action', 'reflection-in-action' and the need for 'sharing' – seem familiar? It may well be, of course, that Schon did not see any link between Reg Revans's ideas and his own. I can find no reference to Revans in *Educating the Reflective Practitioner*. If colleges had taken up Revans's ideas 40 years ago in the way that they are now beginning to review Schon's ideas – much of this present discussion would have become redundant because the theory as taught by colleges and the practice of management would be one and the same. Schon, of course, is aiming his work primarily *at* colleges and education in a way Revans never did. At the conclusion of his book he poses an interesting question:

Is it possible to combine a coherent professional curriculum with the conditions essential to a reflective practicum? For the more we integrate in a curriculum the knowledge and skills that students, in our judgement, need to learn, the more we make it difficult for them to function as reflective designers of their own education (p. 341).[22]

A lot depends, of course, on the students' own background and previous experience of being able to manage their own learning. I have found first year undergraduates straight from school very reluctant to abandon their dependence on 'being taught' rather than learn in small problem solving groups and 'reflect-in-action'. On the other hand, more mature students who have had experience of industry are much more willing to experiment and explore their own experiences. I have found this true of HND students as well as postgraduate students who are doing the DMS or MBA.

We have spent some time now exploring changes in the management education system which will gradually have an impact on the next generation of managers. But equal changes have been taking place in thinking about management development in-company. What has not happened – yet – is for one to influence the other. I am still amazed, for example, that my MBA students see the 'education' process they are going through at the university as being quite separate from any training and development they may have received in-company. Equally I find that industry – despite the increase in company based DMS and MBA schemes – sees these schemes as 'external' to the development process going on inside the company.

Part of the problem is that the MBA still reflects the 'competitive' values that derive from its origins at Harvard; but even the Americans now recognize this image needs to be changed to embrace a 'life-long learning process', 'development of teamwork rather than individual competition'.[23]

The irony is that Schon's 'Practicum' – like open learning – should not depend on being placed *at* a college. It can be formed wherever there are managers willing to reflect-in-action with each other. (Ideally, as Schon intends, it should be the bridge between the practical world of industry and the academic campus.) Self-reflection and self-development have been at the heart of management development thinking over the past 10–15 years.

I remember being struck by both the simplicity and potential of the ideas in Pedler, Burgoyne and Boydell's book *A Manager's Guide to Self-Development*[17] when it first came out in 1978. As with most ITBs at the time, the Hotel and Catering Training Board for whom I was then working had been struggling with the notion of management development and how companies in its scope should be influenced to develop their managers of the future. There was never a clear policy. The thinking then was parallel with the kind of developments we have already explored in this section. In other words, management development was synonymous with a series of programmes for managers who happened to reach certain positions in the organization.

But in one other respect the ITBs did have some influence – in that the process of systematic training was expected to apply to managers as well. Therefore there had to be some kind of appraisal system by which their needs were identified and programmes tailored to meet their needs. The trouble was more attention was given to the programmes than to the system by which the needs had been identified. With hindsight it would have been interesting to create a 'Practicum' around the very process of self- and group-assessment. This would have revealed and facilitated much more about individual skill and competence and company culture than was achieved by the manager attending a series of courses on budgeting, for example.

In the 1970s there was an initiative from Durham University Business School which involved companies carrying out an audit into the way they identified and met managers' training and development needs. The Hotel and Catering Training Board was among those that piloted the scheme in some of its companies. This did not profess to be a management development scheme as such but at the time it struck me that questioning a company about its approach to management development, then collecting information about what happens in practice and feeding it back was a powerful process. Little did I realize then that this was a very good example of 'reflection-in-action'. But, like many schemes before it, it was replaced by another 'flavour of the month'.

But *A Manager's Guide to Self-Development* is different simply because it does not need a system to support it. I had the same kind of eureka experience as had happened to the instructor who suddenly realized the power of separating out training objectives from learning inputs (see Section 3.4). Once a manager has diagnosed the kind of skills needed to be effective in a given organization they can then develop themselves by using structured exercises that the book recommends as appropriate to various skills. (I have already listed these skills in Figure 5.3.) The book offers no less than 42 simply explained exercises to choose from. For example, if 'proactivity' is a skill you needed to develop, then these are the kind of exercises that were recommended:

2 Making contacts
9 Choosing solutions with a chance
11 Planning change
13 Catastrophic contingencies
15 Asserting yourself
17 Practising new group behaviours
21 Looking after yourself
26 Who's the boss
27 Practising change
28 Action planning
29 Imaging

By definition, it is a manual for self-development. It places ownership of the individual manager for their own learning and development. Pedler and Boydell have written another book, *Managing Yourself*,[24] published as a paperback and intended for 'the thinking manager'. This is one in a series aimed at 'the Successful Manager' published in association with the Association of Teachers of Management (now the Association of Management, Education and Development) which has done much to stimulate innovative thinking about management development in this country.

But self-development, as we found with Open Learning, presupposes an enormous amount of commitment and motivation on the part of the self-developer. To succeed they need help and support from the organization

Level 1 No systematic management development (i.e. managers left to develop themselves)

Level 2 Isolated tactical management development (i.e. the organization might arrange an isolated event to meet a particular need)

Level 3 Integrated and coordinated structural and development tactics (i.e. evidence of some coordination of development 'tactics')

Level 4 A management development strategy to implement corporate policy (i.e. there is some central planning of what development will take place to meet central policy)

Level 5 Management development strategy input to corporate policy formation (i.e. results of management development are fed back into corporate policy)

Level 6 Strategic development of the management of corporate policy (i.e. results of management development help to shape nature and direction of future corporate policy)

Figure 5.5 *Burgoyne's levels of organizational management development*

within which they are developing. Therefore self-development has been succeeded by 'self-development in the organization': 'This new horizon extends the implications of this learner-empowering way of doing management development into the broader field of managing and developing the organization' (p. xii).[25]

One of the reasons many well-intentioned management development schemes have never really taken off in-company is that they are owned more by the organization (usually the personnel and training department) than by the managers. The ideal would be a scheme that met the needs of both. Burgoyne developed a model that reflects six levels of maturity of 'organizational management development'.[26] This is summarized in Figure 5.5.

ACTIVITY 5.2
● *Read through the various levels of development suggested in Figure 5.5 and identify at which level your organization is currently operating.*

For someone who has been so involved in freeing up the capacity of the individual manager to manage his or her own development, I find this model *too* embedded within an organization's system and determined, it seems to me, largely by senior management. I prefer Alan Mumford's model which he develops in an excellent overview of *Management Development: Strategies for Action.*[27] He identifies three broad types of management development which are summarized in Figure 5.6.

Type 1 *Informal Managerial*	Type 2 *Integrated Managerial*	Type 3 *Formal Management Development*
(Accidental processes)	(Opportunistic processes)	(Planned process)
Not planned or structured. Based on managerial activities and task oriented. Owned by manager	Planned and structured by both boss and subordinate/ Based on managerial activities but aims to help both task performance and individual development. Owned by manager	Planned and structured by developers. Often outside of normal managerial activity. Aims to help individual development. Owned more by developers than manager

Figure 5.6 *Mumford's three types of management development*

ACTIVITY 5.3
● *Which of the types of management development characterizes your organization?*

Clearly type 2 comes closest to meeting the needs of both the individual manager and the organization. Mumford places emphasis on a multitude of resources that are available within the organization to both boss and subordinate for the purposes of management development. These would include structured exercises found on more formalized management development courses. (A good source for the range of such techniques that are available is Huczynski's *Encyclopedia of Management Development Methods*.)[28] But it also includes most importantly the people within the organization who are crucial to any development activity. Mumford emphasizes the role of the following groups of people:

1 The boss
2 Mentors
3 Specialist advisers (e.g. trainers)
4 Peers
5 Subordinates
6 Network contacts

He also quotes findings from research by Charles Margerison[29] into what were the major influences on chief executives in the UK (which were closely replicated by findings in the United States). These findings are reproduced in Figure 5.7.

If you are looking to develop a chief executive for the future you might be inclined to present them with such a list and make available the necessary resources and facilities in-company. Based on these findings I know that if I had aspirations for a chief executive post I would eschew any suggestion I

1 Ability to work with a wide variety of people	78.4
2 Early overall responsibility for important tasks	74.8
3 A need to achieve results	74.8
4 Leadership experience early in career	73.6
5 Wide experience in many functions before 35	67.6
6 An ability to do deals and negotiate	66.4
7 Willingness to take risks	62.8
8 Having more ideas than other colleagues	61.6
9 Being stretched by immediate bosses	60.4
10 An ability to change managerial style to suit occasion	58.8
11 A desire to seek new opportunities	56.8
12 Becoming visible to top management before 30	56.0
13 Family support (wife/parents)	55.2
14 Having a sound technical training	54.8
15 Having a manager early in your career who acted as a model (from whom you learned a lot)	52.0
16 Overseas managerial/work experience	41.2
17 Experience of leadership in armed forces (peacetime/wartime)	40.4
18 Having special 'off the job' management training	32.8

Figure 5.7 *Reported major influences on chief executives. (From C. Margerison, 'How chief executives succeed', p. 18*[29]

go on an in-company course (or external course for that matter) and start networking fast!

It also provides an indicative list of what is valued in Western organizations. It seems that the way to get to the top is to be in the right place at the right time and to be visible and useful to the right people. It is interesting to contrast Margerison's findings with those of a research study comparing managers and management development in Britain and Japan.[30] The study compared four major British companies (Lucas, NatWest, Tesco and BT) with match-paired counterparts in Japan (Sumitomo, Mitsui, Jusco and NTT) in four major sectors: electrical engineering, banking, retailing and a representative of the privatized sector.

The study has revealed some surprising conclusions, 'not least the fact that British managers spend more time on formal management development courses than their Japanese counterparts and far less time on developing themselves and their subordinates on a day-to-day basis'. Part of the explanation for the surprising fact that Japanese managers seemed to have less full time training than their British counterparts is that:

> In Japan there was much less of a focus on 'management development' *per se*. In fact, many Japanese clearly had difficulty in relating to the concept. Their attention was drawn to general capability development, irrespective of the kind of contribution, technical, or otherwise, which people might be making.
>
> In Japan development was a long-drawn out process, and a wide spectrum of employees were drawn in. Hence when it came to the specific stage of appointment to a managerial position, much of the necessary preparation had already been accomplished (p. 26).[30]

But also, 'the Japanese were relying far more on on-the-job training, self-development and correspondence courses, rather than the singular off-site training course'.

It is also interesting to compare the emphasis in Margerison's rankings of responsibility early on in the high flier's career. In contrast, Japanese managers are expected to serve a long apprenticeship during which time they will have been influenced by role models and mentors. Fifteen per cent of Lucas managers made reference to role models as influencing their development as compared with 70% at Sumitomo Electric.

However, there do seem to be *some* encouraging signs in the British companies surveyed. The survey reports on the percentage of companies who regarded the following as having responsibility for their own management development:

1 Management development department
2 Head of department
3 Individual
4 Personnel

It was clear that Japanese and most British companies ranked the management/department last. Most Japanese and British companies ranked the head of department as having first or second ranking as far as their own development was concerned. But the Japanese generally ranked 'individual responsibility' higher than their British counterparts. The notable exception amongst the British companies was BT: 67% of their managers surveyed saw themselves as being responsible for their own development.

In addition, the survey showed that there was increased interest in management development amongst the British companies. An interesting comment is made about mentoring and coaching, which seems to be increasing in popularity:

> Mentoring and coaching were trends which typically excited much interest among our respondents. These were approaches which, in British eyes, seem to offer a way into on-the-job training. Their installation in Britain reflects, however, the characteristics and fundamental problems highlighted by the study: in the main mentors were regarded as 'bolt-ons' who probably could not do any harm and just might do some good (p. 27).[20]

This last comment perhaps typifies the British attitude to management development in general. i.e. it shouldn't do any harm and might do some good. But management still remains an enigma – in contrast to the straightforward Japanese system through which managers emerge as if by natural evolution. We like our *top* managers to be something 'special'; like the Americans we revere 'star' quality, people who have 'made it' outside the system – people like Richard Branson, Anita Roddick and Alan Sugar.

But what about the rest? This is where it seems to me that a 'competence' approach to management development has much to contribute. There has been much criticism of the approach for the way it inevitably 'limits' management to a finite set of behaviours.[31, 32, 33] But at least it *is* an approach and, as I hope we have already demonstrated when introducing competences in Chapter 3, it need only be as bureaucratic as we choose to make it.

5.3 Management competences

What is available

A new approach to management

The national Forum for Management Education and Development, following major consultations with interested parties and research among practising managers, is establishing a new framework for management and supervisory awards based upon demonstrated ability to manage.

The developing hierarchy has three levels, reflecting major career stages of management:

Supervisor level – for those with supervisory responsibilities
Certificate level – for first level managers
Diploma level – for middle managers and those with more complex managerial responsibilities
Masters level – for senior managers with strategic responsibilities

The proposed structure – based on units of managerial competence – will enable the development of relevant competences at the appropriate time in a manager's career and concurrent with the development of any specialist, professional or occupationally specific expertise. It will require practical managerial experience as well as the acquisition of relevant knowledge and understanding (p. 5).[34]

The above is taken from the MCI Guidelines for the Diploma level. To date standards of competence have been published for the Certificate level (Management I) and the Diploma level (Management II). Details of the units and elements for both levels can be found in the Appendix to this chapter. The next standards to be produced will be for the Supervisor level, which has been added to the original three levels of management. It is likely that standards for the Masters level will depend on extended consultation.

The objective of this section is to demonstrate what is available to you now before considering the arguments for and against competences for managers. The fact is they *have* been produced and in my opinion make available a valuable framework within which *any* company regardless of size or management development resources can review its managerial responsibilities and plan an appropriate programme of development.

In order to demonstrate how the various documents available from MCI can be used we will select one element from those contained in the Appendix and examine:

1 The performance criteria and range indicators that apply.
2 The underpinning knowledge that has been identified for this element.
3 The assessment criteria and evidence of achievement that will be required.

ACTIVITY 5.4
● *Look through the units of competence and elements contained in the Appendix. Are these the kind of activities in which your managers are engaged?*

The key emphasis is on activities, not roles or functions. This presents a problem for colleges who are more used to dividing up a syllabus in terms of content relating to finance, marketing etc. In fact the MCI has grouped the units into 'key roles' as follows:

	Management I units	Management II units
Manage operations	I1	II1
	I2	II2
Manage finance	I3	II3
		II4
Manage people	I4	II5
	I5	II6
	I6	II7
	I7	II8
Manage information	I8	II9
	I9	II10

In addition, there is a separate set of competences relating to the kind of 'Personal Competence' each manager needs to be effective. These are summarized in Figure 5.8. Notice how they cover many of the key skills identified in *A Manager's Guide to Self-Development*.

Planning
- Showing concern for excellence
- Setting and prioritizing objectives
- Monitoring and responding to situations

Managing others
- Showing sensitivity to the needs of others
- Relating to others
- Obtaining the commitment of others
- Presenting oneself positively to others

Managing oneself
- Showing self confidence and personal drive
- Managing personal emotions and stress
- Managing personal learning and development

Using intellect
- Collecting and analysing information
- Identifying and applying concepts
- Taking decisions

Figure 5.8 *Personal competences required for effectiveness*

Another feature that might have struck you as you read through the list in the Appendix is that many of the units and elements at the Diploma level are word-for-word the same as at the Certificate level (particularly units within the function of managing people). If someone has demonstrated evidence of achievement in managing people at the Certificate level do they need to repeat it at the Diploma level? MCI emphasize that the competences at the Diploma level are carried out in a much more complex environment and therefore the manager *still* needs to demonstrate evidence at this level though he or she may have already provided documentary evidence at level MI. This issue reflects a major difference between the traditional approach of taking an exam in 'Man Management', when a first line manager for example, and being considered proficient thereafter, and having to demonstrate that you still have the skills when you reach a higher management position.

At the Diploma level there is a greater emphasis on financial and resource controlling; the underpinning knowledge requires a broader and deeper coverage and there is greater emphasis on the integration of these competences. There is also a greater focus on pro-activity and a move towards strategic decisions.

The way the competences are broken down follows the standard pattern we explored in Chapter 3. Similarly, certification is primarily by demonstration of evidence of achievement against each of the elements for the respective management levels. In Figure 5.9 I have taken one element from the Certificate level – element I5.1 'Develop and improve teams through planning activities' – and reproduce the MCI standards,[34] which is broken down into performance criteria and range indicators and also includes details of assessment criteria. Every element listed in the Appendix has corresponding details of

- Performance criteria
- Range indicators
- Performance evidence required
- Sources of evidence
- Forms of evidence

In addition, research has been undertaken into what knowledge and understanding are necessary to achieve competence at levels Management I and II. For each element there is available a description of such knowledge which is divided into three categories:

- Purpose and context: which is knowledge and understanding of the manager's objectives, and of the relevant organizational and environmental influences, opportunities and values (this applies to all elements)
- Principles and methods: which is knowledge and understanding of the theories, models, principles, methods and techniques that provide the basis of competent managerial performance
- Data: which is knowledge and understanding of specific facts likely to be important to meeting standards

Key purpose: To achieve the organization's objectives and continuously improve performance

Key role: Manage people

Unit 1.5: Develop teams, individuals and self to enhance performance

Element I5.1: Develop and improve teams through planning activities

Performance criteria

(a) The strengths and weaknesses of the team are identified against current and anticipated work requirements
(b) All individuals within the team are encouraged and assisted to evaluate the team's overall development needs and to contribute to the discussion and planning of how these will be met
(c) Any unproductive friction between team members is minimized
(d) Team building and development plans contain clear, relevant and realistic development objectives for the team as a whole
(e) Development activities optimize the use of available resources
(f) Plans are reviewed, updated and improved at regular intervals after discussion and agreement with the appropriate people
(g) Where development activities prove inadequate and/or the resources used are unsuitable or inadequate, realistic alternatives are discussed, agreed and implemented

Range indicators

This activity is carried out with the manager's team and all individuals who form the manager's work team(s) including the manager him/herself

The identification of strengths and weaknesses is against:
● technical needs
● team roles
● interpersonal skills

Development objectives and activities cover all areas in which the teams are expected to:
● produce results
● meet quality standards

Development activities include:
● specially designed work
● activities
● formal training
● informal training

Approval, if required, for the use of resources is sought from:
● higher level manager
● colleagues, specialists, staff in other departments

Figure 5.9 *Occupational standard for Certificate level (Management 1)*

Figure 5.10 gives the Management Knowledge and Understanding Specification[35] which corresponds to the element we have selected. The occupational standards, the assessment criteria and the underpinning knowledge and understanding required, provide a framework within which any organization could review its management strengths and weaknesses and

---

Purpose and context: (taken from the *Certificate Level Guidelines*[36])

Broad understanding of: organizational objectives and plans; organizational policies and priorities regarding productivity and staff development; promotion/development plans and development activities and resources available (training, secondments, etc.)

Principles and methods relating to:

- identifying competence requirements in relation to work demands
- forming and managing work groups and teams
- identifying, defining and assessing the competences of individuals
- establishing and agreeing objectives for team development
- providing praise and constructive criticism to encourage staff and improve future performance

Data relating to:

- content and anticipated work requirements of teams and individuals
- key strengths and weaknesses of teams and individuals, including any audits of individual skills and competences and appraisals
- cost and type of training provision available as required
- previous development opportunities afforded to teams and individuals

---

Figure 5.10 *Knowledge and understanding underpinning element 15.1*

plan an appropriate development programme (whether or not it was seeking accreditation). A sample development programme is suggested in Figure 5.12 at the end of this section.

A *Good Practice Guide*[37] is also available which illustrates the importance of six principles which MCI believe are critical to effective management education and training. For each principle there is a checklist of questions and example of a company which has put the principle into practice. Figure 5.11 gives a description of each of the six principles. In my view, these principles are very much in line with many of the developments we have so far been exploring and provide sound advice for a management development policy – whether or not you support a competence based approach to

---

1 **Open access** Ensure that there is no barrier to manager receiving development
2 **Flexibility and innovation of delivery** Don't rely solely on traditional methods like lecturing but ensure a range of resources, facilities are used
3 **Corporate and individual development** Ensure that individual development is directly linked with the business objectives of the organization
4 **A competence approach** Outcome of any development programme needs to be assessed against national management standards
5 **Credit accumulation and transfer** Ensure that managers can gain credit for competences they already possess
6 **Employer involvement** Ensure that employers are directly involved in the design and assessment of the programme

---

Figure 5.11 *Six principles for good practice in management development*

development. The *Guide for Good Practice* also contains questions for self-assessment which are very much in line with the criteria we examined in Chapter 2 for assessment under the 'Investors in People' initiative. Equally, it demonstrates to those opposed to a competence approach that the competences themselves are only *part* of a total in-company support process.

ACTIVITY 5.5
● *Before going on to the next section review again the complete list of competences at Management levels I and II (in Appendix) together with the kind of back-up support we have illustrated in relation to element I5.1 on team performance and the above principles of good practice. Then select a management programme you run in-company (or indeed from the prospectus of an external provider, e.g. a college) and the skills it covers (or doesn't, as the case may be!) and consider how a competence based approach and/or examples of good practice above could improve its effectiveness. If you cover Team Building you might take this as an example. At the end of the next section we will focus on building a team and suggest a hypothetical development module to illustrate how you can cover a whole range of issues relevant to your company within the framework of a competence based programme of development.*

The case for competences

In general I take the same view of competences applied to management as we explored in Chapter 3 on competences in general. While of course recognizing the danger of a bureaucratic and rigid assessment of standards, my view is still that a competency approach *can* give and add value to both individual and organization alike.

Rather than seeing the unit or element as a fixed entity (which its opponents seem to do), my suggestion is that it be seen as the basis for a process of ongoing inquiry into the kind of behaviours and consequences the elements themselves describe. In this context the ideas of Donald Schon on the 'reflective practitioner' seem to me to be highly relevant. Below I put forward three propositions in support of a competence based approach to management development.

First, management competences of the kind listed in the appendix provide a recipe for 'learning managers', as MCI calls them, to gain 'knowledge-in-action' in the sense we have already discussed in Section 5.2. At one and the same time they act as a *trigger to action* but also provide a *focal point* on which boss, tutor and learner can compare competence aimed for with competence achieved. This could happen in the studio kind of context Schon describes in

Educating the Reflective Practitioner[22] in which the student learns by *practice* the outcome of which is continually being reviewed and adjusted. (Incidentally MCI provides a self-assessment package on floppy disks which can be used by the manager's boss to compare their perception of the manager's effectiveness against appropriate competences.) This leads on, secondly, to 'reflection-in-action' which is what the learner would record in his or her portfolio. I would maintain, therefore, that it is as much the learning from and reflection *on* the competences which are assessed as the competences themselves.

My third argument relates to the notion of 'visibility', which is a theme that emerged in the previous chapter. Rather like 'training objectives', a major benefit of competences, it seems to me, is that it helps learners *recognize* what they can do after they have done it! By the same token, they make explicit goals and possibilities they might never have *conceived* otherwise. Schon notes:

> the paradox of learning a really new competence is this: that a student cannot at first understand what he needs to learn, can learn it only by educating himself and can educate himself only by beginning to do what he does not yet understand (p. 93).[22]

In the context of learning about architectural design, the student

> is expected to plunge into designing, trying from the outset to do what he does not yet know how to do, in order to get the sort of experience that will help him learn what designing means. He cannot make an informed choice to take this plunge because he does not yet grasp its essential meanings and his instructors cannot convey these to him until he has had the requisite experience. Thus, he must jump in without knowing – indeed, in order to discover – what he needs to know (p. 93).[22]

At first sight, learning about budgetary control for the first time might not seem as creative as architectural design – but the manager who has never done it before is in the same predicament as the architectural student. The traditional approach of management training has been to run courses like 'Finance for the Non-Financial Manager', assuming that learning about budgets is simply a question of absorbing information. Maybe if this subject were approached more like teaching architecture, there would be a lower failure rate than there is!

What I believe competences can do is to provide the student who knows nothing about budgetary control with a 'picture' of what it is like to *be* competent at budgeting. If she or he looked at details of element II.4.2, for example, at the Diploma level (Appendix), they would see reference to 'Negotiate and agree budget'. The assessment criteria for this element say as much about negotiating as they do about budgeting. The financial purist may be unhappy about the lack of finance theory in the proposed underpinning knowledge (see below), but it surely reflects much more accurately the picture of the knowledge a middle manager needs in practice, that is:

- Planning and scheduling financial flows over budgetary periods.
- Organizing and presenting financial information to support a proposal for expenditure.
- Possible objections to budget proposals.
- Personnel able to help the proposal succeed.
  [I particularly like this last one!]

One of the great advantages of the MCI management framework is that it does *not* focus on traditional functions (like marketing) and the kind of theory that such a function would encompass. In this context Mumford makes, in my view, a very valid observation:

> Although it may undoubtedly at some level be a useful piece of knowledge for the production manager to know how the marketing manager produces a marketing plan, in real management life the more important issue is how the production manager and marketing manager develop a process for managing the consequences of the plan (p. 26).[27]

This is the kind of issue that the MCI competences *do* address. But equally, this does not (or should not) stop the production manager finding out more about producing a marketing plan or the new department head reading up on budgetary control *if* this is appropriate to the development plan that would be drawn up between boss and provider. The opponents of competences seem to assume that achieving a competence at what they maybe see as a 'trivial' level in some way precludes the individual from building on both the technical knowledge and (more importantly) his or her own *experience* achievement at a basic level.

I would classify all these benefits under the heading of 'transferability' – which is, of course, one of the key reasons underlying competence development. But they also involve, in my opinion, the dimension of visibility in that assessment requires a number of departments being involved. Therefore, by definition, more people in an organization may be involved than would have been the case if it were simply a question of performance appraisal, for example. If you look through many of the assessment criteria you will find that evidence of success requires corroboration from a number of sources. In the final analysis I believe it will be the organizational processes supporting assessment that will be critical if a competence based approach is to succeed. The conclusion of a CNAA report on *The Assessment of Management Competences*[38] puts this very well:

> A feature of good assessment is noticeable where there is a high level of *transparency*; the openness of the assessment is crucial in that all

parties are aware of the what, when, how and why. A shared understanding clears the path, eases the tensions and allows everyone to perform to their best. Lack of transparency suggests one-sided appraisal or even surveillance (p. 17, emphasis added).[38]

It was this kind of 'transparency', 'visibility' which I tried to portray in the scenario at the beginning of Chapter 4. I believe that competences *especially* for managers make them as visible as everyone else in the process of development. Above all, it allows the non-management person to get a picture of just what they need to do to develop themselves and – long before they actually get their foot on the management ladder – to begin to collect evidence of competence. This should, after all, be a feature of a company's Open Access policy.

To end this section I propose in Figure 5.12 a development programme that the XYZ company might make available to existing and prospective managers who wish to improve the effectiveness of their teams of staff *and* to collect sufficient evidence of achievement to be assessed against element I5.1 of the MCI. I have tried to incorporate elements of all six principles of good practice as well as to take account of details of assessment criteria and underpinning knowledge as reproduced in Figures 5.9 and 5.10. The assumption is made that this company has had assessors trained by an approved MCI agency and that the programme is part of a wider development programme that has been endorsed by an MCI agency. If you wish to obtain details about this process, contact the MCI.

ACTIVITY 5.6
● *Read through the approach in Figure 5.12 as an example of good management development practice. Does this meet Schon's conditions for a Practicum?*

5.4 Managers of tomorrow

In this concluding section we look at the lessons we might draw from all the initiatives we have explored in this chapter, many of which were launched as a result of the McCormick and Handy reports. Whatever the outcome, they have certainly focused attention on the role of the manager at a time when organization changes in response to changes in the market place have led to 'leaner' organizations in which the role of the *manager* has become increasingly uncertain. On the other hand *management* has become and will increasingly become a function of *every* job in an organization. This is the scenario Handy predicts of employees of organizations in the future:

Everyone will increasingly be expected not only to be good at something, to have their own professional or technical expertise but

NOTICE TO ALL STAFF IN ALL DEPARTMENTS

IMPROVING EFFECTIVENESS THROUGH TEAM PERFORMANCE

As from next month, between 1500 and 1700 every Monday afternoon for the next five weeks we will be holding a seminar in the Training Room based on the above theme. It is open to all staff to attend and will provide exercises and activities which will enable you to collect evidence which can later be assessed and accredited against MCI level I, element I5.1: 'Develop and improve teams through planning activities'.

Below is a summary of the kind of development inputs planned but this may well change depending on the kind of needs that emerge. You are welcome to attend any of the sessions even if you may not be able to complete the full programme. We hope to repeat the programme in the coming months.

OVERALL OBJECTIVE

To enable you to agree joint objectives with all your team and success criteria by which they will be measured

To enable you to review your current success as a team and plan a development programme to meet success criteria using a wide range of company resources

Session 1: Your team experience

Open session in which you identify criteria for success of your current working team; how clear are you that other members of team have same objectives? Input on how to set objectives and kinds of measurement you might use to assess success

Inter-session exercise: You meet up with members of your team and agree objectives and success criteria to be presented at session 2

Session 2: What is a successful team?

Explore how teams are formed and use Belbin model to identify what kind of a team member you are. Discuss kind of roles your team has/needs. Watch and comment on video 'Successful teams at work'

Inter-session exercise: Check out other members of team using Belbin model. Discuss what kinds of skills you need to develop to be a more balanced team

Session 3: What stops you from being a successful team?

Feedback results of survey. How to measure individual competence. Kinds of resources you need to meet your success criteria

Inter-session exercise: Agree with group as a whole and with individual members technical competences needed and overall resources

Session 4: Formulating the team development plan and budget

Feedback from exercise. Examples of team development plans, resources needed and likely cost (time/money)

Inter-session exercise: Agree group development plan, timescale over which needs to run and likely budget which will need to be allocated

Session 5: Handling group conflict

Video plus some role play. Explore model of Forming. Storming, Norming and Performing. Take away structured exercise to use with group

WORK THROUGH PLAN

Complete structured exercises with group and note down how conflict has been resolved. Implement development plan recording results. Produce final report

FEEDBACK AND ASSESSMENT

These sessions will be arranged when you have worked through your plan and have evidence of how well the team have achieved the targets you set. You will be required to present the report to your boss who will also have spoken individually to team members to assess their reactions to the programme. If the evidence is sufficient to meet criteria in 'Occupational Standards for Managers Level I' (see Dick Hayes for copy) you will get an accreditation certificate for this element

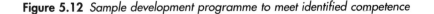

Figure 5.12 *Sample development programme to meet identified competence*

will also very rapidly acquire responsibility for money, people or property, or all three, a managerial task in fact (p. 121).[39]

The implication of this will be that:

> Management ceases to be a definition of a status, of a class within an organization, but an *activity*, an activity which can be defined and its skills taught, learnt and developed (p. 122).[39]

The move to develop the kind of competences listed in the Appendix is an attempt to describe the kind of activities managers carry out and bring them within the potential scope of *everyone*. At the same time, there has been an increasing trend towards what might be called the 'New Age' approach to management which emphasizes what Jacobs calls 'soft qualities'[33] and in particular a move towards 'spirituality'. This is a direction the 'self-development' movement has been leading towards for some time. In developing self-awareness the ultimate state is an awareness of being totally integrated with the world 'outside'. It is a trend which started with Maslow's hierarchy of needs and culminated in 'self-actualization'[9] and ultimately 'self-transcendence'.

How can these two approaches be reconciled within a single approach to management development which an organization can use to grow *all* its staff? A starting point is to look at what is common to what we will call the 'competence development' movement and the 'self-development growth' movement. Both approaches would agree that management should be free of the traditional 'top-down' control model embedded within the typical organization hierarchy and born out of Taylor's scientific approach to management. This is where we came in, with Zuboff's vision of an alternative to 'imperative control'.

In *The Age of the Smart Machine* Zuboff describes the implications of the industrial revolution and later 'Taylorism' in 'rationalizing' craft skills and taking away the craftsman's individuality in 'action-with' such skills and responsibility for output. Instead, a management hierarchy was created and, as we have seen, the division between manager and worker was created. But, as we have also seen, the introduction of information technology, has interfered with this balance giving, as it has, information back into the hands of the workers. Every worker, as Handy has indicated, is not just a *potential* manager he *is* a manager of his own work output. This is what the 'workers' Zuboff spoke to were discovering as they realized through the agency of information technology that they knew as much as management and *therefore* they could 'manage' just as well. But to succeed they needed to develop 'intellective skills'.

Inherent within such skills is the recognition that 'learning is the new form of labour' (p. 375).[4] Garratt calls the outcome of such learning 'intellectual property':

> people are realizing that future wealth lies in the creation of intellectual property as well as the exploitation of it (p. 56).[4]

Another key influence in giving power to the people has been the move towards Total Quality Management. Like Action Learning the underlying principles have been around for a long time; it is only now that a paradigm shift is becoming possible in organizations' attitudes towards their customers. It all started with an American, W. E. Deming, who in 1950 addressed a group of leading Japanese industrialists in Tokyo who had invited him to help them solve their problem – their terrible reputation for quality! His advice was to carry out consumer research, to find out what the customer really wanted and to institute process controls inside the company to ensure goods and service met these expectations. In broad terms this is the essence of Total Quality Management. The Japanese enthusiastically took it on board, the West did not, preferring to focus on Management Control and the bottom-line. The difference between the two approaches and their consequences is simple and stark:

> When quality is increased by improving processes (not by expanded inspection) the better quality will lead to improved productivity. This leads to lower costs, which lead to lower prices. Better quality and lower prices mean the company can expand its market, and can stay in business creating jobs and a greater return on investment.
>
> Management by Control, on the other hand, tends to focus only on the end result – the return on investment; it is like wagging the tail to keep a dog healthy.[40]

The key issue which interests us as far as employees managing themselves is concerned, is that Deming's approach to management was to train everybody in the organization to play a part in operating a quality process which they managed themselves. Managers' roles were not to *inspect* the output from such processes but to ensure the processes worked and had an impact on the organization as a whole. Deming's background was in statistics and his contribution to the workers' 'intellective skills' was to give *everyone* a basic grounding in statistical control techniques so that they could manage the quality process effectively. But, as Pirsig vividly describes in *Zen and the Art of Motorcycle Maintenance*,[41] quality cannot be achieved simply by giving each employee the 'intellective skills' – it is first a question of having the right 'attitude' towards the task itself. After that, it's easy! The problem, of course, is that in the West it is much easier to work on somebody's knowledge base than it is to change their attitude. In the East, as Deming found, they don't see such hard and fast distinctions.

But more and more companies are discovering that management development is not just about the development of a top elite, as the Ashridge Research Group found when they undertook a survey of 150 organizations to discover what was best practice; in particular they wanted to explore the closeness of the relationship between management development policy and business policy and if it could improve business performance. What they found from companies like Nissan, United Biscuits, ICI, NFC, Thorn EMI and Rothmans was that it was all about creating conditions for 'total employee growth'.[32] In this context managers have only one function, according to Colin O'Neill of Rothmans Personnel Function: 'to coach, counsel and enable the team to perform; they really don't have any other function'. Summarizing the findings of the survey in an article entitled 'Should Management Development just be for Managers?' Edgar Willie writes:

> This emphasis on joint responsibility and team-building redefines management development as a collective activity rather than just an individual one and takes it beyond the top echelon into the total company (p. 36).[42]

Similar findings are publicized in a report *The Power of the Open Company*,[43] which compared the management style in top companies with varying levels of performance. The conclusion was that the better performers were more 'open' in their management style; this meant they delegated more responsibility, fostered employee involvement and personal initiatives and provided more effective internal communications.

So, the first issue for the manager of tomorrow is to review his or her role in the light of such new found attitudes towards 'management'. The second issue is to come to terms with the fact that he or she may well not *have* a role in the absence of any supporting hierarchy:

> When organizations operate in a managerial culture the only claim for attention is the value of the role one performs: Absent the role, gone the identity (p. 52).[44]

In *The Managerial Mystique* Zaleznik makes a powerful plea for restoring leadership, rather than management, to business:

> In its pure form managerial mystique is a denial of personal influence. At every level of the hierarchy power is impersonal. Thought and action are directed by some structure, system or procedure, not an individual (p. 229).[44]

But what happens to the manager if that hierarchy of support is no longer there, which is what business gurus like Ros Moss Kanter are suggesting:

> Once high performance is established, once the standards are clear and clearly achieved, the subordinate no longer needs the good will of his boss or her boss quite so much (p. 262).[45]

The same message comes from Megatrends authors Naisbitt and Aburdene:

> The shift from hierarchies to networking means that it matters less who your boss is (or how well the boss manages you) more how well you make the right connections with a supportive mentor or a sponsor to champion your ideas and contributions (p. 84).[46]

In *Re-Inventing the Corporation* they describe a design for the organization of the future that Jay Forrester put forward back in 1965. He strongly opposed the superior-subordinate relationships in the United States and proposed that they be abolished.

> In the new corporation that Forrester envisioned individuals would not have a 'superior' but a 'continually changing structure of relationships' freely negotiated by the individual (p. 41).[46]

They then go on to describe these ideas actually being put in practice in W. L. Gore's as what they call a 'lattice organization'. When a new starter joins the company they are assigned a *starting sponsor* whose job it is to make sure the new employee becomes competent in the job. There are two other sponsors allocated to support the individual: an *advocate sponsor* (whose responsibility it is to know about and appreciate a person's accomplishments and contributions in the organization and speak for them) and a *compensation sponsor* who liaises with the work team members and the other advocates. At the end of three months if the new employee is not performing up to standard he is not fired, just paid a salary which equals his/her contribution – zero!

This may be a trifle idealistic for most UK companies but it raises some interesting issues about the role of the manager in the future. For example he or she may choose to be at the centre of the kind of networks Naisbitt and Aberdene describe. In the report 'Do the Japanese make better managers'[30] Storey reports that there was a lot of interest by British companies in the concept of mentoring. David Clutterbuck has written up the British experience of mentoring in *Everyone Needs a Mentor – fostering talent at work*.[47] It also describes how a company should go about setting up a mentoring programme based on experiences of companies like Pilkington Glass, AMI Healthcare, Cable and Wireless. As to exactly what *is* a mentor he quotes two descriptions gathered by Dr Audrey Collin of the School of Management at Leicester Polytechnic who collected a number of definitions:

> Mentoring is a 'process in which one person [mentor] is responsible for overseeing the career and development of another person [protege] outside the normal manager/subordinate relationship'. Alternatively, mentoring is a 'protected relationship in which learning and experimentation can occur, potential skills can be developed, and in which results can be measured in terms of competencies gained rather than curricular territory covered' (pp. 2–3).[47]

The key phrase is 'outside the normal manager/subordinate relationship'; it might therefore be the boss or someone from another department. In essence it is re-creating the old apprenticeship scheme and some of the 'action-with' qualities that Zuboff claims disappeared with imposition of strict hierarchical accountabilities. In the organization of the future, if such manager/

subordinate relationships are no longer the norm, then perhaps every manager will be seeking to establish such a relationship with one or more protégés in the organization. It is this kind of mentoring network which may very well replace the hierarchy and yet still provide the manager with a *role* within the system.

Finally, then, what kind of skills will the manager of the future need to fulfill this new kind of role? My argument is that all employees from the day they start will be looking to develop not just technical competences (covered in Chapter 3) but the kind of management competences we have explored in this chapter. Therefore let us assume that the manager of the future will have already demonstrated competence in what we might call the more 'hygiene' factors of management (i.e. managing operations, people, resources, information). In any case these same skills will be demonstrated by his or her subordinates. So what does that leave the manager to do?

The answer seems to lie in the word 'leadership' and the kind of personal growth qualities that have come out of the self-development movement. In many respects they seem to be dealing with the same qualities – above all it seems that leadership essentially involves the process of 'transforming' the work of others not by the exercise of power (which was given to a manager by virtue of his or her role in a hierarchy) but by 'empowering' others. In this book *Total Quality Learning – Building a Learning Organization*,[48] Ronnie Lessem considers that the kind of management competences we have explored in this chapter account for less than 50% of the total skills a manager will need. The other 50% are what he calls 'the emerging skills of influencing, learning, facilitating and creating' – these are leadership skills. In particular, it seems to me, it is the 'facilitating and creating' skills that the manager of tomorrow will need above all. Under these headings Lessem identifies the following sub-skills:

Facilitating skills

- Listening skills
- Recognizing potential
- Team-building
- Building alliances

Creative skills

- Envisioning
- Inspiring
- Empowering
- Aligning (aligning people behind the vision)

Lessem develops a model of what he calls 'Total Quality Learning' which revolves around a developmental cycle of 'learning' (inward reflection) and 'innovation' (outward action). It takes an individual manager from the lowest level 'reacting physically' to an event to a point where he or she 'imagines creatively' and translates this level of thinking into action which has an effect on the organization. We will return to these ideas again when we come to the final chapter on the learning organization.

These are the 'soft-skills' of managing which go beyond an analytical description of the external world to one involving feeling and intuition.

These are the qualities which, it is understood, come from the right hemisphere of the brain rather than the left side in which the 'intellective' and analytical skills are centred. These are the skills which have for long been the basis of most management education and training. But, as we have tried to demonstrate, this is rapidly changing.

In 1985 the then MSC sponsored a project to look at 'the qualities of managing', recognizing that management effectiveness was as much about 'qualities' which were difficult to measure.[49] Out of the research evolved a developmental model of managing based around three dimensions: *thinking*, *feeling* and *willing*. Management development programmes have overemphasized *thinking* at the expense of the other two dimensions, which are critical if theory is to be put into practice. The authors of the report identify seven 'modes' of managing, each of which corresponds to different qualities of thinking, feeling and willing. A summary of the model is outlined in Figure 5.13.

---

1 Static, rigid, standard. **Adhering** to rules and procedures. **Obeying** those in authority

2 Responding by **adapting**, modifying or **controlling** rules, procedures, systems and people

3 Sensitive, **aware**, in tune with what is happening, thus **relating** to norms and conventions

> In modes 1 to 3 my behaviour is basically controlled by outsiders – by rules and procedures (1 and 2) or – at 3 – by established 'right' thinking in the form of other peoples' theories, or norms of 'right' or 'good, correct' ways of behaving or doing things. Normative, correct, conforming behaviour

4 **Experiencing** things and prepared to learn from this experience

5 **Experimenting** and deliberately trying to find out more, to add to the stock of knowledge, to improve on the status quo, to advance the 'state of the art'

6 **Connecting**, making large scale links, leading to much wider understanding, including the realization that most things are somehow connected. Sense of oneness

> In modes 4–6 I now move away from doing the approved thing, as defined by established rules,norms, principles, conventions. I now start to find out and decide for myself what is true, right, correct. Thus I control my behaviour from within myself; I learn to find out for myself, to do things my way – even though this may mean deviating from norms, being different, being myself

7 **Integrating** yourself with the outside world and with the task of the times. Making part of this your own life task, and **dedicating** yourself with full commitment to it

> Now, in addition to the new type of holistic consciousness that comes with mode 6, at mode 7 we find an additional quality – changing the world, doing something important and constructive, that needs to be done at this particular time; finding my life task

---

Figure 5.13 *Seven modes of managing, from the MSC report on* The Qualities of Managing *(pp. 46, 46a, 47)*[49]

The report also contained a questionnaire which managers could use to identify the mode of managing they were currently practising. I believe this is a powerful model that deserves to be more widely explored and built upon. I remember in 1986 being given my copy at the end of a conference on self-development but it doesn't seem to have had much wider circulation (though Tom Boydell and Gloria Welshman have used the model as a basis for a paper on modes of being and learning[50]).

So far, we have established that the manager of the future will have to establish him- or herself outside of a formal role in a hierarchy, and that this will require taking on the position of a mentor at the centre of different networks (which will determine the structure of the organization of the future – see Chapter 7). The skills that will be needed to sustain such a role go beyond management competences of the kind listed in the Appendix. If these are the 'hygiene' factors that keep the organization going the 'motivators' that will lead to growth and innovation are the kind of leadership skills and modes of management described above.

The final issue, then, is what *purpose* will the manager of the future serve? The purpose underlying the management competences is 'To achieve the organization's objectives and continuously improve its performance'. This may be sufficient at the level of hygiene factors but the leader of the future should aspire to something more. Ros Moss Kanter introduces the concept of an 'entrepreneurial career'

> in which growth occurs through the creation of new value or new organizational capacity. If the key resource in a bureaucratic career is hierarchical position and the key resources in a professional career are knowledge and reputation, then the key resource in an entrepreneurial career is the ability to create a product or service of value (p. 313).[45]

I would like to suggest that the manager of tomorrow will be assessed in terms of the value he or she adds not to products or services (although that will also occur) but to people. Just as new employees will be negotiating ways of learning and developing (see Chapter 4), including who will be their mentor and tutor, so the manager will seek new ways of adding value to more and more employees:

> Instead of *moving up*, those in entrepreneurial careers see progress *when the territory grows* below them and when they have a share of the returns of that growth (p. 314).[45]

Senge has a similar view of the leader being able to articulate and describe a 'larger story'. According to Senge, the leader in the learning organization of the future will have three key roles: as *designer* of the systems whereby staff can learn (see Chapters 6 and 7), as *teacher* and as 'steward of the vision' that drives the company forward.[51]

The value that will be accrued will be the value of what Garratt has called 'intellectual property':

Central to the intellectual property issue is the ability to capture, codify and diffuse in a useful and profitable form the learning of the organization. This is when the need to develop the role of learning leaders is paramount for the organization to have the chance to survive and grow. Learning occurs all over organizations. The problem is that there are so few systems for valuing it and capturing it (p. 57).[4]

It is to the question of what systems can be established in the organization to value what learning is being realized that we turn in the next and penultimate chapter. The conclusion we reach at the end of this chapter is that the role of tomorrow's managers will be primarily to 'capture, codify and diffuse in a useful and profitable form the learning of the organization' which their own skills will have largely helped to generate. They will be assessed according to the extent to which they add value to staff within their own managerial domain (which will be constantly changing) and as a result to the organization as a whole. In the next chapter we explore how systems can be established to 'capture' this value in the first place.

References

1 Zuboff, S. (1988) *In the Age of the Smart Machine*, Heinemann
2 Constable, J. and McCormick, R. (1987) *The Making of British Managers*, Report for BIM and CBI
3 Handy, C. (1987) *The Making of Managers*, NEDO
4 Garratt, B. (1990) *Creating a Learning Organization*, Institute of Directors
5 Fayol, H. (1930) *Industrial and General Administration*, trans. J. A. Coulborough, Geneva International Management Institute
6 Taylor, F. W. (1911) *The Principles of Scientific Management*, Harper and Row
7 Mayo E. (1945) *The Social Problems of an Industrial Civilisation*, Harvard University Press
8 McGregor, D. (1960) *The Human Side of Enterprise*, McGraw Hill
9 Maslow, A. (1954) *Motivation of Personality*, Harper and Row
10 Herzberg, F., Mausner, B. and Synderman, B. (1959) *The Motivation to Work*, John Wiley
11 Blake, R. and Mouton, J. R. (1985) *The Managerial Grid 111*, Gulf Publishing
12 Schon, D. A. (1983) *The Reflective Practitioner*, Basic Books
13 Drucker, P. F. (1954) *The Practice of Management*, Harper and Row
14 Mintzberg, H. (1974) *Mintzberg on Management*, The Free Press
15 Stewart, R. (1976) *Contrasts in Management: A Study of Different Types of Management Jobs*, McGraw Hill
16 Burgoyne, J. G. and Stuart, R. (1976) The nature, use and acquisition of managerial skills and other attributes. *Personnel Review*, 5(4), 19–29

17 Pedler, M., Burgoyne, J. and Boydell, T. (1986) *A Manager's Guide to Self-Development*, McGraw Hill

18 Blanchard, K. and Johnson, S. (1983) *The One Minute Manager*, Fontana

19 Warner, A. (1990) When Business Schools fail to meet business needs. *Personnel Management*, July, 52–56

20 Revans, R. (1945) *Plans for Recruitment, Education and Training in the Coal Mining Industry*, Mining Association of Great Britain, reproduced in R. Revans, *The Origins and Growth of Action Learning* (1982), Chartwell Bratt

21 Shaw, A. (1991) Power to the People, *Transition*, **91**(4), 14–16 April

22 Schon, D. A. (1987) *Educating the Reflective Practitioner*, Jossey Bass

23 CNAA (1991) *Review of MBA*, CNAA, November

24 Pedler, M., Boydell, T. (1985) *Managing Yourself*, Fontana

25 Pedler, M., Burgoyne, J., Boydell, T., Welshman, G. (1990) *Self-Development in Organizations*, McGraw Hill

26 Burgoyne, J. (1988) Management development for the individual and the organization, *Personnel Management*, June

27 Mumford, A. (1989) *Management Development: Strategies for Action*, IPM

28 Huczynski, A. (1983) *Encyclopedia of Management Development Methods*, Gower

29 Margerison, C. (1980) How chief executives succeed. *Journal of European Industrial Training*, **4**(5), 18

30 Storey, J. (1991) Do the Japanese make better managers? *Personnel Management*, August, 24–28

31 Burgoyne, J. (1988) *Competency Approaches to Management Development*, CSML University of Lancaster, November

32 Jacobs, R. (1989) *Assessing Management Competencies*, Ashridge Management Research Group

33 Jacobs, R. (1989) Getting the measure of management competence. *Personnel Management*, June, 32–37

34 Management Charter Initiative (1991) *Occupational Standards for Managers: Management I and Assessment Criteria*, MCI

35 Management Charter Initiative (1990) *Management Knowledge and Understanding Specifications – Level I* MCI

36 Management Charter Initiative (1990) *Certificate Level Guidelines*, MCI

37 Management Charter Initiative (1991) *Good Practice Guide*, MCI

38 Training Agency (1990) *The Assessment of Management Competence*, Employment Department, Moorfoot, Sheffield

39 Handy, C. (1989) *The Age of Unreason*, Hutchinson

40 Joiner, B. L. and Scholtes, P. R. (1985) *Total Quality Leadership vs. Management by Control*, Joiner Associates Inc

41 Pirsig, R. (1989) *Zen and the Art of Motorcycle Maintenance*, Black Swan

42 Willie, E. (1990) Should management development just be for managers? *Personnel Management*, August

43 Smythe Dorward Lambert (1991) *The Power of the Open Company.* Smythe Dorward Lambert, Julia House, 40–42 Newman St, London WIP 3PA
44 Zaleznik, A. (1989) *The Managerial Mystique*, Harper and Row
45 Kanter, Ros Moss (1989) *When Giants Learn to Dance*, Unwin Hyman Ltd
46 Naisbitt, J. and Aburdene, P. (1986) *Re-inventing the Corporation*, Macdonald
47 Clutterbuck, D. (1991) *Everyone Needs a Mentor*, IPM
48 Lessem, R. (1991) *Total Quality Learning: Building a Learning Organization*, Basil Blackwell
49 Leary, M., Boydell, T., Van Boeschoten, M. and Carlisle, J. (1986) *The Qualities of Managing*, MSC
50 Boydell, T. and Welshman, G. (1990) Modes of Being and Learning. Paper presented at Conference on 'Learning from Experience', Centre for Creative Leadership, Greensboro, North Carolina
51 Senge, P. (1990) *The Fifth Discipline: The Art and Practice of the Learning Organization*, Doubleday

Appendix

Overview of MCI competences at certificate and diploma levels I and II

Key purpose (for both levels): To achieve the organization's objectives and continuously improve its performance

Certificate level – Management I

UNITS	ELEMENTS
I1 Maintain and improve service and product operations	1.1 Maintain operations to meet quality standards 1.2 Create and maintain the necessary conditions for productive work
I2 Contribute to the implementation of change in services, products and systems	2.1 Contribute to the evaluation of proposed changes to services, products and systems 2.2 Implement and evaluate changes to services, products and systems
I3 Recommend, monitor and control the use of resources	3.1 Make recommendations for expenditure 3.2 Monitor and control the use of resources
I4 Contribute to the recruitment and selection of personnel	4.1 Define future personnel requirements 4.2 Contribute to the assessment and selection of candidates against team and organizational requirements
I5 Develop teams, individuals and self to enhance performance	5.1 Develop and improve teams through planning activities 5.2 Identify, review and improve development activities for individuals
I6 Plan, allocate and evaluate work carried out by teams, individuals and self	6.1 Set and update work objectives for teams and individuals 6.2 Plan activities and determine work methods to achieve objectives

UNITS	ELEMENTS
	6.3 Allocate work and evaluate teams, individuals and self against objectives
	6.4 Provide feedback to teams and individuals on their performance
I7 Create, maintain and enhance effective working relationships	7.1 Establish and maintain the trust and support of one's subordinates
	7.2 Establish and maintain the trust and support of one's immediate manager
	7.3 Establish and maintain relationships with colleagues
	7.4 Identify and minimize interpersonal conflict
	7.5 Implement disciplinary and grievance procedures
	7.6 Counsel staff
I8 Seek, evaluate and organize information for action	8.1 Obtain and evaluate information to aid decision making
	8.2 Record and store information
I9 Exchange information to solve problems and make decisions	9.1 Lead meetings and group discussions to solve problems and make decisions
	9.2 Contribute to discussions to solve problems and make decisions
	9.3 Advise and inform others

Diploma level – Management II

UNITS	ELEMENTS
II1 Initiate and implement change and improvement in services, products and systems	1.1 Identify opportunities for improvement in services, products and systems
	1.2 Evaluate proposed changes for benefits and disadvantages
	1.3 Negotiate and agree the introduction of change

UNITS	ELEMENTS
	1.4 Implement and evaluate changes to services, products and systems
	1.5 Introduce, develop and evaluate quality assurance systems
II2 Monitor, maintain and improve service and product delivery	2.1 Establish and maintain the supply of resources into the organization/department
	2.2 Establish and agree customer requirements
	2.3 Maintain and improve operations against quality and functional specifications
	2.4 Create and maintain the necessary conditions for productive work
II3 Monitor and control the use of resources	3.1 Control costs and enhance value
	3.2 Monitor and control activities against budgets
II4 Secure effective resource allocation for activities and projects	4.1 Justify proposals for expenditure on projects
	4.2 Negotiate and agree budgets
II5 Recruit and select personnel	5.1 Define future personnel requirements
	5.2 Determine specifications to secure quality people
	5.3 Assess and select candidates against team and organizational requirements
II6 Develop teams, individuals and self to enhance performance	6.1 Develop and improve teams through planning and activities
	6.2 Identify, review and improve development activities for individuals
	6.3 Develop oneself within the job role
	6.4 Evaluate and improve the development processes used

UNITS	ELEMENTS
II7 Plan, allocate and evaluate work carried out by teams, individuals and self	7.1 Set and update work objectives for teams and individuals 7.2 Plan activities and determine work methods to achieve objectives 7.3 Allocate work and evaluate teams, individuals and self against objectives 7.4 Provide feedback to teams and individuals on their performance
II8 Create, maintain and enhance effective working relationships	8.1 Establish and maintain the trust and support of one's subordinates 8.2 Establish and maintain the trust and support of one's immediate manager 8.3 Establish and maintain relationships with colleagues 8.4 Identify and minimize interpersonal conflict 8.5 Implement disciplinary and grievance procedures 8.6 Counsel staff
II9 Seek, evaluate and organize information	9.1 Obtain and evaluate information to aid decision making 9.2 Forecast trends and developments which affect objectives 9.3 Record and store information
II10 Exchange information to solve problems and make decisions	10.1 Lead meetings and group discussions to solve problems and make decisions 10.2 Contribute to discussions to solve problems and make decisions 10.3 Advise and inform others

6 Evaluation – the hidden accumulator

I would predict that before the end of the century it will be impossible to write a book purely about the evaluation of training. Training, except for certain routine tasks, will cease to be a separate organizational activity in the majority of firms and evaluation (if the word is still being used) will be concerned with the total evaluation of organizational or personal activities rather than training as such. . . . Yet many of the issues discussed in this book will be more important than ever. The overwhelming need in organismic organization is for free-flowing network systems of information sharing and communication; and the creation and maintenance of such systems is one of the basic problems with which we have been dealing (p. 190).[1]

Tony Hamblin wrote this prediction in 1974 in the conclusion of his book *Evaluation and Control of Training* which was to become one of the definitive text books on the subject. There have been other books since and, I suspect, despite his prediction more will surely follow. But if the organizations of the future are going to have to become more akin to 'learning organizations' and, as we have been suggesting throughout this book, individuals are increasingly encouraged to manage their *own* learning, the whole issue of evaluation will need to move centre-stage. In fact, in my view it is the one process that will enable individual development to become part of organization development.

Hamblin's book[1] followed on from a series of seminars on evaluation which he organized at the University of Bath in the early 1970s. I remember attending one such seminar while I was at BEA and experiencing a transformation in my thinking not just about evaluation methods – which was my main reason for attending – but also about the *purpose* of evaluation itself.

At the time, in line with most companies then and now, BEA evaluated its training mainly through collecting information from course participants on the last day of the course on what have since been called 'happiness sheets'. Participants were invited to rate sessions on the course on scales from 1–10 on such dimensions as 'interest', 'relevance of content', 'how well objectives were achieved'; they might be asked to comment on a tutor's approach.

Because the questionnaires were designed by and directed at course tutors, there would also be questions relating to such 'hygiene' aspects as 'course facilities', 'food' etc. They might also be asked to comment on what they had learned from the course.

The design of the evaluation was by trainers for trainers. The findings were primarily aimed at supporting the running of a given programme, though feedback was taken into account to improve sessions; basically they were used to demonstrate that, on the whole, participants found the course satisfactory and that they should continue to run. The Bath seminar made me aware that collecting data on participants' reactions was only the tip of the iceberg, that in addition to participants' own views, much more valuable were the comments from their superiors as to whether their behaviour had changed in any way. But most exciting of all, from my point of view, was the possibility that an individual's improved performance as the result of a course could have an impact on the organization as a whole.

As a result of that seminar I made some changes to post-course questionnaires. This included a final blank box in which participants were encouraged to give details of what 'action' they were now going to take in their own departments as a result of what they had learned on the course. All of a sudden the post-course questionnaire ceased to be the property of the Training Department but became a vital link with the 'real world' out there in the organization. I also began to apply Tony Hamblin's model and to explore just what *evaluation* meant as a concept. This led me to approach Tony Hamblin at the University of Bath and to register as a PhD student under his supervision. In this chapter I have drawn heavily on the doctoral thesis that resulted from that research.[2]

The first part of this chapter explores just what evaluation means, particularly as applied to training and education. In the second part we review the various models of evaluation that have emerged over the past 30 years. I then present the basis for the model I have developed[2] and review these conclusions ten years on in the light of initiatives like 'Investors in People'. Finally, I suggest a method by which evaluation can become a tool for the organization as a whole as Tony Hamblin envisaged it in the opening extract.

6.1 The nature of evaluation

Defining evaluation is rather like defining 'quality'; we all know what it is and can recognize its outcome but when it comes to definitions we get into all kinds of dilemmas (as I was to find). In this respect the official definition of 'evaluation' offered in the then Manpower Services Commission's *Glossary of Training Terms*[3] in 1981 was no different:

> The assessment of the total value of a training system, training course or programme in social as well as financial terms. Evaluation differs

from validation in that it attempts to measure the overall cost-benefit of the course or programme and not just the achievement of its laid down objectives. The term is also used in the general judgemental sense of the continuous monitoring of a programme or of the training function as a whole.

While beginning with what, in my view, is the essence of evaluation, i.e. 'total value', it then prescribes how that value should be measured. Indeed the holy grail of evaluators is how to find *the* way of putting a 'financial' value on training that has been carried out.

It also draws attention to the distinction to be made between 'validation' and 'evaluation'. Validation is about measuring whether the course has delivered what it promised in terms of its published objectives; evaluation is making a judgement about the effect of putting those objectives into practice. I well remember this distinction alone would generate endless debates amongst trainers. Happily, validation has now come to be subsumed under the umbrella term of evaluation.

But the debate has thrown up what have so far been the two main roles or purposes of carrying out evaluations. These were first proposed by Scriven in 1967[4]. One role is 'formative', i.e. concerned with gathering such information that will improve the programme. (This was very much the role it had in BEA, for example.) The second role is 'summative', which is arriving at a judgement about the programme's value from an analysis of its total effects.

Mark Easterby-Smith[5] calls these two roles respectively 'improving' and 'proving'. He also adds a third role, 'learning' which, as he says, 'has received less attention in the literature than either of the above two purposes.' This was very much the conclusion I arrived at.

But there was another issue that was to become central in my exploration of evaluation and this related to the role 'value' played in evaluation. After all evaluation literally means 'extracting, taking out *value*'. But in all my dealings with trainers and training programmes (I was now working for a Training Board) I could see little evidence of 'value' being a central issue.

Evaluation was the final stage of the 'systematic training cycle' (see Chapter 3, p. 42) and had become synonymous with collecting information about the programme itself (i.e. it still had largely a 'formative' role). In reviewing training with companies seeking exemption from levy, I would often put aside the volumes of data 'about' the programme the participants had attended etc., and ask them – 'So what? What value has it been to you as a company to run these programmes?' I rarely got a satisfactory answer. As far as they were concerned, they had followed the system we had laid down and had collected all the information as required. What they were not able to do was reflect on what they had done and *articulate* its value.

It seemed to me evaluation should be less about collection and quantification of information (though that was part of it) and more about the *process* of articulating value. Indeed, might not the very *process* of searching for value itself generate data of its own?

6.2 Models of evaluation

Easterby-Smith[5] has a useful model for dividing up the various schools of evaluation according to two dimensions:

Methodology   Scientific _____ Naturalistic

                      Quantitative methods   Qualitative methods
                      (statistics, pre-determined)   (descriptive, discovery)

Style   Research _____ Pragmatic

                      Rigorous procedures   Based on practical
                      based on a guiding   interests, operational
                      theory   decisions

By putting the two together he is able to categorize where the main schools fall. I have separated out three other schools (marked by an asterisk) in the 'scientific/pragmatic' and 'scientific/research' quadrants in Figure 6.1 below which is an adapted version of Easterby-Smith's model. I have also numbered them in the order in which we will cover them in this section which also reflects the chronological order in which they appeared over the past 30–40 years. Although these schools are dealt with in a historical perspective all eight of them will be being used somewhere in some form wherever companies are seeking to evaluate their training.

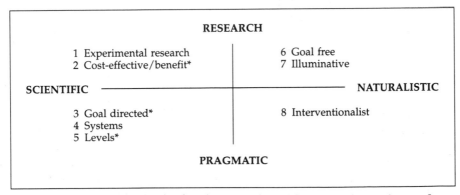

Figure 6.1 *Models and schools of evaluation (adapted from Easterby-Smith, p. 25[5].* *(Reproduced with kind permission of Gower Publishing Co Ltd)*

ACTIVITY 6.1
● *As we cover each one, make a note of whether a particular approach is behind the way your company is currently evaluating training; or whether it reflects the way you would like to evaluate the training.*

---

(1) Experimental research school

The roots of this scientific research approach go back to the 1940s. In their review of evaluation practice,[6] Smith and Piper trace its origins to a report on 'Training within Industry'[7] which advocated a systematic collection of information about the programme covering such areas as:

1 Information to be collected is decided in advance.
2 Methods of collection are devised which permit quantification of data.
3 Data is collected before and after the course.
4 Cross-checking of data is conducted by adding control groups, placebo groups who receive placebo training, varying the measurement and the measurement times etc.

By this means it was hoped to draw a direct correlation between training and the change in performance.

This 'scientific' approach was the ideal of the 1950s and 1960s. One of its most influential proponents was Hesseling[8] who saw evaluation as a research process which could lead to 'a scientific assessment of changes in human behaviour' (p. 301).[8] As a result of surveying how a number of companies reviewed their training he concluded that it was largely a hit-and-miss approach which failed

> mainly because the evaluator attempted an evaluation of a training course as a whole or tried to discover a direct correlation between training activities and an increase of profit and organizational effectiveness (p. 49).[8]

The solution, he suggested, was to be very clear as to *what* was being measured, *who* needed the information and *who* was doing the measuring. As a result he evolved a 'typology' which comprised a matrix of possible decisions which any would-be evaluator can take with respect to *who* is making the assessment and *for whom* the assessment is intended. He identified five possible evaluators each of whom could also be on the receiving end of the information.

● Trainees
● Trainers
● Supervisors
● Policy makers
● Scientists

As a result there were 25 ways by which appropriate information could be collected for a respective client. Despite being a prime exponent of the experimental/research school, Hesseling was also sufficiently pragmatic to make this recommendation, which is good advice to all evaluators:

> An exact identification of the problem is more important than the rigorous application of the methods of measurement (p. 283).[8]

ACTIVITY 6.2
● *How clear are you just what it is you should be measuring and for whom the assessment is intended? What value do you place on how 'rigorous' is the methodology for assessment?*

---

(2) Costing, cost-effectiveness and cost-benefit analysis

As the MSC definition of 'evaluation' makes clear, assessment of total value implies some kind of assessment of a training programme's 'financial' value. But though employers continually cite it as being critical and trainers attempt to produce some kind of supporting evidence, the issue of putting a financial value on the output of training has never been satisfactorily resolved.

Although not strictly a 'school' of evaluation, I have separated it out – and included it in Easterby-Smith's 'scientific/research quadrant' – because it is always an issue in any kind of evaluation, albeit implicit rather than explicit. It is also currently under scrutiny again, as we shall see, in the criteria for the Investors in People award.

I have categorized it as 'scientific/research' because more often than not 'costing' of training is an end in itself. Oatey comes to this conclusion:

> training cost data and budgets, where they exist, are set up more for internal administrative convenience than for the purpose of estimating real economic costs (p. 11).[9]

During the 1960s, prompted by the Industrial Training Act, there were a number of 'Guides' for training managers on how to 'cost' training.[10–13]

Hitherto, there was little awareness that training actually did have *costs* that could be allocated to the training department and which *could* be apportioned out according to how a particular department used the company's training services. Very few companies actually put this into practice but the kind of costs identified by Garbutt in the following list would have made accountants happy:

1 Personnel costs and payment to personnel (e.g. wages, salaries)
2 Personnel costs – other payments (e.g. national insurance, luncheon vouchers, pension fund contributions etc.)
3 Fees paid for external training
4 Building costs and services (e.g. rent, rates, water, gas etc.)
5 Production costs (e.g. machine hire, repairs, maintenance)
6 Administrative costs (e.g. printing, stationery, furniture)
7 Insurance (e.g. employers' liability, accident, fire)
8 Transportation and travel
9 Depreciation (e.g. land, buildings, machinery)
10 Purchasing and selling expenses[12]

For a simple matrix for costing training events see Bramley's work on *Evaluating Training Effectiveness*,[14] where he divides up costs into personnel, facilities and equipment and allocates them according to three stages in a training programme's development: design, delivery and evaluation.

The emphasis was on the costing of formal training. But what about the economic viability of alternatives like formal learning from experience, recruitment of employees who have the required skill, job redesign etc?[9]

There is growing evidence of the 'value' of informal and incidental learning at the workplace[15] and more account will need to be taken of the costs involved in informal as well as formal learning in any evaluation carried out in the future.

So far we have only considered the 'costing' of training and the implications of not training. The next issue relates to what you do with the costs once they have been collected. One form of analysis which ITBs have tried to get companies to adopt – without much success – is cost effectiveness. This involves a *comparison* of the cost of one method of training/learning to achieve a particular objective with other methods. In an ideal world a company would choose the *cheapest* method which enables the same objective to be achieved satisfactorily.

An example of a cost-effectiveness exercise was carried out by Cooper and Lybrand to compare costs of Open Learning with more traditional methods. An extract from an analysis of the costs attributed to a hotel based supervisor course using traditional and Open Learning methods is contained in Figure 6.2.[16] It shows the kind of seemingly dramatic changes that can take place using Open Learning methods. Cost savings were in areas of course fees, loss of trainee productive time whilst away from work and opportunity costs of using the hotel's own conference facilities.

Economist Keith Drake produced a report in 1979 on the cost-effectiveness of a number of British vocational training programmes and came to some interesting conclusions about the nature of cost-effectiveness analysis as a *process* in its own right.

> What emerges as the primary objective is not the production of an exclusive criterion for making decisions about training, but a means of

	Open Learning (20 trainees) £	In-house courses (20 trainees) £
Development	228	228
HCTB material	2040	–
Tutorial Support	840	–
Polytechnic course fees	–	10000
Trainee time and expenses	800	23000
Manager support	600	1800
Hotel conference facilities	–	18000
Head office administration	764	764
	5272	53792

Figure 6.2 *Example analysis of cost of Open Learning compared to in-house lecture course*

improving the accessibility, quality and relevance of the information with which management has to make a judgement. The data of choices are always *imagined* and expected costs and benefits from competing options, not the actual costs and benefits which flow from past choices. Nevertheless the information on cost-effectiveness, timing and risks which is assembled and systemized by a cost-effectiveness analyst can influence the *imagination* of those who are taking allocative decisions (pp. 11–12) (emphasis added).[17]

The use of the term 'imagination' in this context is an interesting one based as it is on the economic concept of imagining 'opportunity costs' rather than accounting for hard and fast cost data. Drake sees the primary purpose of cost-effectiveness as that of improving the decision making process. But secondly he considers the process of analysis 'may stimulate reactions which are beneficial in their own right' and gives these as examples:

- More careful specification of training objectives and of the relative weights attached to them.
- Development of an agreed model of the training activity based on a clearer idea of what it involves.
- Search for feasible competing packages of ways and means of achieving objectives.
- Improved measures of the magnitude and incidence of benefits from training.
- Careful evaluation of rival criteria of choice (p. 12).[17]

Finally he identifies a third benefit as clarifying the 'relationship between training and its organizational and social context'!

Whether training produces easily distinguishable or almost indis-
tinguishable effects, it still needs to be viewed as part of a total
organizational effort in which there exist possibilities (1) for substitu-
tion and (2) for improving complementarity between training and non-
training strategies. Cost-effectiveness analysis can then be regarded
not merely as (i) a means of getting feedback from the improvement of
the training function in isolation but also as (ii) a contributor to the task
of assessing and improving the overall efficiency of the client
organization (p. 15).[17]

This notion of the analysis *itself* leading to the identification of value was
central to my own thesis on evaluation in 1982 and, as we shall see, is even
more valid and applicable in the current developments taking place in
training and development:

The value theory employed in using accounting or non-accounting
costs is as important to make clear as the actual figuring which
delineates it. Value judgements start with the assessment of costs
(p. 22).[17]

ACTIVITY 6.3
- *Consider the decision making process in your own organization. How
could an analysis of comparative methods for achieving learning objectives
reveal underlying values that your organization holds?*

If companies have been reluctant to carry out cost-effectiveness evaluation
they have certainly fought shy of the final 'costing' approach we need to
consider – *cost-benefit analysis*. This is really the key to 'financial' value; it
implies some form of 'pay-back' over and above the original costs of
training and answers the fundamental question at the heart of evaluation:
Was the expense incurred in training/learning *worth it*?

An example of a cost-benefit analysis is quoted by Bramley[14] and is
reproduced in Figure 6.3 below. It is taken from a report by the Training

---

Quality awareness programmes have become very popular and some of these lend
themselves to cost-benefit studies. For instance, Girobank decided to focus on
improving quality in its Operations Directorate which undertakes most of the
processing and data capture functions at the main operational site. A one-day quality
awareness module was developed and delivered through 69 workshops. An internal
publicity campaign maintained the impetus of the process. There has been a 22%
reduction in keying errors, a 28% reduction in stationery re-order, and a reduction in
the scrutiny of customer transaction documents. The estimated saving is about £1
million from an investment of £25,000 in training.

Figure 6.3 *Example of cost-benefit analysis (reproduced from Bramley, Evaluating
Training Effectiveness[4]. (Reproduced with kind permission of McGraw Hill)*

Agency on the national training awards in 1988. The problem of cost-benefit analysis is not the costing side – we have already examined a range of criteria for allocating training costs – but in measuring benefits that can be attributed solely to the training input. In my experience working with companies on evaluation, the issue is more to do with an inability to *think* in output terms other than those of the restricted targets that are operationally set – often to meet internal administrative systems.

I recently completed an evaluation report for a national company based on work I had been engaged on supported by funding from the then Training Agency. A condition of government funding had been the need to demonstrate quantifiable business benefits arising from the training we had designed. Right from the outset we had to commit ourselves to a percentage change in dimensions like market share, customer spend, staff retention etc. The company had well-established systems for collecting information but we found that they were not geared up to collecting the kind of company-wide data the Training Agency were looking for. Therefore new procedures were introduced which enabled the company to collect such information. It is my belief that the very *process* of establishing such new procedures did as much to influence the figures as the training itself (rather like the Hawthorne effect).

It also strikes me now that what was happening was the 'imagining' process Drake was describing. What is needed is for companies to come up with more and more creative measures that reflect benefits that are unique to the company. But we have to start somewhere. Bramley uses a classification developed by Cameron[18] to suggest a wide range of criteria for organizational effectiveness (pp. 71–6)[14] Figure 6.4 gives a summary of

---

1 **Goal directed** definitions focus on the output of the organization and how close it comes to meeting its goals

Examples include: units produced; defects; backlogs; output per person per hour; running costs; amount of overtime

2 **Resource acquiring** definitions judge effectiveness by the extent to which the organization acquires much needed resources from its external environment

Examples include: new markets entered; skills developed

3 **Constituencies** are groups of individuals who have some stake in the organization – resource providers, customers etc. – and effectiveness is judged in terms of how well the organization responds to the demands and expectations of these groups

Examples include: customer complaints; company surveys; incorrect goods received

4 **Internal process** definitions focus attention on flows of information, absence of strain, and levels of trust as measures of effectiveness

Examples include: turnover of employees; job satisfaction

Figure 6.4 *Four ways of defining criteria to measure organizational effectiveness*

Cameron's classification and some of the variables Bramley identifies under each heading.

Perhaps there has been too much emphasis on what Chris Hendry calls 'hard' criteria.[19] He found that companies who were most committed to training were those using 'soft' evaluation measures. In their case the sense of the value of training often gets translated into 'soft' criteria relating to broad human resource goals (to do with recruitment and retention, career management, morale etc.) and there is scepticism (which is entirely rational) about 'hard' cost/benefit evaluation related to bottom-line (financial) outcomes. In other words they look beyond specific training activity at the wider issues of managing people and organizational effectiveness.[19]

His conclusion is that companies should use a combination of hard and soft criteria 'which are intermediate to, or the means to, bottom-line performance'. In other words, we should abandon the attempt to see a *direct* relationship between training and profit. Indeed, it might be said that those companies who require to see evidence of such a correlation have little faith in training as a process for change. In reviewing some of his earlier findings on cost-benefit analysis,[13] Jones comes to this conclusion:

> Early in the research it was assumed that value can be expressed in terms of hard cash and that if hard cash data were presented to decision makers it would modify their decisions. It was surprising that this did not always follow, e.g. small clothing manufacturers, when presented with evidence of possible large savings which they could obtain from a more systematic approach to training, did not leap in the air with joy at this new revelation ... They stated that they did not expect *improvements* but felt that the training was worthwhile in other ways (i.e. they had a different currency from immediate job improvements or cash returns) (p. 139).[20]

A 'different currency' was what the accountants Fielden and Pearson recommended in their report to the then Manpower Services Commission on the feasibility of costing training.[21] They are critical of the attempt to 'cost' training in 'monetary units at an early stage' before identifying what they call the critical 'resource units' appropriate to bringing about a particular change. By resource units they mean

> the natural units in which a change in resource usage can be perceived and measured. Only in a relatively few cases is money the correct resource unit and its use should be restricted, at this stage, to those changes which directly affect the cash flow of the company in the purchase of resources which it does not at present possess or income which it does not at present receive, or a saving in expenditure which it now occurs. In general, resource units are measured such as man days of staff time, a change in the annual percentage turnover, square metres of floor space, days of training and so on (p. 23).[24]

They advise companies to concentrate on the kind of changes they are seeking to bring about by training and the kind of analysis that is *appropriate* to the way decisions are made in that company. 'If a costing approach is to make any real impact it must eventually feature as part of the regular decision making process' (p. 73).[21]

Not only were they critical of a premature costing of training, drawing on their previous work on costing educational practice they emphasize 'the importance of recognizing that many effects cannot be quantified and that *subjective judgement plays an important, and often dominant part in resource evaluation*' (emphasis added).[21]

I find it significant that both economists (Drake) and accountants (Fielden and Pearson) carrying out independent investigations should both emphasize:

1 The importance of the natural decision making process in a company and the need to *improve* that process as part of the evaluation analysis.
2 The recognition of the *subjective* value of judgments that make up this decision making process.

Finally, there is the HRA (Human Resource Accounting) approach which featured in the 1970s (though there may well be a need to revive the concept in view of the Investors in People initiative). Likert and Pyle[22] posed one of the fundamental questions like this: 'How many years of payroll would it take for a firm that has lost all its employees except the President to build back its human organization to the original level of effectiveness of its previous personnel?' This seems to me an 'accountant' approach – though some companies might be tempted to ask themselves this question if only to consider how they might manage things differently a second time around!

Tsaklanganos[23] suggests the economic approach to putting a price on an employee's head:

> The first step ... is to multiply the individual's annual salary and efficiency factor, and adjust this for the probability of mortality and the probability of remaining employed for the rest of the year. The present value of the product of salary, efficiency factor and termination probabilities for each year is discounted using the aforementioned discount rate. The present value result for each year from the present until retirement is then summed to produce the economic value of the individual to the organization (p. 47).[23]

Simple? There's just one snag embodied in the throw away technicality – 'efficiency factor'. What is it and how do you measure it? Bringing the debate up-to-date, Bramley[14] has an ingenious model for estimating employees' worth which is based on a number of assumptions:

1 Start off with a simple definition of 'performance at work'. (As he says 'it is sometimes useful in social science to work with a 'primitive' concept which is inherently somewhat vague and imprecise, as this can make it possible to integrate seemingly disparate ideas' (p. 82).)[14]
2 Before training employees are going to need additional skills, knowledge to perform effectively.
3 After training they should be able to perform more effectively and therefore be of greater value to the organization.
4 At least *some* of this added value could be attributed to training.

The logic is impeccable – an evaluator's dream. Bramley suggests performance is a function of Skills × Motivation × Opportunity. Bramley's starting point is to compare an individual's pre-training performance (using the above formula) with the *average* level of other employees engaged in the same work. To do this he produces a normal distribution curve from which he derives standard deviations from the average (e.g. one standard deviation below or above the mean leads to a noticeable difference whereas two SDs above or below the mean signals a significant difference).

By estimating a person's performance in relation to his or her colleagues before and after training Bramley suggests you have some measure for putting a value on what the training has contributed to the organization:

> For instance, an employee who is considered to have average motivation (1.0) but whose skills are noticeably below average (0.67) is estimated to be performing at 0.7 of what is expected in the job. If training can bring such a person up to the average level of skills, the increment in performance is 0.3 and the value added to the employee by such training is, therefore, 0.3 salary of the salary for the job (p. 84).[14]

I am sure that along with Drake, Fielden and Pearson, Bramley would not look upon his model as *actually and objectively* measuring value. What it does, I suggest, is make explicit the value a company may *unconsciously* put on an individual. Furthermore, however subjective the outcome, as Bramley suggests, it can be backed up with 'hard' data on costs (using the kind of analysis we have discussed) which will give a company at least an indication of the return on its assets.

A conclusion I came to when reviewing these approaches in the late 1970s was that the *content* of the analysis was not nearly as important as the *process of analysis itself* which, as we have suggested with Bramley's model, makes explicit values which otherwise would not have been articulated. As we shall see, companies are increasingly going to have to make decisions, albeit subjective, about the worth of employees and *how to reward that worth*. Ros Moss Kanter[24] has for some time been preparing management for a new age in which they must reward contribution and not status.

We have spent so much time on the 'costing' approach to evaluation because it is central to the popular notion of what evaluation entails. We began by categorizing it as 'scientific/research' in Easterby-Smith's model because that is the way, I suggest, most companies see it, as a paper exercise. (ITBs also tended to reinforce this view, though not intentionally.) However, the conclusion we have come to is that the kind of analyses suggested by Drake,[17] Fielden and Pearson[21] and Bramley[14] provide a much more flexible and essentially 'pragmatic' approach to evaluation.

In this section I hope I have demonstrated that any company *could*, if it so wished, cost out training and put a value on its outcome. But would any company go to that trouble? Certainly the results of the survey *Training in Britain*[25] indicated that very few companies were even attempting to cost training and where they did it was mainly 'external' costs and did not, for example, include participants' wages.

ACTIVITY 6.4
● *Taking account of the various approaches to costing and measuring the benefits of training in this section, what value do you now place on the need to carry out such an analysis? What methods would you use? What value would you expect to get out of such an exercise?*

To conclude this section, I have reproduced in Figure 6.5 a model I have used to open up a debate about the nature of financial value that *could* be attributed to a *given* input of training. I believe that much of the debate about the problems of putting a financial value on training has centred on the inability of companies to identify just what elements make up training. This was why I devoted Chapter 4 to the nature of the resources that make up a training programme. But being clear about training resources is only half the equation. We also have to be clear about the specific outcomes we expect to occur as a result of particular inputs. (This is the subject of the next section.) Given that we can specify both output and inputs of training we can then engage in some imagining as to what might be the possible consequences of a particular training objective being achieved. This is the basis for the evaluation equation in Figure 6.5.

I have deliberately taken a rather mundane subject (with no offence offered to kitchen porters!) to illustrate the point that it does not have to be just management training that can lead to economic benefits to the organization. The exercise is to start with a particular training objective and write it in the top box (see Figure 6.5). *Assuming* the objective is achieved, write down a series of consequences (one being the cause of a further consequence) on which you could put an estimated financial value. To the sum you end up with by totalling this column (see example in Figure 6.5), you then add the sum of the second column which goes one stage further

Description of training objective that has been achieved

> Kitchen porter now able to detect any faulty goods being delivered to kitchen

What series of consequences has/could this bring about which have a financial payoff?		What 'added value' might accrue from these consequences which have a financial payoff?		Cost of training
	£		£	£
1 Food costs reduced by 10%	?			
2 Overall unit productivity improves by 15%	?	1 Your status as Unit Manager improves	?	
3 Your Area Manager's regional figures improve by 5%	?	2 Your Area Manager wins area prize	?	
4 Regional Director's annual figures up by 4%	?	3 Regional Director promoted	?	
5 Company makes improved profit of 12%	?			
6 Improved company figure leads to new business	?	4 CBI cite company as example of good cost-control management	?	
Total financial value	?	+ Total added value	?	− Total costs ?

Figure 6.5 *The evaluation equation*

and asks you to 'imagine' how the consequences you have listed in the first column can lead to 'added value'. For this you really do have to do some upside-down thinking! Finally you deduct from the final sum the cost of training this one kitchen porter to detect faulty goods being delivered to the kitchen.

The answer to the inevitable question 'How can you be sure that such value came *just* from training?' is that you never can. But carrying out such an analysis takes you beyond straight cause and effect conclusions with the result that you just might realize value of which you would otherwise have been unaware.

ACTIVITY 6.5
● *Carry out the exercise in Figure 6.5 on a training objective that has been achieved in your own company.*

An exercise such as Activity 6.5 does make the assumption that you *do have* training objectives. This is the subject of our next section.

(3) Goal-directed school of evaluation

Logically, this school should have come before dealing with 'costing' of training, because without clear objectives of what training should achieve there is no way you can measure or put a financial value on the outcome. It also goes back some way to the work of Tyler in the United States who carried out a comparative study of educational curricula[26] and concluded that 'the process of evaluation is essentially the process of determining to what extent the educational objectives are actually being realized by the programme of curriculum and instruction'. But 'behavioural objectives' did not really get under way until the 1960s – principally with the publication of Mager's *Preparing Instructional Objectives*[27] in 1962; it also falls into the 'pragmatic' rather than the 'scientific' dimension on Easterby-Smith's scale. Mager was writing specifically for instructors to help them communicate what he called 'instructional intent' to the student.

But what started as an exercise in good communication soon became in the 1970s – once the ITBs had got hold of the idea – a prescription for any training programme. I hate to think how many training manuals were rejected out of hand because they did not have 'behavioural objectives'. In Mager's model an objective had three components:

1 Statement of performance:
   there had to be an 'active' verb describing what the learner was expected to *do*.
2 Condition:
   where necessary it should state specific conditions under which the action should occur.
3 Criteria:
   there should be a description of what would be considered 'acceptable' performance (i.e. success criteria).

Thus 'vague' aims like 'student room attendant will be expected to clean room' when translated into the Mager model became: 'Given access to proprietary cleaning brand X (Condition) room attendant will clean all vitreous surfaces (Performance) so that they are free of dust and shiny within total time of 5 minutes (Criterion).

But the approach had a number of benefits for both instructor and student:

For the instructor

1 It enables him/her to measure success in terms of achievement of the objectives (though this is validation rather than evaluation).
2 It enables him/her to choose instructional methods appropriate to how the objective is to be measured. If the objective required the student to demonstrate success by using a particular machine, then the training had to ensure hands-on practice and not rely on simply 'knowledge awareness' of how the machine worked.
3 It removes ambiguity from the instructor's role; everyone is clear what is expected and *all* instructors following a particular programme would be expected to aim for the same results.

For the student/learner

4 It gives a clear indication of what a given programme is about and what is expected of him/her.
5 It enables him/her to direct his/her own learning towards the achievement of the objective.

Having read Chapter 3, it will not have escaped your attention that competence based development owes a lot to the Mager approach. It is interesting (and encouraging) that what started in the 1960s as a prescription for instructors has now become the means of helping learners take ownership for their own development. However, in the meantime, rather like an evangelical movement, goal-oriented evaluation in the form of objectives had both its fanatical supporters and its detractors.

It was deceptively simple and worked best with clearly defined behavioural skills and less well where the outcome was more knowledge based or required an evaluative judgement. This was where Bloom's *Taxonomy of Educational Objectives*[28] was perhaps more useful. It drew distinctions between three kinds of objectives depending on whether an outcome required a cognitive, an affective or a psychomotor response. Whereas Mager's was a reductionist approach which sought to break down any outcome until measurable criteria emerged, Bloom sought to classify different types of response (in this sense it is more a naturalistic rather than research approach).

But it is Mager's rather than Bloom's approach which has had a major influence on the way training programmes are designed. From my point of view this was and is the advantage of the approach. It really does not go beyond the boundary of the design of the programme – which is all that Mager intended. Evaluation requires us to take a much larger picture. But we ought to be grateful to Mager for emphasizing the importance of goals in the first place. Without them, as he said, we might end up someplace else!

But, again, I suggest the *value* is not in the objectives themselves (as it is not in the competence statements that have now taken over where behavioural objectives left off) but in the *process* which the very definition of the goals has started:

> Goals are rational abstractions in non-rational systems; they are the rational expression of a highly subjective process. Statements of goals emerge at the interface between the ideals of human rationality and the reality of human values. Therein lies their strength and their weakness. *Goals provide direction for action and evaluation but only for those who share in the values expressed by the goals.* Evaluators live inside that paradox (p. 147, emphasis added).[29]

One of the issues I explored while working on my model of evaluation was on the 'ownership of goals'; taking very much to heart Patton's words which I have highlighted in the extract above. Objectives of programmes that are published have been set by professional trainers, designers. Why not describe the outcome of programmes in the way former participants would describe their *own* outcomes? I used this approach by asking one group of participants at the end of a management course to articulate the kind of objectives they felt best described the outcome of the course. If they were recommending the course to a colleague how would *they* describe the course goals?

I then used these goals to reflect what I saw as the 'values' of the previous group to the next group who were to attend the same course. This, of course, cuts right across the benefits of objectives describing a standard, unambiguous product. But the goals the participants came up with tended not to be that different from the objectives of the programme. It was just that they were expressed in a way which reflected the values as perceived by the group. In the end it still achieved what was Mager's intention for an objective, that it 'conveys to others a picture of what a successful learner will be like' (p. 19).[27] In the second edition of his book, Mager was sensitive to the kind of witch-hunts that his original text had sparked off to seek out and eradicate all 'loose' descriptions of objectives (e.g. words like 'awareness' and 'understand'). He calls these 'false criteria' and affirms:

> Frankly, I don't care what words you use ... Use *whatever words will communicate what you have in mind well enough for others to understand your intents as you understand them* (p. 40, emphasis added).[27]

ACTIVITY 6.6
- *Next time you attend/run a training programme, compare the objectives you would set with those that are published. Is it more appropriate to have a selection of objectives chosen by former participants which reflect the kinds of outcome both you and the students agree are appropriate?*

(4) The systems school of evaluation

The model of 'systematic training' was introduced in Chapter 3, when we investigated the way training needs have been traditionally identified and how the 'systems' approach adopted by the Training Boards was able to institutionalize the process. I also alluded to the same approach at the beginning of this chapter in the context of the inability of companies to put a value on their own training. Their response was that 'they followed the system'. It was like being caught in a trap and it was largely as a consequence of this 'feeling' that I started my research into evaluation to find a way out of the trap.

In order to do so I tried to analyse what it was about 'systems' approaches to evaluation that was helpful or unhelpful. To recap, the basic four-stage feedback model that most ITBs adopted in the 1970s and 1980s was as follows:

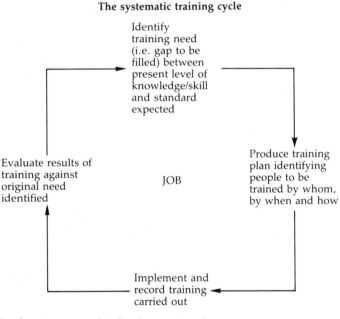

The systematic training cycle

Identify training need (i.e. gap to be filled) between present level of knowledge/skill and standard expected

Produce training plan identifying people to be trained by whom, by when and how

JOB

Evaluate results of training against original need identified

Implement and record training carried out

Evaluation was the final stage in the process.

My reservations were threefold:

1 It focuses attention on the internal process of the system itself rather than what the system is there to achieve.
2 The underlying principle is that of control, whereby information is fed back to maintain the system itself. In this context evaluation can only have a 'formative' role.
3 The role of the learner in the system approach is a passive one.

My experience of companies following a systematic approach for the purposes of exemption from levy was that they used it simply to collect information which they rarely even used to improve the system let alone reflect on what it had achieved. How did one break out of the system?

During the 1970s there were a number of studies into the 'transfer' of management skills from training courses into the real world of the organization.[30-32] In different ways they all sought to modify the basic systematic feedback model to take account of both individual learning needs and, most importantly of all,[30] of organizational factors that would help facilitate transfer. What they did was to add more 'mediating' boxes and control systems within control systems. The mediating boxes were becoming more sensitive to individual needs and the real world of the organization *but* the outcome was the same – the information that these boxes collected never went anywhere, except to feed the model itself.

In the midst of all these models I felt trapped too, until I happened on the work of Stafford Beer.[33] It seems ironic that it should take a distinguished expert in cybernetics to shed some light on why traditional systems thinking is not much help when it comes to putting value on social systems. *Platform for Change* is a collection of papers out of which I derived three notions that changed the way I thought about evaluation in organizations and, in particular, sprung me free from the systems trap. These notions, very broadly stated, are as follows:

1 The illogicality of controlling the real world by a model which is out of date (what Beer calls a 'surrogate').
2 This would be bad enough if the world was static but it is constantly changing and generating 'variety' which the system has somehow to control; it can only do this by Ashby's law of 'requisite variety' which states that only *variety* can absorb variety.
3 Within the stereotype of the system there are issues which cannot be decided within the language of the system but require a meta-language which is the property of a *meta*-system.

Despite the jargon, these ideas seemed to describe the dilemma I found in a systems approach to evaluation. Thus, the first proposition recognizes the redundancy of adding more and more boxes to a control model which can never capture 'the real world'. The second proposition is one we will come back to in the final chapter when we look at the learning organization. Its relevance for evaluation is that a systems model has tended to simplify and control rather than *generate* variety.

But it is the concept of a meta-system that I believe is the real breakthrough. The proposition is that by definition value cannot be described within or by the language of the system itself; it lies in a system that is outside ('meta') the system but which can only be reached *through* the system.

As an example, in a paper called 'Questions of Metric' Beer considers the problem of how we can measure public worth. He concludes it is by 'utility', though he uses the Greek word 'eudemony' which describes a state of 'public satisfaction'; this can be gauged only by measuring 'changes in potential'. To take a simple example, he considers how a government might measure just how secure the average citizen feels. This could be answered by simply asking at a point of time 'Are you more or less secure than the last time I asked?' This is measuring what Beer calls 'eudemonic potential'. It is literally being able to pick up the voice of the people even though the people may not be conscious of any system which is collecting such information. This is where the systems approach to evaluation breaks down – it is ostensibly collecting information which is out-of-date and out-of-touch. It will continue to be so *until* we can find a way of asking the kind of question that captures 'eudemonic potential'. This will not be the existing models, of which we could make the same criticism that Beer uses against 'most of the models of social utility':

> they deal in the accepted measurements by which social institutions are already stably governed. But *the choices we have to make lie only ostensibly within those systems* and are determined only ostensibly on the scales of their accustomed metrics. *The choices are really made at the meta systemic level in terms of eudemony*; and here our institutions are wildly unstable because the required servo controls do not exist and no-one knows what the metric may be. Instead of measurement *we have a value system* (p. 171, emphasis added).[33]

That value system is based on and around what Beer calls a 'focus of meaning' whereby each of us makes judgements about the world outside from within a 'judgemental *n*-space'. *That* is the proper data any evaluation system should be collecting. But though it has its roots in the present system, its *value* can only be described in terms that come from another, 'meta' system.

When I asked course participants to describe the course they had attended in terms of objectives *they* had identified for the benefit of the next course, I was tapping into what Beer calls 'eudemony'. As a result the descriptions they came out with comprised the meta system which, Beer would argue, is a more appropriate 'metric' value of that course. On the other hand, if we had simply asked them to comment on the objectives as set by the course designers, we would simply be perpetuating the systematic chain we have already criticized.

In practice, of course, we should maintain both systems. We do need information of the 'systematic' kind to sustain the system but it will never grow and change until we compare it with the perspective from a 'meta' level as well. A similar argument has been put forward by Taylor.[34] He includes the traditional systematic cycle within an 'outer loop' which more appropriately describes the 'circumstances of many organizations today, as they struggle to move progressively out of purely rational management systems towards those with greater emphasis on intuition, initiative and some degree of shared values'. But it is not clear how one moves from the inner systematic cycle to the outer one which embraces vision, mission, unstructured experimentation leading to vision. One solution is provided by Senge in *The Fifth Discipline*.[35]

The fifth discipline is 'systems thinking'. It is called the 'fifth' discipline because, Senge argues, it integrates four other disciplines all of which are needed to bring about the learning organization of the future. (These are reviewed in Chapter 7). Systems thinking, Senge argues, enables you to recognize and articulate patterns in events which lead to 'metanoia', a literal 'change of mind'. Senge uses diagrams to describe what he calls 'Systems Archetypes'. These enable you to describe reality in circles of 'feedback loops' rather than in a traditional linear cause and effect mode.

He identifies two primary types of feedback which enable our subconscious to become used to seeing the world in a circular rather than cause and effect way; in this world we are not separate but are *part* of the system and indeed our actions have a 'reinforcing' and/or 'balancing' impact on the system itself. Reinforcing feedback 'amplifies' cumulative effects and balancing feedback brings about a stable state. In diagrammatic form Senge illustrates how systems diagrams can enable us to stand outside the system in which we are trapped and see patterns that would otherwise have not been made explicit.

In many respects Senge's approach is similar to the concept of the meta-system propounded by Stafford Beer. Indeed Beer's use of his concept in a very practical way in Allende's Chile seems very close to the kind of pragmatic approach Senge is advocating and it is noticeable that no reference is made to Beer's work. (Like Senge, Beer was very fond of simple systems diagrams to illustrate what Senge calls 'dynamic complexity'.)

We have again come a long way from the original description of a systems approach to evaluation. The lesson for the evaluator for companies using a systems approach is to open up the process whereby data are collected so that it can capture something of what Beer calls 'changes in potential' and Senge 'metanoia'.

Suppose one of your managers recently attended a training course. How would you review whether the course had made any difference? Would this be at the time of formal appraisal? Would you feed back to the trainers what changes had occurred? How would they know that their course is relevant?

This is the 'formal' approach, which fitted in well with the systematic approach to training. It was also 'tidy' and enabled ITBs to check the system at critical points, though I have yet to find a company that regularly reported back to its training department in this way.

Evaluation

Suppose now you are at a meeting with the manager who was on the course and notice how well she is tackling a particular question. You remark on this. She tells you about a particular session on the course that had helped her develop assertiveness. You think about other managers who could do with the same help. You make a point of arranging for some training on assertiveness with the training department.

This is the informal route. It is also an example, I suggest, of a meta-system in the making. It reflects the way real choices are made on value within the organization. It would be up to the trainers how they use this to build on the 'eudemony' you have chanced to identify. Maybe it would simply be to encourage you to keep in contact, to show that they can design any change programme appropriate to your needs. They might suggest they spend more time in your department to identify similar needs. You both become aware of the value of increased contact – a meta-system is born.

ACTIVITY 6.7
● *Consider how you currently collect information about the impact of development on your organization. Does it follow the systematic training cycle? Are there other ways in which you get feedback on development activities? Which methods best reflect the way your organization makes decisions?*

---

(5) Levels of evaluation

Bramley[14] includes this approach under 'Goal based' evaluation while Easterby-Smith[5] and Smith and Piper[6] include it under a 'Systems' approach. I have chosen to separate it out into a class of its own. It is *goal* based in so far as it advocates objectives being set at different levels depending on the kind of outcome you want to achieve and measure. It is also part of a systems tradition in that it provides a systematic way of collecting feedback at each of the respective levels. But I maintain it is also qualitatively different in that it can be used in what Hamblin called a 'discovery approach to evaluation'. In this sense, I believe, it occupies a watershed position between the 'scientific' methods we have explored so far and the more 'naturalistic' approaches we look at next.

Though its origins go back to 1939,[36] it is generally accepted that Kirkpatrick[37] was the first to put forward a practical approach aimed at trainers. His intention was to demonstrate to trainers that evaluation was not as elusive a problem as they imagined. He put forward four steps which enabled trainers to pose key questions at what were to become four critical levels of evaluation:

Step 1–*Reaction*   How well did course participants like the programme?
Step 2–*Learning*   What did they learn?
Step 3–*Behaviour*   What changes in job behaviour resulted from the programme?
Step 4–*Results*   What were tangible results in terms of reduced cost, improved quality etc?

The next model to appear was CIRO.[38] This was essentially a conceptual framework which identified the following levels of evaluation:

Context evaluation   Obtaining information about the operational context in which the prospective trainee works
Input evaluation   Obtaining information about and comparing different resources that will contribute to training input
Reactions evaluation   Obtaining information about trainees' reaction to the training in order to improve it.
Outcome evaluation   Obtaining information at three levels
   Ultimate   What are the particular problems in organization that training is trying to resolve?
   Intermediate   What changes in the trainee's work behaviour would be necessary for ultimate objective to be achieved?
   Immediate   What new skills, knowledge, attitude will trainee need to change his/her behaviour?

Hamblin[1] put all the models together and proposed a 'cause and effect chain' linking five levels of training effects as follows:

           TRAINING
leads to   REACTIONS
lead to   LEARNING
leads to   CHANGES IN THE ORGANIZATION
lead to   CHANGES IN ACHIEVEMENT OF ULTIMATE GOALS

This chain may snap at any of its links. A trainee may react correctly but fail to learn; or he may learn but fail to apply his learning on the job; or he may change his job behaviour but this may have no effect on organizational variables; or the organization may change but this may have no effect on profits or other ultimate criteria. The task of the evaluator-controller is to discover whether the chain has held through all its links. If it has not he should be able to say which of the links has snapped and for what reason. He should also be able to make suggestions on how it should be mended (p. 18).[1]

Hamblin's model helps the evaluator *plan* a strategy. I believe this goes beyond the purely systems approach which was measuring effects at designated stages. Hamblin's model invites the evaluator to set objectives beforehand appropriate to the level of evaluation at which he subsequently intends to measure change. I used this approach to help *structure* managers' expectations of what they could expect out of a particular course. But first let's review the total model, which appears in Figure 6.6 together with different measuring techniques that I suggest might be appropriate to collecting data at the respective stages.

Hamblin's model takes account of the fact that the evaluator may want to consider and plan for activities other than training to meet his or her objectives; hence the arrows in Figure 6.6 which shoot off to the left and enter the model from the right at the appropriate level of evaluation.

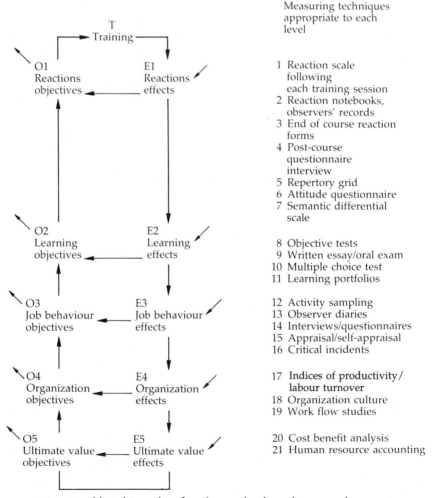

Figure 6.6 *Hamblin's hierarchy of evaluation levels and suggested measuring techniques*

Another feature is that the manager or trainer using the model can start or end at whatever stage is most appropriate. But once he or she has entered the cycle, Hamblin sees a fixed causal link connecting up the intermediate stages.

For example, let us suppose you set objectives and intend to measure change at the JOB BEHAVIOUR level. You would follow this route: the starting point is to set 03 objectives. Let us suppose you want a member of your staff to learn how to chair meetings successfully. It may be this objective is achieved by sending him or her on a course; but it might be achieved by other means, e.g. by sitting in on more meetings (hence the arrow on the left). Whether you achieve the objective by training or not you also need to measure the effects at the appropriate level (in this case E3) by using an appropriate technique (for example asking staff attending meeting to fill in a comment sheet about the chairperson's competence).

If you follow the 'training' route, the next step is to set objectives at level 02 (LEARNING). Hamblin would argue your manager will be unable to achieve the job behaviour objectives until he has also achieved appropriate learning objectives (for example, you might expect your potential chairperson to be able to tell you what are the three most important functions a chairperson has to perform; you could test this simply by questioning him or her or asking him or her to produce a report reflecting on what has been learned. If their response fails to identify the critical three points you will have identified, Hamblin would argue, a key fault in the chain).

Finally, following the logic of the model, you would also have to set and measure 01 (REACTION) objectives (for example, by expecting the person to have a positive reaction to the role of chairperson which you might assess by interview or asking individuals to keep notes of his or her reactions in meetings).

Putting the training chain together, Hamblin would argue that *unless* your chairperson has a positive reaction to the role of chairperson he or she will not be able to take on board what are the key functions of a chairman which will mean that he or she will not be able to achieve the job behaviour objectives you have set. Each step has a consequence for another and in this way you can identify where and why the cycle breaks down.

Whether you agree with the logic or not, you would certainly have a high degree of control over the outcome of the training. But I suspect that the model has more often than not been used as a conceptual model rather than in the way Hamblin intended it to be used (which we have just illustrated). But even as a conceptual model it provides a useful overview of potentially what could be the result of training. I would argue it helps you 'imagine' possibilities which you may otherwise not have envisaged. Furthermore, if you accept that achievement at level 04 is potentially more valuable to the organization than achievement at, say, 02, then you have a metric for assessing potential *scale* of value. The problem is that most managers tend to be conditioned to have expectations at levels no higher than E2 (see

Whitelaw)[36] because that is their experience of what is the outcome of a course, i.e. change in knowledge/learning.

ACTIVITY 6.8
● *Select any training or development objective and use Hamblin's hierarchical model to explore consequences and implications of its being achieved at each of the five levels.*

I have used Hamblin's model to stretch managers' expectations to 'imagine' achievement at 'higher' levels. Personally, I have found the model a useful way of becoming liberated from a purely mechanical way of looking at training which, as we saw, was one of the adverse consequences of following a purely 'systems' model. In the final analysis Hamblin's model is about discovery:

> If we adopt this more open-ended approach to evaluation we can hardly ever set up a scientifically controlled research experiment, which has a beginning, a middle and an end, and at the end of which we can confidently state that certain statements have been proved true and others false. It is necessary to adopt a much more discursive, exploratory approach to evaluation, in which we are not trying to prove anything but simply to find things out (p. 72)[1]

This is a good cue to move from the essentially 'research' based methods of evaluation we have been considering so far to the 'naturalistic' approach. However, I have found that in many cases so-called research methods that began on a 'predetermined path' very often led me off in all directions. What took over, I would argue, was the process of change that is at the very heart of *any* evaluation method.

This was the conclusion I arrived at in 1982 after reviewing the kinds of models of evaluation we have so far been exploring:

> The methods and models described are essentially a *means* of projecting the evaluator *beyond* what the respective models are describing to make explicit a *new* order of value that has hitherto been implicit. To 'capture' the essence of this 'metalanguage' we need to be equipped with new methods; we need to rethink assumptions about evaluation. In short we need a new 'paradigm' which, in the sense that Kuhn uses it is not so much defined by its content as by its underlying process which draws together a wide range of views (p. 206).[2]

The concept of a 'paradigm' (see Kuhn[39]) reflects the way new ideas/ theories are developed and which is anything but a systematic accumulation and extension of *existing* data/theories. It requires what Kuhn describes as 'a reconstruction of the field from new fundamentals'.

As a result we arrive at a point when we recognize that in sharing in one paradigm we are rejecting another. This seemed to me to reflect the need for a *qualitatively different* approach which is not simply an extension of existing models. I found this paradigm in the 'naturalistic' approaches to evaluation which we now explore, starting with the 'Goalfree' approach to evaluation. The source for what was for me a new-found revelation was a collection of papers brought together in *Beyond the Numbers Game*.[40]

(6) Goal free evaluation

We have already explored the goal based approach to evaluation and Mager's recipe for behavioural instructional objectives which swept through the world of training in the 1960s and 1970s. But, like any evangelical approach, it also promoted fierce opposition. The first warning shot came from Belasco and Trice in 1969,[41] who drew attention to the fact that in addition to the prescribed and intended outcomes a programme of training could also have *unanticipated consequences*. Regardless of whether these were desirable or not, an evaluator should be aware of such outcomes. Essentially, critics of the prescribed objectives approach had two reservations:

1 Emphasis on measurable objectives can prevent us seeing or describing the *actual outcome* of a particular programme.
2 The description of measurable objectives cannot do justice to the *complexity of the process* that makes up a training or educational programme.

The main advocate for what he called 'Goal free evaluation' was Scriven.[42] In comparing different programmes he came to the conclusion that the difference between them had nothing to do with the 'defined goals'. He therefore began to work on an alternative approach which focused on actual effects against defined *needs*. His conclusions were as follows:

> The so-called 'side effects', whether good or bad, often wholly determine the outcome of the evaluation. It's absolutely irrelevant to the evaluator whether they are 'side' or 'main' effects; that language refers to the *intentions* of the producer and the evaluator isn't evaluating intentions but *achievements* (p. 135).[42]

In fact, Scriven takes a very extreme view in that he advocates that the evaluator should not only remain *unaware* of what the 'intended' goals of the programme are but he or she should not even have any contact with the programme designers lest they 'contaminate' the evaluator's judgement, which should be *solely* based on *actual* effects. Scriven's loyalties lie with giving credit for *what* has been achieved, which ties in very much with the current competence approach and accreditation of prior learning.

> I don't want to penalize them for failing to reach over ambitious goals. I want to give them credit for doing something worthwhile in getting halfway to these goals (p. 138).[42]

The second reservation about goal based evaluation is that it cannot do justice to the complexity of what is the essence of a training or education programme. (We explored this diversity in Chapter 4.) But whereas Scriven would advocate that the evaluator should have no part in the programme itself, this particular approach to 'goal free' evaluation immerses itself fully in the programme to express objectives which reflect the process that is the essence of the programme. It was Eisner who suggested that curriculum designers should use objectives to 'establish a direction of inquiry' rather than prescribe an outcome. These kind of objectives he called 'expressive objectives':

> The expressive objective is intended to serve as a theme around which skills and understandings learned earlier can be brought to bear, but *through which* those skills and understandings can be expanded, elaborated and made idiosyncratic. With an expressive objective what is desired *is not homogeneity of response among students but diversity* (p. 94, emphasis added).[43]

In this context the evaluative task 'is not one of applying a common standard to the products produced, but *one of reflecting upon what has been produced in order to reveal its uniqueness and significance*' (p. 94, emphasis added).[43]

Although his words are aimed at the teacher in school, Eisner's description above seems to me to capture just what training and development and its design should be about. It is also very relevant to a number of the arguments I am seeking to develop in this book.

First, Eisner's description of 'expressive objectives' comes close to the approach I was advocating in Chapter 3 for building on competences. Rather than being prescribed by the words in the element, performance criteria etc., why can't we use them as a means 'through which . . . skills and understandings can be expanded, elaborated and made idiosyncratic'.

Second, they reflect the need for *variety* which was so much missing from the systems approach to evaluation but is central to the generation and construction of a metasystem (we will return to this theme again in the final chapter).

Third, there is an element of Schon's 'reflection-in-action' argument which we explored in the last chapter.

Finally, it takes us towards the next school of evaluation, illuminative evaluation. In a sense Eisner is more representative of this school than he is of 'goal free evaluation'.

(7) Illuminative evaluation

The term 'illuminative evaluation' was introduced in a paper presented at the University of Edinburgh in 1972 by Parlett and Hamilton.[44] The authors contrasted two approaches to educational research.

> Dominant is the classical or 'agricultural-botany' paradigm which utilizes a hypothetico-deductive methodology derived from the experimental and mental testing traditions in psychology. Almost all evaluation studies have resided within this traditional paradigm (p. 7).[44]

Though a parody, their description of what they mean by an 'agricultural-botany' paradigm, still reflects the 'scientific' approach to evaluation, some of whose models we have explored:

> students – rather like crop plants – are given pre-tests (the seedlings are weighed or measured) and then submitted to different experiences (treatment conditions). Subsequently, after a period of time, their attainment (growth or yield) is measured to indicate the efficiency of the methods (fertilizers) used (p. 7).[44]

In sharp contrast, they point to studies from the fields of social anthropology, psychiatry and sociology which reflect a 'contrasting paradigm with a fundamentally different research style and methodology'. This paradigm is what Easterby-Smith has classified as naturalistic (though *still* research-oriented). Rather like an anthropologist trying to understand a new culture, the evaluator makes no assumptions about the programme being evaluated; his or her role

> is to provide a comprehensive understanding of the complex reality (or realities) surrounding the programme: in short to illuminate. In his report, therefore, the evaluator aims to sharpen discussion, disentangle complexities, isolate the significant from the trivial and to raise the level of sophistication of debate (p. 21).[44]

On the other hand an evaluator is faced with a defined programme, syllabus and predetermined objectives. But does this reflect what Parlett and Hamilton call 'the complex reality . . . surrounding the programme'? Is this the way programmes *really* work? They suggest an alternative model which is much closer to reality and which they call the 'learning milieu'.

> This is the social-psychological and material environment in which students and teachers work together. The learning milieu represents a network or nexus of cultural, social, institutional and psychological variables. These interact in complicated ways to produce in each class or course, a unique pattern of circumstances, pressures, customers, opinions and workstyles which suffuse the teaching and learning that occurs there (p. 11).[44]

We have already explored some of the implications in Chapter 4, when we looked at the variety of resources and skills that go to make up a training programme. Consider what greater complexity there is when we come to look at the learning experience within and of the organization as a whole.

ACTIVITY 6.9
- *How would you go about compiling a realistic picture of the 'learning milieu' in your organization?*

But though the 'naturalistic approach' presents an authentic picture, it did not necessarily help an organization take action. This is what the 'interventionalist' school of evaluation sought to tackle.

(8) The interventionalist school

Another source on which I drew in 1982 was the work emerging from a group of social scientists who made up the 'New Paradigm Research Group'. The basis of their thinking was to question the 'objectivity' of the researcher when engaged in social research (i.e. research on and with other people). Peter Reason puts the case for 'cooperative research', which is

> a way of doing research in which all those involved contribute both to the creative thinking that goes into the enterprise – deciding on what is to be looked at, the methods of the inquiry, and making sense of what is found out – and *also* contribute to the action which is the subject of the research. Thus, in its fullest form the distinction between researcher and subject disappears, and all who participate are both co-researchers and co-subjects.[45]

It seemed to me there was a close relationship between the role of the social researcher and the evaluator of training; furthermore, this approach offered a more *practical* outcome than illuminative evaluation in which the researcher tended to play a lone role; although totally immersed in the process his role was to *report* on what he or she observed rather than *influence* it. My position was the same as Robert Stake's[46]:

> Evaluation studies should be a service rather than a research function, to provide needed assistance and useful information to a clientele or audience. These studies may or may not be attentive to the aims and concerns of those developing or operating the programme (p. 160).[46]

Stake developed an approach which he called 'responsive evaluation' which put primary emphasis on the requirements of stakeholders in the organization who have a vested interest in the outcome of a programme. For them the evaluator plays a crucial role because:

It is difficult for many clients to perceive the scope and movement of the programme. The programme director's perspective is partially observed; the outsider's is evanescent. They need to see more, to share more in the experience. If the programme glows the evaluation should reflect some of it. If the programme wobbles the tremor should pass through the evaluation report (p. 161).[47]

To convey the complexity of the programme and to do justice to it requires more than a report, it requires what Stake calls a 'portrayal':

The responsive evaluator prepares portrayals. Some will be short, featuring perhaps a five minute script, a log or scrap book. A longer portrayal may require several media. Narrations, maps and graphs, exhibits, taped conversations, photographs, even audience role playing (p. 164).[48]

Does this ring any bells? Isn't such evidence the kind of material we were suggesting individuals collect as evidence of achievement of competence? For portrayal, read portfolio.

Stake was a big influence on my thinking, as was the last contributor to this section, Patton and his *Utilization Focused Evaluation*. Like Stake, he saw evaluation as being a service to a stakeholder; it must have 'utility'. Patton sees evaluation as a process of negotiation between evaluator and stakeholders. The 'goal' is not predetermined, but worked out and negotiated with the decision makers during the process of evaluation itself. Indeed it *is* the process of evaluation. Central to it is

this moving back and forth – action, reaction, adaptation until the evaluator *finally focuses* on central issues of relevance to the identified and organized decision makers and information users (p. 143).[29]

Doesn't this bear some resemblance to Schon's concept of 'reflection-in-action'?[49] The final outcome of the evaluation, though, doesn't come just from the evaluator:

Utilization-focused evaluation brings together evaluators, decision makers and information users in an active-reactive-adaptive process where *all participants share responsibility for creatively shaping* and rigorously implementing an evaluation that is both useful and high quality (p. 289, emphasis added).[29]

This brings us to what I would regard as the optimum outcome of an evaluation, a long way away from where we started – with an analysis of the scientific school of evaluation. The purpose for such a detailed review of theories and models over the past 30 years has not been to overwhelm you with jargon but to *illustrate* the wealth of thinking and ideas that abound. As we shall see later, there is scant evidence that very much of this thinking has been taken into account when it comes to advocating approaches to evaluation for the future.

The model of evaluation at which I finally arrived[50] had six primary principles:

1 Evaluation is above all a *dynamic* process which *generates* value in its own right.
2 This process can be triggered by *any* of the schools of evaluation we have examined. What they do is provide a *perspective* from which to examine and describe a wide range of data.
3 In the context of programmes of education and training the data to be collected are complex and diverse. In order, therefore, to generate the *maximum* value a given programme of training/development could have for an organization, the 'programme', its resources and context of use has to be *fully described* (using the kind of techniques illustrated in the 'illuminative' approach to evaluation).
4 But this description has no value in itself; it can only be *given* value by the various stakeholders in the organization for whom the outcome of the programme can have potential value.
5 This 'ultimate' value will not be *automatically* realized but requires an essentially *personal* judgement (what I would now call 'reflection-in-action') on the part of each stakeholder based on the information with which he/she is *confronted*.
6 The ultimate value for the organization is when *all* stakeholders are able to *reflect* on this information together and arrive at a consensus of value which lies outside of the systems, of the information sources which gave rise to it (i.e. a meta-system).

There were three key stages in the process, which I called 'Description', 'Focusing' and 'Confrontation'. In the final section in this chapter I have sketched out a scenario of how this process might be used for the benefit of the organization as a whole. But first we review the extent to which current initiatives have taken account of any of the developments we have been discussing.

6.3 How evaluation is currently perceived

When I saw the consultative document for the TDLB Training Standards in September 1990[51] I was encouraged to see that the section on evaluation referred to 'Evaluate the effectiveness of HRD strategies, plans and systems', i.e. it was not limited to the evaluation of training and development *per se*.

I was even more encouraged to read details of two of the elements in the evaluation section:

● Identify and assess changes in *organizational capability* which result from the process of identifying organizational training and development requirements and strategies.
● Evaluate effectiveness of the *organizational learning* process (emphasis added).

There was also a final section devoted to 'Establish and maintain effective communications and feedback systems', one element of which was to

● Promote and support communication systems and relationships which make it possible for the *organization to learn from its own experience and that of others* (emphasis added).

All of this, I thought, boded well for a radical review of evaluation so that it was not exclusively concerned with measuring effects of 'training' *per se* but was more akin to the processes described in section 6.2 whereby the organization set up mechanisms to get feedback on how well it was succeeding in becoming a learning organization. But the published standards in 1992[52] have no reference that I can see to:

● Organizational capability
● Organizational learning
● An organization learning from its own experience

Perhaps these issues will be taken up in the development of standards appropriate at level 5. For the moment the Evaluation Section of the TDLB standards aims to 'Evaluate' the effectiveness of training and development' and its elements refer mainly to collecting information on how well the 'training and development function' has met its objectives. Though 'function' can be interpreted widely, it seems to me a lost opportunity for making closer links between the role of the trainer and *organizational* learning.

The Investors in People initiative, which we reviewed in Chapter 2, is likely to have a significant effect on the way evaluation is organized. Figure 6.7 summarizes the five indicators that are intended to cover evaluation and the kinds of questions you will need to satisfy.[53]

ACTIVITY 6.9
● *How does your training match up to these criteria? Which criterion do you find the most difficult to fulfil?*

An Investor in People evaluates the investment in training and development to assess achievement and improve future effectiveness.

Principles
- The investment, the competence and commitment of employees and the use made of skills learned, should be reviewed at all levels against business aims and targets
- The effectiveness of training and development should be reviewed at the top level and lead to renewed commitment and target setting

INDICATORS

4.1 The organization evaluates how its development of people is contributing to business goals and targets

Key questions
- How is training and development evaluated?
- Is training evaluated in terms of its contribution to business goals and targets?
- Does evaluation involve line management?
- Does evaluation influence subsequent action?

4.2 The organization evaluates whether its development actions have achieved their objectives

Key questions
- Does the evaluation make it clear whether the objectives of training have been achieved?
- What methods have been used?
- Do managers review whether the skills developed through training are used in practice?

4.3 The outcomes of training and development are evaluated at individual, team and organizational levels

Key questions
- How is individual achievement of competence assessed? (Use of external standards and NVQs)
- Does the organization assess commitment and enthusiasm?
- Where training claims to change attitudes, how does the organization assess whether this has been achieved?

4.4 Top management understand the broad costs and benefits of developing people

Key questions
- How are costs identified?
- How are the benefits of training identified?
- What evidence is there of senior management understanding of these?
- How does this information influence future plans?

4.5 The continuing commitment of top management to training and development is communicated to all employees

Key questions
- How does management communicate on a continuing basis?
- Are employees made aware of major training and development achievements?
- When the organization faces a difficult period of trading, what are people told about training and development?

Figure 6.7 *Investors in People – criteria for evaluation*

Undoubtedly, these criteria are a vast improvement because they are business led and not trainer led. They encourage the manager to think strategically in how he or she is to deploy training resources to meet business needs. In so doing they also reflect some of the schools of evaluation we have explored. Thus, Indicator 1 tackles straight away the issue of training being seen to be *effective* and measurable against criteria of value to the organization. As stated in the guidelines to employers: 'relatively few employers evaluate their investment effectively' (p. 44).[53]

Indicator 2 then picks up what used to be called 'validation', i.e. has the training met the objectives it has set itself?

Indicator 3 has a tenuous link with the 'hierarchical levels' school of evaluation we examined in Section 6.2, drawing attention to the different kind of evidence required depending on whether the outcome is at the level of individual, group or organization.

Indicator 4 tackles the fraught area of costing training and quantifying benefits. At one time it was thought that achievement of the Investors in People standard would depend very heavily on the extent to which the company was able to quantify and cost out the benefits from training. But it was soon realized that on this basis hardly any companies would ever qualify! Interestingly Indicator 4 is a rather 'diluted' attempt to encourage companies to cost and quantify training by merely requiring that 'top management should *understand* the broad cost and benefits of developing people' (my emphasis). In my view companies will never succeed in this area as long as they separate out training for special treatment and institute special systems to collect special data – this time for TECs rather than ITBs. Remember the advice of the accountants Fielden and Pearson: 'If a costing approach is to make any real impact it must eventually feature as part of the regular decision making process' (p. 73).[21]

As such it should also identify the costs of 'informal' as well as 'formal' learning.[15] This is not only part of the model we discuss in Section 6.4, it is *central* to any evaluation approach which seeks to put a value on every member of the organization.

The other observation I would make about Indicator 4 is that 'benefits' and 'costs' could be catalogued separately and submitted as evidence without one necessarily being seen to relate to the other. In the final analysis stakeholders have to put a *value* on the investment based on confronting both sides of the equation (costs and benefits) simultaneously (see Figure 6.5).

I hope that the detailed discussion of 'costing' of training in Section 6.2 has helped in giving you an overall *feeling* for the subject and will enable you to think deeply about what systems will work best for you before embarking on any 'quick fix' to collect financial data.

Indicator 5 is perhaps the most interesting in that it does not relate to any particular school of evaluation – but seeks to emphasize the way the organization communicates details of training and its outcomes; but, again, the responsibility seems to lie with 'top management' for such communication. This is where a criterion in the first draft of TDLB Training Standards (already discussed above) would be appropriate:

> Promote and support communication systems and relationships which make it possible for the *organization to learn from its own experience and that of others* (emphasis added).[51]

I believe that this is the essence of the evaluation process at the level of the organization in which *every* member of the organization is involved, not just top management (see Figure 2.6). Perhaps as the Investors in People programme develops this indicator will assume greater importance.

Because the criteria for evaluation in Investors in People are 'Business goal led' they do not take account of the fact that 'value' is being given to the organization by all kinds of people all the time. Though this must ultimately affect business goals I suggest we need a wider net within which to capture such data. In other words, by concentrating on the business goals we may overlook the investment that is being made elsewhere. (See arguments of 'goal free evaluation' in section 6.2 above).

The evaluation criteria also reflect the 'top-down' focus of Investors in People, which we have already commented on in Chapter 2. While it is understandable that TECs should want to see evidence of top management being directly involved in the costing and evaluation of training, there is the danger that bureaucratic controls will take the place of what, I believe, should be an organization-wide process of inquiry; this is in line with the arguments outlined in the 'interventionalist' approach to evaluation in Section 6.2 above.

What evidence is there that such a model exists or will work? The reason we have explored a wide range of schools of thinking on evaluation is to demonstrate what a rich source of theory there is. As Smith and Piper conclude:

> The overview of evaluation theory ... demonstrates that a body of knowledge exists and that it is not static but is continuing to evolve ... having said that our research into evaluation practices of major institutions gives the impression that evaluation practices are exceedingly limited. We have a body of knowledge but in very few places is it being used (p. 7).[6]

Interestingly, they too emphasize the need to identify and *involve* the 'stakeholders' who will be doing the evaluating:

1 The purchaser of training whom we shall refer to as the patron.
2 The training agency whom we shall call the provider.
3 The trainee whom we shall call the participant.
4 The independent contracted assessor or researcher whom we shall call the agent.

They also recognize that rarely do all four parties 'jointly collaborate':

> The authors are of the opinion that openness and discussion, with the purpose of the evaluation being made clear, may well lead to (1) the exercise being approached more seriously and positively by all parties, and (2) the results contributing to further action. By this means *evaluation becomes part of a framework adding to organization development* (pp. 8–9 emphasis added).[6]

This is very much the same conclusion I formed[50] and I hope that such approaches become the norm in the future.

In the final part of this chapter I identify the key steps of what I would call an 'Organization-wide' approach to evaluation.

6.4 A model that meets the needs of both individuals and organization alike

In this section I have tried to bring together what I consider to be the critical issues underlying the evaluation debate which has been aired in detail so far in this chapter. It also refers you back to points made in previous chapters which have all been preparing the ground. Let's start with an issue introduced at the end of Chapter 5 raised by Garratt:

> Learning occurs all over organizations. The problem is that there are so few systems for valuing it and capturing it (p. 7).[54]

The conclusion we reached at the end of Chapter 5 on management was that a key role, if not *the* role, of the manager of the future would be to 'capture, codify and diffuse in a useful and profitable form the learning of the organization'. What we have tried to explore in this chapter is the nature of the systems within which such value could be captured.

The reason I have gone back to the roots of all the various schools of evaluation is because I believe that we are still creating 'systems' for evaluation which are based on outmoded concepts. These are just some examples:

1 That training and development can somehow be isolated within a separate function and costed and valued accordingly.
2 That 'management' should be in charge of evaluation and decide what information should be collected and to whom it is to be disseminated.

Against this model, is the conclusion that evaluation is a dynamic, creative process in its own right which *everyone* is capable of exercising. However, it *does* need facilitation and guidance as to where its impact should be directed. In other words, somebody has got to start the process off. Because it must be organization-wide (if the organization is to derive maximum value from the process) this person/s has/have to be top management. By definition – taking the conclusion of Chapter 5 – the senior manager has the role of putting a value on everybody else! In practice, I suggest, his or her role is to set up a system within which such value would *accumulate*. It is not his or her role to say what kind of information should be collected – that must come from open negotiation with all the stakeholders involved; this is likely to be the learner, the boss, the developer/trainer. But it *is* his or her role to put a value on the outcome which in turn is fed into the system to be further debated and reflected on and thus accumulate added value.

Until such a system becomes as natural to organizations as agreeing the annual budget, they will need some specialist help in putting this picture together. To do this they will need a person/s whose designated role, I suggest, is solely to collect evidence of *human value being accumulated*, to feed it back to the stakeholders involved and continually invest the dividends. For want of a better name, we will call this person the *Evaluator*.

So where do you start, company goals or individual values? In actual fact one doesn't preclude the other and, as we shall see, the aim of the process is to bring both together anyway. So, let's start with company goals but let's look upon them not as fixed targets but in the way Eisner described objectives, as *directions for enquiry*.

Below we look at a step-by-step process of how evaluation can work as an 'accumulator' within the organization. We make the assumption that the organization has taken on board the themes that have emerged from the previous chapters and has initiated processes in the company which support the following principles:

- Everyone (including the chief executive) is a learner.
- Everyone (also including the chief executive) acts as a resource to each other (see Chapter 4).
- Everyone has his/her own Development Log with details of competences to be achieved and resources needed to attain them. We also assume that the appropriate computer technology is in place to record the process (again, see Chapter 4).
- Every manager sees his/her role as increasing the value of their staff in terms of increasing range of skills.

ACTIVITY 6.10
- *As you work through this extended piece of 'upside-down thinking' consider how the process might work in your organization.*

Stage 1 Contracting

Senior manager convenes a meeting of the management team and briefs the group on the goals to be achieved. Note this doesn't follow the usual practice of manager setting out the goals and expecting individual managers to go away and meet their respective targets. Remember that in this organization each manager is responsible for adding value to his subordinates. So this is how this senior manager tackles this stage:

1 The goals are used as 'directions of enquiry' to enable the managers to voice their hopes, concerns and comments. The aim is to arrive at a clear vision of what has to be achieved which everyone shares because they've each contributed to it. (See Senge's description of 'team learning' and dialogue, p. 40.)[35] This means being very clear as to what the organization will look like when goals are achieved, who will be doing what, how they will recognize it, how they will measure its success. (See the kind of criteria outlined in Figure 6.4.)
2 They then explore as a group what skills will be needed to bring these changes about. This includes themselves. What will they and their staff need to do differently? Each manager makes a note (or inputs direct into Development Log). The senior manager does the same.
3 But they also identify what skills, competences, experiences they already have that will be critical for success.
4 They identify as a group the kind of resources they will need to draw upon to bring about the new skills, experiences, competences. (Again, this is recorded.)

The role of the Evaluator during this stage is to help the group be clear about its vision, to ensure they can visualize both the kind of behaviour they need to demonstrate, the benefits it will bring and the kind of resources needed to bring it about. He/she may also need to remind them of the range of resources available (see Chapter 4). He/she agrees a timescale within which the programme will be implemented and by which he/she will 'portray' the results.

Each manager goes away to carry out the same CONTRACTING stage with their own staff at which the Evaluator assists in the same way as above. He/she also agrees a time to come back and check out the process.

Stage 2 Description

This stage aims to help learners become fully aware of the aims that have to be achieved and the range of resources available to achieve them. It requires a 'full' and open description of what illuminative evaluation calls the 'learning milieu'. It also requires learners to make us 'visible' as possible the process of learning they are to undergo and the outcomes (see Chapter 4).

It may not involve the Evaluator directly but he/she will advise each of the learners (which is everyone) how to cover each of the following steps:

1 Follow through the development programme agreed with the evaluator. (An example of a possible format that might be used to record the process is illustrated in Figure 6.8.)
2 Record the resources used to develop each skill, attain each experience (see Figure 6.8).

Goal To improve speed of getting orders out			
Skills needed	**Resources**	**Time**	**Outcome**
Negotiation	Off-job course; individual project	3 days 2 days	Changed mind of boss to support JC plan
Assertiveness	In-house work shop; use AK as mentor	2 days 3 days	Stuck out for computer in stores – which we've now got!
Time management	Tutorial with BL + ongoing feedback	2 days	My desk is now clear!

Overall outcome   Average time to get orders out reduced from 4 days to 1

Description of learning   Increased confidence in capability of doing job, in agreeing and keeping to deadlines

So what?   (i)   It's all about planning ahead
So what?   (ii) It means I'll have more time for myself in the future
So what?

Ultimate value for you personally   I'm going to take more risks in the future

Figure 6.8 *Example of individual Development Log*

3 *Record the outcome (see Figure 6.8).*
4 *Record the overall outcome of what has been achieved.*
5 *Describe the value they place on learning they have realized from what they can now do. (This is what I would call 'first order reflection'. In the example in Figure 6.8 this leads to realization of 'increased confidence in ability to do the job'.)*

Stage 3 Focusing

This involves the Evaluator helping the learner draw together common themes from the DESCRIPTION stage and focus on the meaning for him/her. In the example in Figure 6.8 the common link is an awareness of the importance of 'planning' as a consequence of which the learner will have more time for himself/herself in the future. Note we haven't called it focusing – it's about reflecting on what has gone before by asking 'So what?'

It may not be feasible for the Evaluator to carry out such transactions on a one-to-one basis. It may be more appropriate in a group. In fact the Evaluator should follow up such individual focusing with a session with a whole team so as to get a 'group' picture within which the value can be accumulated. It is the cumulative 'picture' from each work group that the Evaluator takes forward to the CONSOLIDATION stage (see below).

Stage 4 Confronting

There is a grey line between FOCUSING and CONFRONTING. It is up to the Evaluator to help the learner 'milk' the learning experience for all it is worth until the eureka point is reached when he/she makes a personal breakthrough towards a new level of meaning. (This is why we've called this stage 'Ultimate value for you personally' in Figure 6.8). There is no way of telling how many FOCUSING cycles it will take to get to this point. Again, the value is that much greater if the breakthrough comes through a team CONFRONTATION.

In the case of the example in Figure 6.8, focusing has gone through two cycles – one arriving at 'planning' as the meta-competence, as it were, the other with the realization that he/she can now 'buy time for the future'. One kind of clue, I have found, to when breakthrough is imminent is that there is some evidence of dissatisfaction, conflict in the learner, i.e. some emotive response. In the example in Figure 6.8 such an emotive response precedes a declaration that he/she is now going to take more risks in the future. It is for the Evaluator to confirm that the learner has reached 'maximum' value (for the time being). It is this picture – augmented at the team meeting with the learner's colleagues – that the Evaluator takes forward to the final stage.

Stage 5 Consolidation

This is where the Evaluator comes into his/her own. The task now is to put together a total picture from all the signs of change so far portrayed – remember Beer's 'eudemonic potential'? – and feed it back to the senior management group which came up with the original goals (see CONTRACTING stage). Of course, in the process of DESCRIPTION, FOCUSING and CONFRONTATION the Evaluator would have met each of the senior managers individually. This is now the opportunity to feed back the picture so far to give the senior manager and his/her team the opportunity to CONFRONT, respond as a group. The Evaluator carries on with this process until all parties are confident they have captured as much learning as can be derived which reflects the learning of the organization as a whole.

For the sake of argument let us suppose the essence of this learning lies in what was the final learning realization of our learner in Figure 6.8 – the confidence to take risks. Let us suppose this was a common theme the Evaluator found throughout the organization at all levels. The resulting message, then, for the senior group is not just that the original goals were achieved – we've taken that as given! – but that the organization is now perceived (as a direct result of the kind of learning processes we've described) as an organization capable of taking risks in the future. This has particular significance for this organization, as it happens, because while all this learning was going on market opportunities have occurred which the organization can take advantage of – if it is capable of taking the risks.

Perhaps the biggest learning value is that the organization can be confident not just that managers can take the risk but that everyone in the organization is now a potential risk taker.

Stage 6 Dissemination

It just remains for this final picture to be fed back to everyone in the organization who has been involved in putting it together. In doing so the Evaluator will draw upon all the information he/she has received and can reflect it back taking account of all the schools of evaluation we looked at in Section 6.2. So it will reflect what objectives have been achieved, what resources have been used, at what cost; it will reflect the different levels of individual, group and organization evaluation as well as the 'ultimate' value which the organization puts on the final result. It will also reflect goals that have been achieved that were not foreseen and 'portray' every high and 'wobble' in the way Stake suggests. Finally and most importantly, in its turn it becomes the source for the next *cycle of learning. The process can then happen all over again – this time it will not need the trigger of company goals to sustain it.*

I believe the scenario set out above achieves what was the stated aim of this final section of this chapter – to evolve a model which meets the kind of requirements for evaluation set out in the Investors in People initiative as well as the wider implications for value assessment which I have tried to describe in my three-stage approach to evaluation (i.e. Description, Focusing and Confrontation).

As to Investors in People, I would submit every one of the five indicators (see Figure 6.7) has been met. Thus the whole approach starts and ends with company goals (though I suggest this should only be seen as the trigger for what should be an ongoing process of evaluation). Evidence is collected as to what are the 'learning' (rather than training) objectives and the resources used to achieve them (see Figure 6.8). Evidence is also collected on individual, team and organization-wide learning.

As regards costs of the exercise, the information can be computed from the analysis of data in everyone's Development Log (see Figure 6.8). In addition, I did make the assumption that the company would have taken on board the kind of ideas introduced in Chapter 4, which means that in addition to keeping a Development Log (of consumption, if you like) each person also records time allocated to develop another. So, for example in Figure 6.8, AK and BL would log down their time spent *developing* as well as learning. Hours will be translated into pounds by the Accounts Department so that when the Evaluator produces his final report (see Dissemination) he or she will be able to include up-to-date costs.

The advantage is that this approach does not just reflect formal training (the three days off-job course on negotiation for example) but the informal learning time and the informal time spent on development. This is rarely – if ever – included in evaluation reports.

Finally, as opposed to just 'top management' knowing about costs, everyone in the organization knows about costs because they realize they are part of them as well as being part of the value that accrues from them.

When it comes to Investors in People Indicator 5 (see Figure 6.7), the scenario we have painted is *all* about feedback; the reports that the Evaluator compiles are *accumulated* through feedback and the final report is then sent to everyone to share in the success of the total process.

But in the final analysis the organization will not have proved only that training can make a contribution to company goals – a company with the systems in place we have described will take that as given – what they will have derived is a statement of just what value such development has added to their corporate capability. I would accept that such a process as we have described is time consuming on the part of the 'Evaluator'. After all, it is he or she who puts it all together – the rest of the organization is just carrying out its normal function, albeit with more attention given to recording development inputs.

Who in your organization could take on such a role? Existing trainers? Existing managers? The personnel manager? It really does not matter *who* does it – though of course he or she will need to acquire new skills, which are mainly to do with facilitation (see Chapter 4).

In the end it is *managers* who should be putting value on their staff (see Chapter 5) and I would see the Evaluator spending at least some of his or her time developing the managers of the organization to take on such a role with ultimately the senior manager taking over the Evaluator's role of putting together the final 'portrayal' of the organization as a whole. This is what the learning organization of the future will look like.

The degree to which the organization becomes a learning organization will be a function of how well the total picture is focused and then fed back. Evaluation is the process whereby the organization is able to see its own image, learn from it and identify the potential for change in the future. This is the subject of our concluding chapter.

References

1 Hamblin, A. C. (1974) *Evaluation and Control of Training*, McGraw Hill
2 Critten, P. W. (1982) The nature of evaluation with reference to programmes of education and training. Unpublished Doctoral thesis, University of Bath
3 Manpower Services Commission (1981) *Glossary of Training Terms*, HMSO
4 Scriven, M. (1967) The methodology of evaluation. In E. R. House (ed.) *AERA Monograph Series in Curriculum Evaluation*, 1, Rand McNally
5 Easterby-Smith, M. (1986) *Evaluation of Management Education, Training and Development*, Gower
6 Smith, A. J. and Piper J. A. (1990) The tailor-made training maze: A practitioner's guide to evaluation. *Journal of European and Industrial Training*, **14**(8), 3–28

7 Manpower Commission (1945) *The Training within Industry Report (1940–1945)*, Washington DC

8 Hesseling, P. G. M. (1966) *Strategy of Evaluation Research*, Van Gorcum

9 Oatey, M. (1970) The economics of training with respect to the firm. *British Journal of Industrial Relations*, **VIII**(1), 1–21

10 King, D. (1964) *Training within the Organisation*, Tavistock

11 Talbot, J. R. and Ellis, C. D. (1969) *Analysis and Costing of Company Training*, Gower

12 Garbutt, D. (1969) *Training Costs; with Reference to the Industrial Training Act*, Gee and Company

13 Thomas, B., Moxham, J. and Jones, J. A. G. (1969) Cost benefit analysis of industrial training. *British Journal of Industrial Relations*, **7**(2), 231–264

14 Bramley, P. (1991) *Evaluating Training Effectiveness*, McGraw Hill

15 Marsick, V. J. and Watkins, K. E. (1990) *Informal and Incidental Learning in the Workplace*, Routledge

16 Coopers and Lybrand (1990) *A Report into the Relative costs of Open Learning*, report to training agency

17 Drake, K. (1979) The cost-effectiveness of vocational training: a survey of British studies. Unpublished study, University of Manchester

18 Cameron, K. (1980) Critical questions in assessing organisational effectiveness. *Organisational Dynamics*, Autumn, pp. 66–80

19 Hendry, C. (1991) Corporate strategy and training. In *Training and Competitiveness*, Kogan Page

20 Jones, J. A. G. (1974) Progress in evaluation and cost benefit research. *Industrial and Commercial Training*, 107–111

21 Fielden J. and Pearson, P. K. (1979) *An Approach to costing Training – a Feasibility Study*, Peat, Marwick and Mitchell

22 Likert, R. and Pyle, W. C. (1971) Human resource accounting: a human organizational measurement approach. *Financial Analysis Journal*, Jan–Feb

23 Tsaklanganos, A. (1980) Human resource accounting; the measure of a person. *CA Magazine*, May, pp. 44–48

24 Kanter, Ros Moss (1989) *When Giants Learn to Dance*, Unwin and Hyman

25 *Training in Britain: Employers' Perspectives on Human Resources* (1989), HMSO

26 Tyler, R. W. (1949) *Basic Principles of Curriculum and Instruction*, University of Chicago Press

27 Mager, R. (1962) *Preparing Instructional Objectives*, Fearon; 2nd ed, 1975

28 Bloom, B. S. (ed.) (1956) *Taxonomy of Educational Objectives*, Longman

29 Patton, M. Q. (1978) *Utilization Focused Evaluation*, Sage

30 Hastings, C. (1978) *Systematic Evaluation of Transfer from Management Training Courses*, Department of Occupational Psychology, Birkbeck

31 Huczynski, A. A. and Lewis, J. W. (1980) An empirical study into the learning transfer process in management learning. *Journal of Management Studies*, May, 227–240

32 Burgoyne, J. (1973) The evaluation of managerial development programmes. Unpublished PhD thesis, University of Manchester
33 Beer, S. (1975) *Platform for Change*, Wiley
34 Taylor, H. (1991) The systematic training model: Corn circles in search of a spaceship? *Management Education and Development*, **22**(4), Winter
35 Senge, P. (1990) *The Fifth Discipline: The Art and Practice of the Learning Organisation*, Doubleday
36 Whitelaw, M. (1972) *The Evaluation of Management Training*, IPM
37 Kirkpatrick, D. L. (1967) Evaluation of Training. In *Training and Development Handbook; American Society for Training and Development* R. L. Craig and L. R. Bittel, McGraw Hill
38 Warr, P. R., Bird, M. W. and Rackham, N. (1970) *Evaluation of Management Training*, Gower Press
39 Kuhn, T. S. (1962) *The Structure of Scientific Revolution*, 2nd edn, Chicago University Press
40 Hamilton, D., Jenkins, D., King, C., Macdonald, B. and Parlett, M. (eds) (1977) *Beyond the Numbers Game*, Macmillan
41 Belasco, J. A. and Trice, H. M. (1969) *The Assessment of Change in Training and Therapy*, McGraw Hill
42 Scriven, M. (1971) Goal free evaluation. Reprinted in Hamilton et al (1977) *Beyond the Numbers Game*, Macmillan
43 Eisner, E. (1969) Instructional and expressive educational objectives; their formulation and use in curriculum. In *Instructional Objectives* (ed. J. Popham), AERA Monograph Series on Curriculum Reflection, No. 3, Rand McNally. Reprinted in Hamilton et al (1977) *Beyond the Numbers Game*, Macmillan
44 Parlett, M., Hamilton, D. (1972) Evaluation as illumination: A new approach to the study of innovatory programmes. Occasional Paper 9, Centre for Research in Educational Sciences, University of Edinburgh. Reprinted in Hamilton et al. (1977) *Beyond the Numbers Game*, Macmillan
45 Reason, P. (1988) *Human Inquiry in Action*, Sage
46 Stake, R. (1972) The seven principal cardinals of educational evaluation. Handout, AERA Annual Meeting, Chicago. Reprinted in Hamilton et al. (1977) *Beyond the Numbers Game*, Macmillan
47 Stake, R. (1972) An approach to the evaluation of instructional programs (program portrayal vs. analysis). Paper delivered at AERA meeting in Chicago 4 April 1972. Reprinted in Hamilton et al (1977) *Beyond the Numbers Game*, Macmillan
48 Stake, R. (1972) To evaluate an arts program. Reprinted in Hamilton et al. (1977) *Beyond the Numbers Game*, Macmillan
49 Schon, D. A. (1987) *Educating the Reflective Practitioner*, Jossey Bass
50 Critten, P. (1982) Evaluation as a process of revelation. Paper presented to Conference on Management Education and Development, University of Lancaster, September 1982

51 TDLB (1990) *Training and Development Standards*. Draft consultative document. Employment Department, Moorfoot, Sheffield
52 TDLB (1992) *National Standards for Training and Development*. Employment Department, Moorfoot, Sheffield
53 Employment Department (1991) How will we gain recognition? Brochure 5 in *Investors in people – The Route*, Employment Department, Moorfoot, Sheffield
54 Garratt, B. (1990) *Creating a Learning Organisation*, Director Books

7 Corporate capability – putting a value on the learning organization

The loss of the stable state means that our society and all of its institutions are in *continuing* processes of transformation. We cannot expect new stable states that will endure even for our own lifetimes.

We must learn to understand, guide, influence and manage these transformations. We must make the capacity for undertaking them integral to ourselves and to our institutions.

We must, in other words, become adept at learning. We must become able not only to transform our institutions, in response to changing situations and requirements; we must invent and develop institutions which are 'learning systems', that is to say, systems capable of bringing about their own continuing transformation (p. 32).[1]

The notion of a 'learning system' as envisaged by Donald Schon in his BBC Reith Lectures in 1970 was one of the earliest references to the idea of a system, an organization being able to *learn* and thereby bring about its own transformation. Schon saw it as the antidote to what he called the loss of the stable state, as reflected in what he saw as a gradual dissolution of public institutions in the face of mounting social change.

If it was true of 1970, how much more critical is it now, which may explain the spate of books on the subject of the 'learning organization' over the past few years.[2-7] To quote from just one, Ronnie Lessem's *Total Quality Learning: Building a Learning Organization*:[6]

It is my view . . . that over the next 25 years the learning organization will supplant the business enterprise as the critical entity within the national and international economy, if not within society as a whole (p. x).[6]

In the course of this final chapter we will examine some of the models that emerge from these developments which offer different perspectives on how to build your own learning organization from scratch. In the final analysis I am not going to suggest any new blueprint, believing, like Pedler, Burgoyne and Boydell, that

We can't take you to visit a Learning Company or bring in a blueprint of what worked elsewhere – it's not like that. The magic of the

Learning Company *has to be realized from within*. The key word is 'transformation' – a radical change in the form and character of what is already there (p. 2, emphasis added).[7]

If you have stayed with me so far (and haven't jumped to take in only the last chapter!) you should already have a picture of your own as to what is a learning system, organization, company. It has emerged as a concept in every chapter so far and as an underlying integrating theme. This has been intentional, to build up a base from which at this stage you should yourself be ready and able to form a perspective about your own organization as to whether it is or could become a *learning* organization; as Pedler et al. suggest, this will be quite unlike any other, emerging, as it should, from within the kinds of initiatives, developments we have explored so far in this book.

A key message, which should be very familiar to you by now, is that there are no definitive steps towards the learning organization – it is more akin to the *meta* systems we explored in the previous chapter which can only be *triggered* somewhere along the way. In this chapter I want to lay down some last milestones on this way, and start off with my own journey and explorations in this still relatively uncharted territory. We then look at the conclusions from the latest works on the subject and out of these and other observations built up over the course of this book leave you, I hope, with a better idea of your own *corporate capability* which, in the final analysis, I believe is the tangible evidence of a learning organization's worth.

7.1 First steps towards a learning organization

It was in 1988 when a copy of the *Learning Company Project*[3] arrived on my desk. Though I had heard about the idea before and had attended conferences on self-development when Mike Pedler and John Burgoyne had introduced and discussed its implications, this was the first time I had seen in print the description of the goal, the vision I had been working towards for the past 20 years in training and development. If you have shared the journey through the last six chapters and even more, if these experiences match your own, then you will fully realize the impact this description of a learning company had on me:

an organization which facilitates the learning of all its members *and* continuously transforms itself (my emphasis).[3]

In particular, I was delighted to note the authors were careful to point out it was *not* the same as a company which does a lot of training! So how would you recognize it? In Figure 7.1 I have extracted five key features which the report describes as being typical of a learning company.

A Learning Company is one which

1 *has a climate in which individual members are encouraged to learn and to develop potential:* people perform beyond competence, taking initiatives, using and developing their intelligence and being themselves in the job; and which . .

2 *extends this learning culture to include customers, suppliers and other significant stakeholders* wherever possible; . . . but which also

3 *makes Human Resource Development strategy central to Business Policy* so that the processes of individual and organizational learning become a major business activity; e.g. as in IBM where the CEO is reputed to have said 'Our business is learning and we sell by-products of that learning'; which involves . . .

4 *a continuous process of organizational transformation* which harnesses the fruits of individual learning to make fundamental changes in assumptions, goals, norms and operating procedures on the basis of an internal drive to self-direction and not simply reactively to external pressures

5 in which *learning and working are synonymous*; is peopled by colleagues and companions rather than bosses, subordinates and workers; where both inside and outside are continuously searched and examined for newness – new ideas, new problems, new opportunities for learning

Figure 7.1 *What is a learning company? Adapted from the Learning Company Project (emphasis added)*[3]

ACTIVITY 7.1
● *Pause a while and consider whether this describes your company. To what extent would the policies and initiatives so far described in this book help you become a learning company?*

Following on from the characteristics described in Figure 7.1, the report also identified nine conditions against which it suggests any organization could be tested for claims to be a learning company. It struck me at the time that such conditions could be used by ITBs to assess not systematic training but the extent to which an organization was sufficiently open to learning and development. I would make the same plea now for the Investors in People programme. If you look back at Figure 2.6 you will see that the framework we suggested for assessing companies for the Investors in People award picks up many of the characteristics from Figure 7.1. The nine conditions have been taken by the authors of the report[3] and become the basis for '11 characteristics of a learning company' which in turn form the basis for their book,[7] the ideas in which we will explore later.

Back in 1988, armed with the vision outlined in the report of the Learning Company Project, my immediate thought was what could I do, as Management Development Manager in the Hotel and Catering Training Company, to help companies realize the same vision, i.e. achieve the goal of *becoming* a learning company. What follows is a description of two initiatives which took me a little further along the road. I reproduce them here for two reasons:

1 Each in its own way reflected what Argyris and Schon would call a 'theory-in-use',[8] i.e. a 'theory' which governed my actions at a particular time. Depending on what is your own current 'theory-in-use' they may therefore trigger off some associations.
2 Comparing my current 'theory-in-use' with those held at the times of the respective initiatives (1989 and 1990) there is much learning I have derived from undertaking these projects. It is this 'reflection-in-action' I would finally like to share with you.

Step 1: Learning organization as collective competences

This I saw as a way of tackling the first half of the learning organization description, i.e. 'an organization which facilitates the learning of *all* its employees'. For some time I had contemplated a way of bringing together all the separate developments at the Hotel and Catering ITB into a coherent model which an organization could use like a template to assess its own level of development. Over a period of five years the HCITB had been prominent in pioneering a number of developments which applied to most levels in any hospitality and catering company.

Thus there was Caterbase, one of the first schemes for enabling staff at craft level to gain professional recognition for competences achieved in the workplace. Then there was an Open Learning scheme leading to accreditation of supervisors and middle managers. Finally we had developed a route for middle managers to get a BTEC Diploma in Hospitality Management which could lead on to a DMS accredited through Middlesex Business School which itself could lead to exemption from the foundation year of the MBA. In theory, therefore, the HCITB was able to offer a step-by-step development route from craft to MBA, but the programmes were marketed separately and not within what I saw as a *strategic company-wide* approach.

The Learning Company Project made me think that one way of facilitating the learning of all employees within the hotel and catering industry would be to implement a company-wide scheme using the full range of resources developed by the HCITB (see above). But it was one thing outlining the route and quite another to project a picture of a company which had followed such a route. I produced a slide presentation based on a national company – a contract catering company which was, in fact, using *all* the HCITB resources (described above) but had not put them together in the way I was envisaging. My intention was to feature five people, each representing a separate level in the hierarchy of the company. Thus there was a catering assistant, a chef, a unit manager, an area manager and an operations director. Each was undertaking a separate development programme. The catering assistant was undertaking caterbase, the chef the supervisor programme, the unit manager the Open Learning programme leading to a BTEC Certificate, the area manager the Diploma programme and the operations director was following an MBA programme.

I featured all five *together* round a coffee table and posed the question: How many competences do these five people *between* them contribute to the organization as a whole? The aim was to shift the emphasis away from the separate programme each was following individually and focus on the value to the *organization overall* of the *outcomes* from such programmes. On reflection, it was rather mechanical, but it did serve to get the company to question the value each development programme contributed to the whole organization. One way to facilitate this process, I argued, was for the 'manager' of each of the staff represented to be a tutor and resource to his or her subordinate. This would be facilitated the more because each was also a learner. Thus we have a picture where every level of staff in the company could be developed in this way and each would be a resource to the other. This was my first step towards a learning company but it remained simply as a model to illustrate the process – in itself it had not generated any action and far less had it led to the organization *transforming* itself as a result of the learning of all its employees being facilitated in this way. This was the trigger for the second initiative.

Step 2: Creating a learning organization

The model for Step 1 had been achieved through collaboration with the Training Director of the national contract catering company. He shared my enthusiasm for the Learning company Project and in 1989 there was an opportunity for funding from the then Training Agency to explore the consequences of using particular techniques not just to facilitate learning amongst company staff but to ensure that the results of such learning had a direct and (as far as the Training Agency was concerned) a *measurable* impact on the organization as a whole.

But first we had to decide on a particular technique that would trigger such reactions. During 1989 I had cause to collaborate with Warren Redman, from Kenilworth Consultancy Associates, who had experience of the design and application of 'learning portfolios'. It was decided that such a technique might be one way to enable *all* members of the organization to capture and record individual learning which could then be shared with peers and superiors and in this way *potentially* have the opportunity of influencing decision and policy making throughout the organization as a whole. In this way, so we argued, both parts of the 'learning organization' definition would be met. Thus *all* members of the organization would be involved in the learning process, the consequences of which could potentially *transform* the organization itself once they had been shared.

Our perception of 'transformation' was fairly limited. We were looking for evidence that the consequences flowing from the sharing of particular learning could be traced right through to a particular change of policy or procedure (for example a modification of rules governing purchasing, new procedure for dealing with customer accounts etc.) Though this was limited, it would indicate the potential for change at an organizational level. The Training Agency, on the other hand, was looking for more 'hard' evidence, such as a 10% increase in market penetration, a reduction in staff turnover of the order of 20% etc.

In our experience it would be necessary to provide the learners with a particular *focus* on learning. Thus it would not be sufficient to pose a general question like 'What did you learn today?' It was decided that the focus of learning would be the *customer*. It was made clear that this could be either an external customer (e.g. staff from client company eating in restaurant) or an internal customer (e.g. colleagues, superiors). At the time this seemed to serve two purposes: one was to provide a focus for learning, as we have explained, but secondly for a service organization it would have intrinsic benefits of its own leading, hopefully, to better quality service. Subsequently the Training Director of the company has written up the results as part of an MBA dissertation and makes the observation:

> If an organization seeks the ability to continuously transform itself, in terms of keeping up with constant changes in the market place at least, then, surely, nothing could be more effective than to actually connect up all of its learning processes *to* customers (p. 60).[9]

Stage 1 **The nature of the experience**

Who is the customer?
What happened?
Why did it happen?

Stage 2 **Learning from/sharing the learning**

What have I learned from this?
How will I deal with this in the future?
What can others learn from this?

Stage 3 **Group discussion**

Group comments?
How has the group's reaction changed my understanding?
What action has been agreed?

Stage 4 **Results**

What has happened to improve things?
How can I demonstrate these improvements? (Give examples)

Figure 7.2 *Example of format of a 'learning portfolio' designed to collect data that can be shared and followed through to measure organizational learning*

The portfolio itself comprised one A4 sheet folded in two to produce four A5 sides each of which summarized responses to questions under four headings. These are reproduced in Figure 7.2. In hindsight, what we were trying to get *every* employee to do was carry out 'reflection-in-action' (see Chapter 5). Thus in Stage 1 they were focusing on the experience itself and reflecting on its cause. Stage 2 moves the reflection process to the point at which the learner is encouraged to articulate learning. We suggested at this stage that it would be useful to have a dialogue with a colleague who would not only help them articulate learning but also indicate *what* they had learned which others might find of value.

This was the basis for what was shared at Stage 3 with their peers at a meeting chaired by their boss (see below). The intention at this stage was also to 'add value' to the original learning experience as well as to lead to specific action. The consequences of this action in terms of the results that accrued from it was the basis for Stage 4. It also tied in with the need to collect evidence which could be the basis of a continuing record of achievement and also lead to subsequent accreditation (if appropriate).

Examples of the kind of details that might be written in under each of the headings and the direction such a learning process might take are illustrated in Figure 7.3. In this case the learner is a General Assistant (GA) in the staff restaurant.

The scenario in Figure 7.3 was an example we included in the briefing to the respective groups of staff involved so that everyone had a picture of the total process and what it could lead to. All we then needed to do was agree the boundary of the organization within which we would introduce and measure the results of such a process. As the particular organization had national outlets it was not thought practical to cover the entire organization. Another factor was the time constraint set by the Training Agency. The process had to be initiated and conclusions drawn within a year. We had also committed ourselves to producing a development package to publicize the findings supported by a video to illustrate the process. We agreed to launch the project in one operating company comprising 800 staff covering 70–80 units.

The method of delivery was to introduce the concept to the top management group comprising the Operations Director and his Area Managers (AMs). In their turn the Area Managers were helped to introduce the project to their immediate subordinates, the Area Catering Supervisors (ACSs). In their turn the ACSs were helped to introduce the process to the 70–80 Unit Managers who introduced it to their staff. Thus by a 'cascade' process every member of the organization would be involved. Furthermore it was introduced by the managers themselves (with help from myself and Warren Redman). The Training Director was anxious that it be not seen as an initiative emanating from his training department.

Each group decided to include Stages 3 and 4 of the process (i.e. share of learning within groups) as part of their normal progress meetings which

Stage 1   **The nature of the experience**

   1 Who is the customer?
External customer: 'Terry from Accounts who comes in for lunch every Tuesday and Friday.'

   2 What happened?
'Terry, with his arm in plaster had difficulty in carrying his tray and held up the queue. He said "It's a damn nuisance having to do this when all I want is a sandwich."'

   3 Why did it happen?
'We only serve full plated meals and they're all from one servery.'

Stage 2   **Learning from/sharing the experience**

   4 What have I learned from this?
'Why don't we offer a choice of snacks from a separate servery? I thought afterwards I should have said something to Terry.'

   5 How will I deal with this in the future?
'Suggest to manager that we open a separate snack bar. Talk to customers more'.

   6 What can others learn from this?
'That we can always get ideas from customers if we keep our eyes open.'

Stage 3   **Group comments**

   7 Group comments
'Joan asked why Terry only comes in twice a week. Sadiq said that Terry has to go to another branch the other days and didn't have enough time to eat his lunch in.'

   8 How has the group's reaction changed my understanding?
'Why didn't I ever think to question why Terry only came in twice a week? Perhaps we could make up sandwiches for him to take with him for the rest of the week.'

   9 What action has been agreed?
'Unit manager will discuss with area manager the possibility of a separate snack bar. We all agreed to find out if customers would be interested. I will have a word with Terry when I see him next.'

Stage 4   **Results**

  10 What has happened to improve things?
'Terry thought it was a good idea and wanted to know if he could order sandwiches in advance each week. We are trying out the scheme by having an assortment of sandwiches by the cashier.'

  11 How can I demonstrate these improvements? (Give examples)
'Terry ordered sandwiches for each Monday, Wednesday and Thursday over the past two weeks since we started. My boss has asked me to keep a record of sandwich sales and shown me how to record sales on a graph.' (Copy of sales figure on graph attached)

Figure 7.3 *Sample entries in the learning portfolio of a General Catering Assistant*

were on average once a month. The process took much longer to percolate down than was planned (no surprise here!) with the result that when an evaluation report was produced in February 1991 the unit managers had only had the opportunity of two or three meetings with staff to collect data.

By virtue of the cascade approach the upper echelons had more time to prepare.

Evaluation was both quantitative (against the Training Agency targets) and qualitative (based on questionnaires and selected interviews with representative groups from each level). Plus there were examples of the kind of learning that was shared at meetings and the action that had resulted. A sample of these is reproduced in Figure 7.4.

As to the quantitative data collected over the period the project was running, there was a slight increase in average spend. But there was a big reduction in staff turnover (20%). However, I believe this was as much a

---

- Inadequate briefing of relief manager who is not aware of peculiarities of client in requesting special sandwiches being sent to her in the middle of serving lunch and therefore is not sympathetic to strange voice making such a request at such a time: Need for better briefing, relief to meet client or at least have list of such 'peculiarities'.

- Senior manager complains through AM, ACS about quality of sandwich in particular unit: manager carries out survey of customers to get their opinion and sends results to senior manager.

- Relief manager comments about how unprepared she was for taking over particular unit: leads to discussion about correct procedure and whether units have 'the yellow book' and how well it is kept up-to-date.

- When AM absent, call from Sales Department direct to ACS giving 'the good news' about new contract that has to be serviced quickly; ACS, given operational load, does not respond as enthusiastically!; discussion about procedure of informing about new contracts in absence of AM and need for Sales Department to have better understanding of position of ACSs and pressures they're under.

- 'We ran out of rolls today'. Suggestions: to survey why more people came in today; to organize a permanent reserve; to establish better contact and communication with the client. The last was seen to be the root of the problem and arrangements made for more regular contact to keep track with customer movements and likely demands.

- The cashier noticed salad sales reducing (during a hot summer period). The team agreed she should ask customers why they weren't buying salads over the course of the next week. She did so, with the response that they were the same and 'boring'. The chef changed the salad presentations more frequently and sales shot up.

- Drinks vending machines were being abused by customers. Suggestions for action: clearer notices on use; better bins for waste. As a result there was a changed attitude in the team who began to see things from the customers' point of view instead of regarding them as awkward people. They agreed to talk more to customers whenever they were around the drinks vending area and help with any problems.

Figure 7.4 *Examples of learning outcomes and consequent action (action agreed is underlined)*

consequence of developing a different form of record keeping. In the final analysis the period of the project just happened to span a time when there was not only a national recession but the company was also undergoing organizational changes. The upshot of this is that it would be very rash to attribute these changes directly to the project. We are forced to rely, therefore, on the qualitative data, on the picture that emerged from interviews with representative parties involved in the process. Figure 7.5 summarizes some of the main benefits as well as some of the main constraints that were reported.

Benefits

Feedback from questionnaires and interviews identified the following key benefits

● Greater 'openness' to ideas from subordinates.
● Closer and stronger teamwork.
● Subordinates more likely to come up with suggestions, ideas which in turn led managers to be more aware of their subordinates' potential contribution.
● Improved communication.
● Greater awareness of tendency to make assumptions and of consequent need to check out individual capabilities and clarify procedures.
● Clearer, more positive and enabling management role undertaken by ACSs.

Constraints

At the same time the following points were identified which tended to constrain and inhibit progress:

● The structure of the portfolio was too complex and restrictive.
● Reluctance to write down incidents (especially at level of GAs).
● The fact that so few special meetings were convened to discuss 'Learning from Experience' meant that it tended to be yet one more item on an increasingly long agenda especially at the level of ACS, GM and Operations Director.
● The pressure of work being 'fed down' the normal organizational communication channels considerably limited the scope for ideas from the 'Learning from Experience' process to 'flow upwards'
● A further consequence of being tied to the existing reporting structure was that the potential success of the 'Learning from Experience' process would be either positively or adversely affected by the effectiveness of such meetings in the past. Experience suggested a degree of scepticism (especially at the level of ACSs) based on past evidence of being involved in the decision making process.

Figure 7.5 *Summary of benefits and constraints from the Learning from Experience process*

The overall conclusion we arrived at was that the company had met half the learning organization definition, i.e. there was evidence that all employees (or at least the vast majority) were being helped to learn from experience. The trouble was that there were not the mechanisms available to both translate *and* reflect upon action agreed at a local level and at an organizational level. One clear reason for this was the fact that we had made the mistake of embedding the whole process within the existing and normal reporting hierarchy and, as the comments make clear, this led to suspicion as to whether the message was getting through to the next level up based on past experience. The conclusion we reached was that in the absence of some radical restructuring the outcome could be no better than arriving at a list of useful suggestions (see Figure 7.4).

A key recommendation, apart from simplifying the details needing to be recorded in the portfolio, was therefore radically to change the mix of the sharing groups. Another key step is then to arrive at an *appropriate* organizational mechanism whereby the results of such questioning and learning are shared with other parties in the organization who are in a position to recommend action which will eventually have an impact on the organization as a whole. This means ensuring that the entire project has the commitment of senior management. Given these pre-conditions are present, there are then six key steps I suggest you should follow. These are summarized in Figure 7.6.

The aim is to enable and encourage *every* member of the organization to:

1 Take a few minutes out of every day to *reflect* on some work experience.
2 *Question* what happened and why it happened.
3 Plan to *take some action* or form an opinion of *what needs to be done*.
4 *Share* the outcome of step (3) with a colleague, boss or subordinate.

and then to

5 Provide the *organizational mechanism* for others in the organization to *share* what has been learned from individual experiences (the outcome from the four steps described above).
6 Ensure that the outcome from the above process leads to *action* to bring about change affecting the *whole organization*.

Figure 7.6 *Six steps towards building a learning organization*

ACTIVITY 7.1
● *Consider how currently equipped your organization is to meet the six preconditions in Figure 7.6.*

I believe these are *practical* steps which I have illustrated in some detail with reference to the work carried out in one particular company. But I also believe it is important to recognize the *kind* of learning that is happening in this process. There are three types of learning you need to distinguish between; they were introduced by Chris Argyris and Donald Schon in their book *Organizational Learning: A Theory of Action Perspective.*[10]

They describe three different types of learning. The first type they call 'single loop learning', which is the normal type of learning that goes on all the time. For example, walking past the Accounts Department on your way into work you notice that Betty is using an outdated form even though you had a meeting with her last week to introduce the new form. You therefore draw the matter to her attention. Betty realizes her error and conforms to the norm that has been agreed.

It is single loop because it works like a closed system: a deviation from a norm is identified, corrective action is taken and everything returns to normal. An analogy that is often used to explain single loop learning is that of a central heating system that is regulated by a thermostat. When the temperature falls below the desired level the thermostat reacts to start up the boiler until the correct temperature is reached at which point the boiler cuts out.

Such learning goes on all the time in most organizations. But by definition it can only serve to reinforce existing norms and existing systems. What if the norms were inappropriate, what if Betty did know about the new form but drawing on her experience questioned its design?

This 'questioning of established norms' is what Argyris and Schon called 'double loop learning'. But it is not enough for Betty simply to change procedures herself – that would merely be single loop learning. For double loop learning to occur Betty would have to draw her questioning of the procedure to the attention of 'the boss'; if, as a result of this process, the procedure was changed in some way that would be true double loop learning, i.e. a questioning of the norm had led to corrective action being taken. (In the case of the central heating system analogy double loop learning would occur if we began to question whether the set temperature was appropriate and then changed it.)

This second kind of learning, Argyris and Schon argued, was the most useful for organizations to acquire; the process would enable them to question procedures continually and as a result they would be more able to respond to change. In the current climate where quality is increasingly becoming a factor in an organization's search for excellence (e.g. increasing popularity of BS5750) there is an even greater case for organizations to engage more in double loop learning.

But Argyris and Schon also identified a third level of learning which they called 'deutero-' or 'double order learning'. They borrowed this concept from Geoffrey Bateson[11] who introduced the term to describe the process of 'learning to learn'. In other words, at this level of learning an organization reflects on how it learns to learn and ensures that the mechanisms are in place for this process to continue into the future. These theories – despite the jargon – are very powerful and really provide the blueprint for how the learning organization should behave in practice.

Argyris and Schon commented that the normal process of learning in organizations tends to be of the single loop kind. This is reinforced by training which, as we have seen, confirms and communicates and tests that these norms are observed in practice. But what about the kind of learning we have described in our six steps which are illustrated in Figures 7.4 and 7.5? Is this single loop, double loop or deutero-learning?

The clue is in the second step – we encouraged staff to *question* an experience, an incident. Have a look at the kinds of experience that were questioned in Figure 7.4 and the action that resulted. If staff had merely identified a fault and the outcome from the 'share' meeting was simply to confirm a standard which the individual member of staff agreed to follow in the future the process would have been single loop learning. In some cases this was the kind of incident that was reported but in the majority of cases staff began to question an experience and this process was continued and extended in the 'share' meetings. The problem was, however, that the process was not 'reflected upon' at the next share meeting in the hierarchy which would be in a position to coordinate and implement action that might affect the organization as a whole.

What was lacking was 'Deutero-learning', the ability to value and learn from the process of learning which would lead to improvements in the process itself. If you look back to the end of Chapter 6 you may well see a parallel here with the role of the 'Evaluator' whose very position is like this central process of putting value on organizational learning.

So far we have explored the findings and lessons from working with one company to create a learning organization. The net result was evidence of examples of a double-loop learning process which were never transformed into lasting change that could benefit the organization. In this sense, though the *process* was one of double loop learning, the outcome was no different from single loop learning: the procedures and norms that were questioned remained largely in place. What was lacking was an organization-wide vision and will to use the change process that had been intitiated to transform the organization itself. We now look at what are the limiting factors that block an organization from becoming a learning organization using both the example of the company we worked with as well as drawing on other sources and models.

7.2 What stops an organization from learning?

One of the images in Gareth Morgan's book *Images of Organization*[12] is of organizations as brains. He starts by looking at one interpretation of the brain as an information processing system and links it with the way many organizations are run as 'bureaucracies', simplifying and standardizing procedures in order to make the whole enterprise more manageable. This approach derives from the scientific approach to management that we explored in Chapter 4.

But there is another image of the brain, taken from cybernetics, which regards the brain as a self-organizing system which is capable of learning and adaptation. It is in this context that he too explores the ideas of single loop and double loop learning and concludes that very few organizations have any incentive for engaging in anything more than single loop learning. The whole basis of bureaucratic accountability rewards conformance to norms and looks on any challenging of established procedures with suspicion. So why should any member of an organization rock the boat? He concludes as follows:

> Learning and self-organization generally call for a re-framing of attitudes, emphasizing the importance of activeness over passiveness, autonomy over dependence, flexibility over rigidity, collaboration over competition, openness over closedness, and democratic inquiry over authoritarian belief. For many organizations this may call for a 'personality change' that can be achieved over a considerable period of time (p. 109).[12]

In retrospect it was very naive to assume we could create a learning organization within a year! I had selected this company because it had well-established training and development programmes but also because its training director I knew to be in favour of innovative approaches to learning and development. What I had completely underrated were what Morgan calls the 'realities of power and control'. In his MBA dissertation, the Training Director in question, Peter Dixon, concludes with a number of generalizations about the conditions needed for a learning organization based on the experience in his own company. Three of these are reproduced below:

1 An improvement in an organization's *ability* to learn is not sufficient in itself to create a learning organization, even if all of its members have that ability.
2 A tide of learning is not enough in itself to overcome the barriers to learning that exist. These barriers to learning must be broken down before organizations can learn and change as a result. These barriers include hierarchy, fear and lack of reward.
3 The organization must have processes that enable it to acquire sufficient inputs for it to adjust to its environment. It must be able to 'learn from the future' as well as from the past, in terms of being able to anticipate future changes in the business environment and be proactive towards them (pp. 87–88).[9]

The last point is a reminder that organizational learning depends as much on adapting to changes in the environment as to generating internal change. It is well described in an equation from Reg Revans, $L \geq C$, where L is the rate of learning and C is the rate of change in an organism's environment. In order to survive, Revans argues, the rate of learning must be equal to or greater than the rate of change in the environment. (Note this has parallels with Ashby's concept of 'requisite variety' (see page 175).)

Dixon also sees some lessons as to what happened in his company in a paper entitled 'Camping on Seesaws: Prescriptions for a Self-Designing Organization'.[13] This paper has become something of a classic in the literature of learning organizations. It introduces six characteristics which a

---

1 **Minimal consensus**: 'Cooperation requires minimal consensus'

In order to generate new ideas and practices organizations should encourage an appropriate amount of dissension: 'Balance implies that consensus does not become regimentation and dissension does not become warfare' (p. 56).

2 **Minimal contentment**: 'Satisfaction rests upon minimal contentment'

Too much contentment will 'incubate crises' while 'sufficient discontent to induce people to speak up about what they think is wrong provides crucial insurance against surprises' (p. 56).

3 **Minimal affluence**: 'wealth arises from minimal affluence'

Whereas affluence is often a key goal of most companies it can lead to complacency and a blindness to what is happening outside. 'An organization requires reminding that its environment is partly unknown, evolves and sometimes turns hostile' (p. 59).

4 **Minimal faith in planning**: 'goals merit minimal faith'

It is important for an organization 'to plan its future but not rely on its plans' (p. 59). Plans can very soon be revealed for what they are: 'Unexpected strategic reorientations remind members that explicit plans and goals are merely images of evolving aspirations' (p. 60).

5 **Minimal consistency**: 'Improvement depends on minimal consistency'

Most organizations avoid change until it is too late when they are imposed by revolution rather than evolution. More beneficial is an 'incremental' approach to change: 'When each increment is small enough to leave intact most of the activities and perceptions of most people, and small enough to uncover only partial conflicts of interests and only marginal contradictions among goals and responsibilities, an organization avoids the mammoth losses that revolutions impose' (p. 61).
    This applies equally to situations where everything seems satisfactory: 'Even in the face of apparent optimality, incremental experiments are needed to sharpen perceptions to test assumptions and to keep learning processes vital' (p. 61).

6 **Minimal rationality**: 'wisdom demands minimal rationality'

Finally, the authors are sceptical of the goal of 'rationality' which has often led to oversimplistic models of complex reality and rational answers to the wrong questions [compare with Revans].
    'The usual organization pursues a superficial image of rationality which understates the value of imperfection ... An optimal degree of imperfection ... converts imbalances into motivators and uses unclear goals to keep an organization as ready for change as the environment is' (p. 63).

Figure 7.7 *Extracts from B. Hedberg, P. Nystrom and W. Starbuck, 'Camping on a seesaw'[13]. Reproduced with kind permission of Administrative Science Quarterly)*

company must learn to acquire if it is to survive in and adapt to a rapidly changing environment. The authors warn that 'Designers who erect an organizational palace had better anticipate problems caused by shifting subsoils' (p. 44).[13] A much more appropriate structure for 'residents of changing environments' is a tent!

The authors then paint a picture of what they call a 'self-designing' organization (which we would now call a learning organization) as needing to 'balance' six attributes. Too much or too little of each attribute could constitute a blockage, so they talk of having a 'minimal' degree of each attribute. Extracts from some of the 'aphorisms' they use to describe the degree of balance required are outlined in Figure 7.7, but the paper is well worth reading in full for the homilies alone.

There is a lot of practical good sense in these criteria. More than anything else they encourage a healthy scepticism of any kind of 'planned' intervention of the kind we were trying to make to *create* a learning organization. Was the organization in question *too* affluent to want to change, *too* locked into established plans and procedures to recognize that they were no longer appropriate in a changing world. In seeking to establish a new process of learning and communication we had omitted to take enough account of the need for what Hedberg et al. call 'unlearning':

> The first step toward new behaviours is unlearning old behaviours. The effectiveness of existing activity programs and traditional strategies is disconfirmed, and the processes binding the organization to today's behavioural patterns are disengaged (p. 51).[13]

Rather like 'a paradigm shift' an old paradigm has to be *replaced* completely in order for a new one to be established. But this does not need to happen all at once; indeed one message that is coming over more and

---

1 Regard any new idea from below with suspicion – because it is new and because it is from below.
2 Insist that people who need your approval to act first go through several other levels of management to get their signatures.
3 Ask departments or individuals to challenge and criticize each others' proposals.
4 Express your criticisms freely and withhold your praise (that keeps people on their toes). Let them know they can be fired at any time.
5 Treat problems as a sign of failure.
6 Control everything carefully. Count anything that can be counted, frequently.
7 Make decisions to reorganize or change policies in secret and spring them on people unexpectedly (that also keeps people on their toes).
8 Make sure that any request for information is fully justified and that it is not distributed too freely (you don't want data to fall into the wrong hands).
9 Assign to lower-level managers, in the name of delegation and participation, responsibility for figuring out how to cut back, lay off or move people around.
10 Above all, never forget that you, the higher-ups already know everything important about the business.

Figure 7.8 *Ten rules for stifling initiative*

more strongly is that a learning organization *cannot* be achieved by some kind of radical intervention. It is more subtle than that, as Pedler et al. imply.[7] In the next section I will try to unravel some of these subtleties so that you can more easily identify them in your own organization. But to conclude this section on what stops an organization from learning I have reproduced in Figure 7.8 a list from Ros Moss Kanter's *The Change Masters*[14] of ten rules for stifling initiative. As Handy maintains in *The Age of Unreason*,[15] if a company wishes to become a learning organization these are rules that need to be broken 'frequently'.

ACTIVITY 7.2
● *Pause a while before going on to the next section to consider how your organization matches up to what we might call the Theory X model of organizations described in Figure 7.8.*

7.3 Recognizing the learning company

As an antidote to the Theory X organization of Figure 7.8 we start this section with a picture of policies that should inform the Theory Y organization of the future. Below we list and discuss 11 characteristics which Pedler et al.[7] consider typify the learning company. As indicated earlier, they are based on their original work reported in the Learning Company Project report.[3]

(1) A learning approach to strategy

> By this we mean that company policy and strategy formation together with implementation, evaluation and improvement are consciously structured as a learning process (p. 18).[7]

In contrast to what Hedberg et al. would call 'excessive rationality', this approach allows business decisions to be continually revised and feedback processes established to ensure plans are continually being improved. The processes needed to bring about Total Quality Management (see Chapter 2) would be an example of such a characteristic.

(2) Participative policy making

This means ensuring *everyone* who makes up the company is involved and is potentially able to affect company-wide policy (see Figure 2.6). But, as we shall see, a company also has a wide range of stakeholders who are not direct employees, i.e. customers, suppliers, members of the community. Means have to be found of involving them in such a way that they can affect company policy.

One of the underlying themes in Chapter 2 was the role of the TEC in being a kind of 'clearing bank' in human resource assets to the local community. By the same token they may help companies take a community view of their business and identify stakeholders who can have an impact on their company policy.

(3) Informating

This reflects the fact that information is power, and, as we have already seen in exploring Zuboff's conclusions about introduction of computers in Chapter 4, information technology now has the capacity to put that power in the hands of everyone. A learning company would seem to informate, that is empower people through the freer use and dissemination of information through more creative uses of information technology.

(4) Formative accounting and control

I believe these are very significant characteristics. In my experience the power, mystery and terror budgets and financial controls impose on managers and departments are the greatest barriers to the company becoming a learning organization. This is in no way to minimize their importance and necessity in the normal day-to-day management and control of a business. It is not so much the figures and accounts themselves which are the barrier but the way they are used and communicated.

Because money will ultimately decide whether the organization stays in business it is not surprising that forms and procedures are instituted from the top downwards to monitor and account for how money has been allocated at every level. This in itself generates vast volumes of paperwork which is often out of date as soon as a new form has been printed. But, as we have seen before, as a nation we have a curious love-hate addiction to systems and to forms in particular. This is a *key* area for much 'unlearning'.

I think it was significant that during the 'Learning from experience' project described in section 7.2 middle managers were sceptical about any change in the decision-making process that would involve them more. As an example of how they felt they were being kept apart, they all cited a recent instance when the accounts department had contacted the managers' own clients informing them of an increase in charges. The middle managers had not been informed and were faced with angry clients who could have been mollified if they had had the opportunity to personally introduce and explain the charges themselves. Accounts departments (like the Inland

Revenue) are not noted for their personal touch – and yet money has the most personal of implications.

In our report to the company we also noted that new forms had been produced by senior managers to record new data which the Training Agency had requested. In our view the company had missed a great opportunity by not involving everyone in the design of such forms to collect information for which *they* would be responsible.

In exploring the various 'costing' approaches to evaluation in Chapter 6 we have already questioned the value of systems which consist largely of collecting historical data. Much more useful would be to recognize the value of the *process* itself of collecting such data which may involve department talking to department for the first time. I am currently involved in a project producing a standards procedure manual for a company. Their interest is in having a standard, uniform set of procedures at the end of the process of data collection and debate. I have tried to refocus their interest on the process itself which in my view has been and *would continue to be* more valuable than the output at the end, which will be out of date as soon as it is published!

I may have extended Pedler and his colleagues' use of 'formative accounting and control' beyond what they intended; but I would argue that within the administrative systems by which a company measures and controls its inputs and outputs lie both the constraints and the challenges which any company seeking to become a learning organization must confront.

(5) Internal exchange

Members from different departments are encouraged to see each other as 'internal' customers and to establish processes and procedures that will facilitate service between each other. The culture is one of 'win:win'; the departments are not in competition with each other. In the future there may well be a focus of attention on what Kevin Thomson calls 'corporate internal marketing'[17] which we have already hinted at before (Chapter 2) in questioning why a company always looks for its market 'outside'.

(6) Reward flexibility

This picks up a theme which Ros Moss Kanter[14] and Lawler[16] have been emphasizing, that organizations of the future have got to arrive at more flexible ways of rewarding contribution than by providing a graduated base pay scale. This might include performance pay, profit sharing, employee ownership. But what is more important, Pedler et al. maintain, is 'to question some of the assumptions we make about payments'. For example: *Why* do we pay some people more than others? Why do we *pay* people at all – To encourage them to work harder? To buy their skills?

Pedler et al. are saying that as long as people are *aware* of the assumptions on which reward is made *and agree with them* they will be happy – but all too often companies do not make such criteria explicit. They also recognize that of the 11 characteristics this one is probably the most difficult to implement 'since it is likely to involve changing not only the distribution of reward but also the distribution of power' (p. 22).[7]

(7) Enabling structures

This too involves a recognition that the structure of the company – the way roles are defined, accountability and the impact of one role on another – has to change to encourage the empowerment and sharing which characterizes the learning organization. Because of the way decisions had been taken and communicated in the past through a 'hierarchical' structure in the company we studied it had led to scepticism as to just how free a learning organization the company could become. Much more appropriate would be a structure depicted in which there is no hierarchy but autonomous work groups that feed into some central process. The structure is more akin to a network and may well characterize the 'form' learning organizations will take in the future. The central core is more like the Central Processing Unit (CPU) of a computer rather than a senior board of management.

> The message is that both technological and social considerations now lead to the view that organizations can be usefully treated as a net of semi-autonomous work groups linked by an information network (p. 77).[18]

One possible sign that an organization is really taking on the form of a learning organization will be when its structure is decided not by the senior board but as a consequence of the decision processes that need to be in place to serve the best interests of the company's customers.

(8) Boundary workers as external scanners

By 'boundary workers' Pedler et al. mean any member of the organization who comes in contact with the organization's 'business environment' and is able to feed back information into the company decision making process. The obvious example is sales people but more and more companies are using technicians, maintenance engineers as their ears and eyes in the outside world. (Again see the increasing importance of using every member of staff as part of 'marketing'.[17])

In any service organization where potentially every member of staff is in contact with an external customer, then *everyone* is capable of feeding back information. In fact I would define a service organization as the *interface* between staff and customer. I would also maintain that its *structure* should be determined by the way staff and customers interact.

The Learning from Experience process used *the customer* as the]
for learning. By definition we were encouraging each member (
scan his or her environment and directly use that information to /
decision making process. As we have already observed we could have ,
more emphasis on the importance of this factor. It is central to Revans's
equation $L \geq C$ where successful organizational learning depends on
learning being equal to or greater than changes going on outside. We could
have made that link more explicit. I suggest that all staff become aware of
this factor right from their induction and are encouraged not just to keep
their 'eyes open' for opportunities in the environment but are positively
rewarded for so doing (see characteristic 6).

(9) Inter-company learning

This reflects the growing number of collaborations between different
companies, even competitors, in order to pool experience and learn from
each other. There is evidence that the secrecy and autonomy that
competition engenders is changing to a much more open market.[19]
I am involved with a group of hospitality and leisure companies in Surrey,
most of whom are competitors of each other, who meet regularly to discuss
issues of quality. We have instituted a Quality Audit where each is paired up
with another and, unbeknown to the other, makes regular visits and sends
back a standard audit on quality.

(10) Learning climate

In a learning company managers see their primary task as facilitating
members' experimentation and learning from experience. It is normal
to take time out to seek feedback, to obtain data to aid understanding.
Senior managers give a lead in questioning their own ideas, attitudes
and actions (p. 23).[7]

This is the kind of climate we tried to create in the company described in
section 7.2. But it cannot be established by implementing a procedure. It
goes much deeper than that. It requires, above all, the kind of management
development we explored in Chapter 5 where the manager of the future will
be a mentor, facilitator and primary resource to his or her subordinates.

(11) Self-development opportunities for all

At the heart of a learning organization is an individual learner who from the
very first time he joins the company will be encouraged to take ownership
for his or her own development and will be provided with the resources to
be able to do so:

A whole range of resources will be required. These will include
courses, workshops, self-learning materials, but in addition there will

be others, such as development groups, one-to-one coaching/mentoring, peer-level one-to-one counselling. Databanks will provide information on what is available, together with, on a voluntary opting-in basis, details of individuals who are working on specific developmental issues and who are ... willing to give support and mutual guidance (p. 23).[7]

Compare the above description with the scenario I introduced at the beginning of Chapter 4.

This completes a brief review of the 11 characteristics Pedler et al. introduce in *The Learning Company*.[5] In the same format as their previous work on management self-development, the book is then devoted to what they call 'glimpses', which illustrate each of the 11 characteristics applied in practice. There are 101 glimpses which the authors call 'a collection of short stories'. There is a matrix indicating which 'glimpses' apply to a particular characteristic.

The Learning Company[7] is a very useful starting point for anyone trying to make sense of the concept 'learning organization'. Incidentally, the term 'learning *company*' they took from a speech given in 1986 by Geoffrey Holland, then Director of the Manpower Services Commission:[20]

If we are to survive – individually or as companies, or as a country, – we must create a tradition of 'learning companies'. Every company must be a 'learning company'.

The authors prefer to use the term 'company' rather than organization because they consider it is 'more convivial'.

'Organization' is a mechanical sort of word, sounding somewhat abstract and lifeless, and the prospect of dealing with it is perhaps intimidating. 'Company', on the other hand, is one of our oldest words for a group of people engaged in a joint enterprise. In everyday terms we 'accompany' others and talk of doing things 'in company' (p. 1).[7]

While understanding the reason for their preference for 'company', I prefer to use 'learning organization' because I have a picture of organization as being anything *but* mechanical (in fact I see a 'company' as being more associated with a legal and bounded entity). Organization, on the other hand, I associate with internal energy and drive! Anyway, whatever word you choose to use I hope you are becoming clearer as to what this concept refers.

Most writers on the subject try to illustrate the concept in the form of a 'dynamic' model. Garratt,[4] for example, depicts the learning organization as the product of two sets of forces: one from the external environment which leads to organizational effectiveness and one from the internal environment which contributes to organizational efficiency. Each of these influences are depicted as two feedback loops informing the centre which is seen as a kind of 'business brain'.

Pedler et al.[7] experimented with five models before the sixth one emerged (from out of the previous five 'transmutations'). They describe it as 'an energy flow model' and in format it appears like four cog wheels driving each other. Each wheel represents the four sources of energy they see at the heart of the learning organization: Policy, Ideas, Operations and Action.

Their advice as to where to start I think is eminently sensible: 'The Learning Company is about aligning and attuning flows of energy so start where the energy is (p. 49).'[7] This could be with the board of directors or it could equally well start with one department or by running a series of workshops on the subject.

The danger with any kind of model as with any set of steps is to suggest that there is *a* way of describing this 'thing' called a learning organization, or at least how to arrive there. But reality, as Hedberg et al. confirm, is very messy. We need, therefore, messy models to describe it. One of the best messy models of a learning organization I know is depicted by Tom Peters.[21] In seeking a new model of organization 'to respond to wildly altered business and economic circumstances' (p. 103), Peters contrasts two models: the first is 'the inflexible, rule-dominated, mass producer of the past'. This is depicted as a circle – the only break with tradition – with a thick line describing the circumference which is the boundary between the firm on the inside and its environment outside, i.e. its suppliers, customers, distributors, franchisees etc. At the centre of the circle is another tiny circle, also with a thick boundary. This is what Peters calls 'the traditional, invisible, impersonal, generally out-of-touch corporate hub' out of which come rules and procedures which are filtered through middle managers (each of whom he depicts as a 'lumpy, substantial square'). The picture is of straight line communications radiating outwards from the centre until they meet the impervious boundary and of strict functional roles.

In contrast, there is a second model, 'the flexible, porous, adaptive, fleet-of-foot organization of the future' in which 'every person is "paid" to be obstreperous, a disrespecter of formal boundaries, to hustle and to be engaged fully with engendering swift action, constantly improving every-thing' (p. 106).[21] This model resembles a living cell (roughly circular in circumference) though with a boundary which is uneven, and thin and porous enabling customers, suppliers and everyone in the 'outside' environment to cross the boundary and be involved inside the organization's internal structure. That structure has a thin circle at the hub which Peters describes as a 'glowing, healthy, breathing corporate centre' into which

> People from below regularly wander . . . without a muss or fuss and those at the top are more often than not out wandering. Customers and suppliers are as likely to be members of the executive floor (which happily doesn't really exist as a physical entity) as are the members of the senior team. But above all the glow comes from management's

availability, informality, energy, hustle and the clarity of (and excitement associated with) the competitive vision, philosophy or core values. (p. 107).[21]

Do you get the picture? If you are familiar with Peters's *Thriving on Chaos*[22] you can perhaps imagine the embodiment of turning an organization inside out and upside down. (This is similar to the process we were trying to depict in Figure 2.6 on page 28.)

But does it have to be so anarchic? Peters would say there is no alternative. Drastic times of change and uncertainty call for drastic changes and challenges to the old, traditional order where a hierarchy of formal accountability could satisfactorily cope with a stable environment (and workforce). But if at this very moment you are sitting on top of or somewhere inside such a hierarchy in which and/or for which you do have formal accountability, you may feel somewhat uncomfortable with these images of anarchy. In fact I *do* believe that's what they are and that's what the learning organization is, *an image*.

In the final section, before we pull together all the threads in this book, I shall address this issue of image and how the image you and your colleagues and your staff have of the organization can make it a learning organization however hierarchical and traditional it might seem.

7.4 How to realize and reinforce the image of the learning organization

Images and pictures have been a regular theme in this book. They have been introduced, usually, at a point in the text when we were about to do some 'upside-down thinking' or depict a concept which was difficult to pin down in a logical and systematic way. Here are some of the images that have been used in each chapter so far:

Chapter 2 ● The image of a TEC as a local clearing bank for local talent, competences
● The focusing of two different pictures to arrive at an organization-view of 'Investing in People' – the view of each employee (bottom-up) and the company view (top-down)

Chapter 3 ● Using the detail in a statement of competence to 'picture' what a particular job entails
● The three-dimensional picture/model of corporate capability which reflects not only every competence within an organization but the transforming effect such capacity has on the organization as a whole

Chapter 4 ● The 'Brave New World' scenario in which every employee is 'logged' into an organization-wide network of learning resources
          ● The breaking down of each learning resource into its basic elements and recombining the elements in a model we called the 'Learning Mix'
          ● The making visible of the learning process in any organization so that it is more accessible to all
Chapter 5 ● The 'picture' of the manager of the future identifying and 'adding value' to each of his/her employees
Chapter 6 ● The concept of a meta-system which can only be arrived at by a projection of an image beyond the existing system
          ● The concept of the Evaluator being the focus of literally 'accumulating' organizational values and being able to feedback to the organization an overall view on which they can take action

These images reflect a way of looking at the world (and in particular the world of training and development) which has resulted in this chapter in further pictures of the learning organization that grew out of activities described in section 7.1. The practical consequence of being able to describe and above all *share* such images is that of being able to focus energy into particular action being taken to *realize* the image so described. This has powerful consequences at the level of the organization:

> Organization is always shaped by underlying images and ideas; we organize as we imaginize; and it is always possible to imaginize in many different ways.
> When we think about organization in this way we are provided with a constant reminder that we are involved in a creative process where new images and ideas can create new actions (p. 343).[12]

The central theme of Gareth Morgan's *Images of Organization* (which is a marvellous and vivid introduction to organization theory and practice) is that there is a direct relationship between the way we think and imagine the world to be and the way we act. By identifying and articulating the different ways in which people 'imagine' the organization of which they are a part, and making them aware of *other* ways in which the organization *could* be viewed, 'we are able to manage and design organizations in ways that we may not have thought possible before' (p. 13).[12]

I wish I had been introduced to Gareth Morgan's text when I was struggling with my picture of evaluation (see Chapter 6) because this was the conclusion I arrived at: that evaluation is essentially a process whereby people are made aware of what are the *possibilities* of value to be derived from any situation. To arrive at this insight they need different ways of describing (imagining) the situation and of interpreting it.

Morgan would argue that an organization actually *becomes* what its members (and in particular its senior management) imagine it to be. Thus if your view of an organization is of a hierarchy of accountabilities, that is what it will become. If you conceive of it as a brain acting as a cybernetic system, on the other hand, then that is what will be realized. The conclusion we reach, therefore, is that if you, your colleagues, superiors and staff imagine your organization *as if it were* a learning organization, then that is what it *can* become. I hope the images and pictures in the preceding chapters have given you a basis from which to project your 'imagining'.

However, I appreciate you might well be able to take in these ideas and images at a purely 'conceptual' level but find it difficult to *imagine* how they might be realized in practice within your own organization. As the saying goes, there really is no answer to this dilemma *except* through action. I do not believe there are a series of steps you can take along the way. I tried this with the Learning from Experience process described in Section 7.1 only to come to the conclusion that though there was evidence of individual learning and potential organizational value, one could only be transformed into the other by a radical attitude change on the part of the organization itself. In many ways it is an innovative organization, but it has a structure which *reflects* the image of organization as the accumulation of compartmentalized and functional roles which prevent innovative ideas seeping out from one level to affect another. (Compare this with Tom Peters's second model described earlier.)

The solution, as Tom Peters claims in his article,[21] 'lies within – that is, within the heads and hearts of our own managers'. The addition of the word 'heart' is significant. Look back to Figure 5.13, where we explored the results of an MSC sponsored research project into 'qualities of managing'. This identified three dimensions, *thinking, feeling* and *willing*. Most managers are developed to think and analyse but not to feel and, what Lessem calls 'grasp wilfully'.[6] Lessem, as we saw in Chapter 5, describes a 'developmental cycle of learning' which starts with 'reacts physically' and progresses through a series of stages including social response and reflection until the ultimate stage of learning and development is reached which he describes as 'imagine creatively'. He then describes how the individual can use such learning in what he calls a journey of 'innovation and transformation' starting with 'envision creatively' and ending with 'enact things'. He also attributes the same qualities to organizations which he says go through the same stages. A learning organization would be the embodiment of what he calls 'learningfulness' which would encompass the self-skill and knowledge development of all its members.

I would recommend Lessem's book *Total Quality Learning*[6] to help on this journey from conception, through envisaging to action. Alternatively, the same kind of issues are summarized in Figure 5.13. What is certain is that the learning organization will not be realized by making plans alone. It goes much deeper than that:

> If people want to change their environment, they need to change themselves and their actions – not someone else ... Problems that never get solved, never get solved because managers keep tinkering with everything but what they do (p. 152).[23]

Karl Weick (above) is quoted again in an extract from a paper by Smircich and Stubbart[24] in which they put forward an alternative view to the one which suggests that organizations should adapt to their environments. According to them, organizations can *enact* their environment, that is to say, they can shape it by the way they think and act. The process they describe in which managers can be helped to 'reflect on the way in which managers' actions create and sustain their particular organizational realities' is one we want to focus on:

> With the development of a greater capacity for self-reflection, corporate officials, governmental policy makers, and all organization members can examine and critique their own enactment processes. By maintaining a *dual focus of attention – an ability to transcend the momentary situation in which they are entangled and to see and understand their actions within a system of meaning that is continually open to reflection and assessment* – strategic managers can challenge the apparent limits and test the possibilities for their organizational existence (p. 95, emphasis added).[24]

If you recall the discussion that revolved around a meta-system from Chapter 6, the passage in italics above should ring some bells. Again, unfortunately, the language is rather obscure but the concept is the same – organizational learning is a dynamic process, like evaluation, which involves using what Schon calls the 'here and now' as a 'projective model' for the future.[1] Senge refers to the same process as 'creative tension'[5] which is caused by, on the one hand, holding a vision of what needs to happen while on the other hand (and *just* as necessary) having a clear awareness of reality through which the vision has to be achieved.

It seems to me significant that a number of writers on learning in organizations and in particular public institutions (like Donald Schon in *Beyond the Stable State* and Stafford Beer who worked with Allende in Chile, for example) all focus on what Marsick and Watkins call an 'ongoing dialectical process of action and reflection'.[25] Because what Schon calls 'public knowing' has never been made explicit before, the language used to describe it takes some getting used to, but I suggest it is critical to understanding what is at the heart of a learning organization, what Schon calls 'existential knowledge'. This kind of learning is quite different from what comes from rational/experimental systematic 'knowing'. In existential knowledge 'The here and now provides the test, the source and the limit of knowledge'.[1]

Hedberg was making very similar points in the article in *Administrative Science Quarterly*[13] (again, a source for public institutions). Finally, just to give one more instance, the corporate strategist Igor Ansoff includes a paper by Lindblom in his book of readings on *Business Strategy*.[26] The title of the paper is 'The science of muddling through' and Ansoff includes it in his collection more as a warning against what he holds to be 'a widely prevalent state of practice in business'. Lindblom is concerned with examining just how the public administrator comes to adopt one policy rather than another and he compares two approaches: one is the rational-comprehensive approach which he calls the 'root' approach. This is the analytical approach whereby objectives are first defined and policies selected as to which one will best achieve the goals.

Lindblom contrasts this with what he calls the 'successive limited comparisons' or 'branch' approach whereby

> Policy making is a process of successive approximation to some desired objective in which what is desired continues to change under reconsideration (p. 55).[26]

This he thinks is more appropriate in the uncertain world of 'public knowing'. Furthermore, he considers that the *test* of a good policy is not that is has met the objectives but that those who have to undertake it *agree with it* as a policy. This has strong parallels with Beer's measurement of eudemony, i.e. 'changes in potential'.

All these writers, I believe, however much the language may disguise it, are putting forward the same message – in public life (i.e. organizations) policy is made, decisions taken and learning realized in what might seem from the *outside* as being a very random and unsystematic manner. This is, for example, in stark contrast to the way MBA students are taught to analyse and prepare business policy or what trainers expect course members to achieve on a problem solving course. But on the *inside*, as Schon describes, there is only the 'here-and-now' which is different from any situation that has ever occurred before. In practice the manager is using past experiences to see how they compare but though they may have worked in the past they can never *exactly* match what is required now. It is in this state of uncertainty – otherwise known as the natural state of reality – that Schon's concept of 'existential knowing' comes into its own. It is in such circumstances

> Where we cannot establish controls we form judgements most effectively about 'what has happened' or 'what has led to these effects' by noting processes *internal* to the project (p. 232).[1]

So, what practical use is all this? The first thing is that after all this if the learning organization is still what you want to achieve – you had better start looking for it 'by noting processes *internal* to the project'. In other words, it doesn't exist *out there*, it cannot be created by following a series of steps – in my opinion it is the *embodiment* of a thousand 'incremental changes' that occur every day in every department but which we are not attuned to because we are looking for consequences of learning we can recognise against standards we have used before. As we discovered when looking at evaluation in the context of Beer's use of 'eudemony' in Chapter 6, we do not have an appropriate 'metric' for these kinds of 'potential change'. All we are left with is judgement (Schon) and value (Beer).

Do you remember Ada in Chapter 3? In order to demonstrate the concept of 'corporate capability' we envisaged what we *knew* about Ada as far as her competences were concerned as an accounts clerk (see p. 78). We have the measurement to recognize and put a value on these kind of skills. But what about other things Ada does that goes beyond what we would *normally* expect? When prompted, this is what she said:

Well, there was this telephone call last Thursday. It was from Mr Francis asking about the weekly B33 figures. Normally my supervisor, Mrs Jones, would deal with it but she'd been called away. Anyway, I knew all about the figures and gave Mr Francis the information he wanted. He was a bit unsure of how they'd been calculated so I explained it to him. He said it was the first time he had understood what they were about!

Isn't this a good example of what Schon calls 'existential knowing'? It is also a good place to begin mapping the origins of a potential learning organization. In doing so we will compare it with the findings from the Learning from Experience process and see what is different.

If you turn back to Chapter 3 (p. 79) you will see that we followed up Ada's revelations of what she was capable of doing by first getting Ada to recognize that she *can* achieve competence at a higher level and then to reflect on how she *could* utilize these skills further with organizational support. With the hindsight of what we have been discussing in the past few pages we can now recognize that what we have done is give Ada a new 'meta-competence' which, though she will not know it, enables her to engage in a

> dual focus of attention – an ability to transcend the momentary situation in which [she is] entangled and to see and understand [her] actions within a system of meaning that is continually open to reflection and assessment (p. 95).[24]

Put another way, we are helping her to engage in 'double loop' learning.

Let us now suppose we follow the same process with each member of the Accounts Department. In each case we are trying to inhabit the world as lived by that person and understand their competences and capabilities in the context of the world as it is. As a result of this exercise we can then compile a picture which gives us what Schon would call a 'projective model' from three perspectives:

What does happen   *(the reality now).*
What should happen *(the above picture compared with our view of reality).*
What could happen   *(a new 'meta' reality which reflects what we have called 'corporate capability' in Chapter 3).*

Suppose we find that the Accounts Department is following unorthodox procedures and using forms which are out-of-date. (This is the result of comparing the two pictures in stage 2). Most organizational audits would report back to Head Office and memos would follow thick and fast bringing back Accounts to the straight and narrow. In other words, the organization engages in single loop learning. The Accounts Department would also learn something new, not to be open in the future about the way it conducts its business!

But supposing we went on to stage 3 and drew a picture based on the kind of capabilities we found Ada had displayed. Putting it all together we find that the Accounts Department, in reality, acts not just as a control centre but as a centre for advice and counselling. Ada is not the only member of the department who has been helping other departments understand the information analysis. In addition you identify at least two members of staff who have redesigned procedures to meet particular managers' requirements which, on reflection, are much simpler than those proposed by Head Office and yet achieve the same objectives in half the time.

One technique that is very useful for reviewing the purpose of departments, roles and depicting visually how decisions are taken and who reports to whom, is Soft Systems Methodology (SSM) – a technique developed by Peter Checkland to try to capture the complexity of 'Human Activity Systems' (as opposed to 'Hard Systems' thinking which measures systems 'out-there', in the real world – for example, engineering systems). SSM, by contrast, is 'a process of inquiry' which begins with a 'root definition':

A root definition expresses the core purpose of a purposeful activity system. That core purpose is always expressed as a transformation process in which some entity, the 'input' is changed or transformed into some new form of that same entity, 'the output' (p. 33).[13]

This root definition is arrived at by taking into account factors like customers, the staff, who owns the problem, the environment, the nature of the transformation process. A root definition that might arise as a result of our new view of the Accounts Department for example might be:

The purpose of the Information Systems Department (previously known as the Accounts Department) is to take each of the company's goals and in association with respective Department Heads produce an appropriate framework for measuring output and identifying appropriate cost factors that will need to be controlled to ensure output is on target.

The process also involves the drawing of 'process' diagrams which connect up who is involved with whom to produce what. These contribute to the final definition of purpose and the kind of monitoring system that is needed to ensure it is achieved. Senge also uses systems diagrams[3] to help an organization see 'circles of influence rather than straight lines' (see Chapter 6).

Checkland and Scholes observe:

> What is in short supply in organizations is an organized sharing of perceptions sufficiently intense that concerted action gets taken corporately. Enacting the process of SSM can help with that (p. 79).[18]

One way that it can assist is in providing tangible evidence of the *outcome* of the process in which the members of the Accounts Department have been involved. Thus the 'root definition' can become *their* mission statement which each owns because each member of staff was part of the process that produced it. The various flow diagrams and pictures describing transactions between department members and outside staff can also serve as 'external' reinforcement of the learning process. In fact this constitutes 'deutero-learning' because it enables members to reflect on the processes that gave rise to it in the first place and improve on them as necessary in the future. Built into the system would be opportunities for group review, feedback that would ensure the whole process is informed and improved.

Many of the processes for change we have explored in this chapter have been brought together by Senge[5] in his description of five core disciplines *all* of which need to be used together to build the learning organization of the future. We have already explored 'the fifth discipline', Systems Thinking, in which all of the others can be integrated. The other four disciplines are as follows:

1 Personal mastery: having a clear personal vision but also being clear about current reality and being able to focus the energy that comes from what he calls 'creative tension' (the gap between the vision and current reality).

2 Mental models: the capacity to recognize and share with others the underlying 'mental models' that shape our assumptions and often prevent us from entering true dialogue with others (see Team Learning below).

3 Shared vision: the process whereby separate personal visions become shared by the whole organization and become 'its' vision rather than emanating from any one individual.

4 Team learning: the process whereby a group goes beyond mere discussion of events and enters 'dialogue' in the original Greek meaning of the word – allowing meaning to flow through and affect the whole group.

Senge's vision of a learning organization is one which is 'continually expanding to create its future'. The core disciplines provide the means whereby everyone in the organization can bring this about.

In retrospect, we now review the conclusions we arrived at from the Learning from Experience project (see Figure 7.5) in the light of the ideas we have explored in this section.

As we have already discussed, there was sufficient evidence of individual and even group learning and proposed action for change (see Figure 7.4). What *didn't* happen, as compared with our hypothetical exploration of an Accounts Department, was for the conclusions to become embedded in some organizational policy and fed back to the participants as evidence of double loop learning being transformed into deutero-learning. The reason, as we have discussed before, was mainly that the whole process was enacted within an existing hierarchy of accountabilities which made it difficult to take an overall 'meta' view. How different *could* it have been?

A key message from this section based on an analysis of writers on organizational and public learning and on decision making is that organizational learning is messy; it does not follow laid down procedures. In this respect it was a mistake to insist on a particular method for participants to record their learning. Based on an extrapolation of the Ada saga I would tend to first encourage a chosen 'group' to engage in double loop learning by freely questioning (with a cross-representation of peers, subordinates and superiors) the procedures they currently operate in relation to the purpose of their particular units/departments as they see them. Part of this process would also attempt to get them to articulate their 'image' of the organization ('theory-in-use'). Encouraged to make proposals for improving the system, they would be provided with organizational *resources* (e.g. outside help, expertise, training) to produce proposals. In their turn these proposals would be fed back to them incorporating changes and additions and also providing a mechanism by which such 'learning' would continue and for monitoring the outcome of the proposals.

One of the constraints of a contract catering organization is that its units are geographically dispersed. Therefore systems for setting up interactions *between* units would be difficult. Exchange of staff between units would also be difficult because clients tend to want to keep the same staff in a particular unit. But once the problem is *articulated* in this way and staff are given an opportunity freely to critique the system it might lead to *alternative images* of just how a contract catering organization should be structured in the future and what should be its contractual relationships with staff and clients alike. This is the potential a *learning* organization offers, to change and extend the boundaries of organization itself and reveal the extent of its corporate capability.

The first step is to be sensitive to processes of learning and image formation *within* the organization. We made the mistake of thinking that a planned intervention would start the process off. We omitted to look more closely at how staff communicated with each other and with other levels in the hierarchy. If we had probed deeper we would have found obstacles to communication which would have to be removed first to allow free flow of ideas from one level to another.

As a general rule I recommend the advice of Pedler et al.[7] that you 'start where the energy is'. It could be wherever there is a potential meta-system in the making which is wherever you notice what Beer calls 'changes in potential' (see Chapter 6). It might be triggered by someone going on a course or workshop which leads to particular changes; it might be a chance remark you overhear which alerts you to the potential of change. Wherever it is, your task is then to open it up further by helping participants engage in 'double-loop' learning and providing the necessary organizational support. This leads to step two.

The next step is to make *explicit* and visible to all concerned the fruits of the organizational learning and action that results. This could take a number of forms. In the case of our Accounts Department we have suggested there be a clear 'mission' statement that serves to communicate clearly the principal purpose which all the participants should feel they now own. This would be further backed up by a visual description of the processes they have undertaken (and will continue to undertake). It is important that any visual display is not seen as simply historical, it must also be a guide to the future.

Other ways of *externalising* the support process might be as follows:

- Progress chart which encourages comment not just from within the department but from outside as well. If you follow the Peters model you might want to extend this to customers and suppliers.
- Computer based reports, models, pictures. Zuboff reports on staff creating their own 'universal mind that would span time and distance'; this was a programme staff could log into to express what they felt about any issue and generate inter-departmental debate.

In my view, corporate capability is the combination of both processes. There must be a continual search for opportunities to add value to experiences and competences *within*, but this must be matched by some kind of *external* evidence which is tangible, integrative and in which everyone can share, i.e. a 'shared vision'.

7.5 Corporate capability – people power pays off

Organizations which have the *capability* to anticipate and respond to their environment will be prepared for future change. This capability is delivered by: creating an appropriate culture; designing management systems to integrate functional needs; building strategic management capability; creating a workforce capable of handling change (p. 1).[27]

The above is taken from a report from the Prospect Centre which describes itself as a management consultancy 'specializing in organizational capability'. This report[27] is an indictment of 'demand based' training, which becomes redundant as soon as it has been implemented, and the absence of 'supply capability' to prepare us for the future. Its authors contrast the UK approach with that of Japan: *'Capabilities first, strategies follow.'* They do find some examples of a change of approach, citing, for example, Alan Sugar of Amstrad who realized that in going up-market he lacked the necessary 'capability to manage inventories for both costs control and quality'. This led to the recruitment of a number of people to fill a range of *new* roles aimed at the future.

The Prospect Centre report is critical of organizations who complain they are victims of circumstances when what is lacking is 'senior management capability to anticipate changes in critical success factors and their organizational capability implications' (p. 32).[27] Senior managers, by the decisions they take, can *create* a potential for business performance. (Compare our discussion on how thinking within organizations can *enact* the environment.)

To counteract this weakness, the Prospect Centre report calls for a 'quantum-shift change in Training Needs Analysis (TNA)' away from focusing on *current* best practice and towards focusing on performance measures of 'the business process':

> This makes it possible to identify current performance and also those aspects of future performance which are *extrapolations, or projected changes*, of present performance (p. 48, emphasis added)[27]

This means asking questions which anticipate future trends (change in technology, implications of opening up global markets etc.) The report argues that such questions should begin to be addressed during an employee's induction stage so that he or she is not only prepared for the requirements of today but can anticipate the kind of service that will be needed in the future. (We have already drawn attention to the power of the induction stage when the company can learn much from the *employee* about their perceived capability as an organization.)

The Prospect Centre report is a timely reminder of the need to address training and development to the needs of the future and not just to the past. But some changes, I would suggest, have to grow from *within* the existing culture. Because we do not have the same culture as the Japanese and the East, which builds up capability as a matter of company policy *before* strategic decisions are taken, we have to find other ways to stimulate the debate. In this chapter we have explored ways in which companies can begin instituting processes of *questioning* throughout the organization which otherwise would have been hidden.

We have also spent some time examining the nature of 'images' and the process of 'imagining' which (like Gareth Morgan and Donald Schon) I believe can enable organizations to 'project' possibilities for change in the future based on current performance and current trends. But when we *talk* about organizations whom are we addressing? It isn't just the senior managers (though they have a crucial responsibility as the Prospect Centre report makes clear). It isn't even just every single person who works for a company (though it is often forgotten just how powerful a contribution each of their individual perceptions makes to the kind of organization it becomes). It *also* includes outside stakeholders – customers, distributors, suppliers, community members etc.

The ideas of Tom Peters might be a little extreme for this country's natural and inbred conservatism, but just imagine what might be achieved if you convened a meeting with representatives from all levels, departments within your organization and a selection of customers, suppliers, distributors, and a representative from the local TEC and invited everyone to address the question: 'What business should we be in in five years time?' The kind of answers you get – and more important the *process of debate* that is started – I venture to suggest would be priceless and certainly cheaper than employing outside corporate strategists to come in and report.

The irony is that such approaches seem *too* simple. But they also involve the kind of upside-down thinking that we have indulged in throughout this book. There is also the question of time. Most companies are so involved juggling with the day-to-day complexities of the business that they do not have (or make) the time to ponder or reflect on such questions. It requires what systems theorists call 'redundancy' being built in, i.e. sufficient 'space', spare capacity to allow everyone to carry out the kind of 'double loop' learning we have discussed in this chapter.

The whole of this book has been about giving *everyone* in the organization this kind of 'reflective' capacity, not just the managers. For some reason most articles and papers that are written on training and development assume that the subject for change is management. If managers change then it is assumed everything will be fine. This reflects, I believe, a particular 'image' people have of organizations and the hierarchy of control. It still smacks of Taylorism (see Chapter 5) which assumes that only the managers need to think; employees are paid to follow instructions.

One of the benefits of the competence intitiative we explored in Chapter 3 is that it allows us to put a value on what people do and in particular to identify the management functions that are part of every job. Right from induction every new member of an organization should be encouraged to see him- or herself in a management role. The only difference between the level at the bottom and that of the top should be one of scope not of content. This implies, of course, a very radical change in the way we *think* about organizational power (and how it is rewarded).

I believe the learning organization will be the natural consequence of these kinds of changes. But it also needs an organization-wide focus to describe its boundaries as you proceed, otherwise neither you, nor your staff, will be able to recognize it. Indeed *being* able to recognize it is part of the process as Peter Dixon observed after our attempt to create a learning organization within his company

> It would seem that learning *how* to create a Learning Organization is a necessary component of actually creating one and it *helps if one's own understanding of what a Learning Organization really is can stay at least one step ahead of the stages of the project's development* (p. 58, emphasis added).[9]

I suggest it is this process of creation (which Senge calls 'creative tension') which should be made explicit and shared and owned by all the participants. The essence of this process is this 'dual focus of attention' which we tried to unravel in the previous section. It means simultaneously keeping one eye on the present (the standards that have to be achieved, the resources that need to be managed etc.) and yet also *questioning* what you are doing and making a mental note of how it might be changed and improved (double loop learning).

Traditionally, training and development have been aimed at reinforcing the existing norms of an organization (i.e. single loop learning). While this is still important, the underlying message of this book is that it *isn't enough* if we are to develop the kind of capacities to cope with the uncertainties and opportunities of the future. Therefore, in each chapter we have suggested ways in which you can continue to meet the demands of the present but at the same time use the experience gained through these processes literally to *create* the future. This is what we mean by corporate capability – the capacity of an organization to add value to *all* of its members and for everyone to *recognize* the difference. It is something over and above achieving existing objectives and demands. In this sense it equates to the Prospect Centre's call for development that is not simply 'demand based' but provides 'supply capability'.

Yet it can also go deeper still than becoming more capable of coping with the future by investing in skill development now (valuable though that is). Just how deep it can go was explored in an AMED (Association for Management Education and Development) Conference which addressed 'Joining Forces: Working with Spirituality in Organizations'. In one of the papers delivered at that conference Peter Hawkins addresses the issue of 'The Spiritual Dimension of the Learning Organization'.[28] He reviews single and double loop learning theories which equate to Bateson's Level I and Level II learning.[11] But Bateson also introduced a Level III learning which involves what Hawkins calls 'a transcendence of the ego-world' – the spiritual dimension.

Any 'transcendent' state is always going to give us problems when it comes to using language to describe it, as we found with the concept of the 'meta-system'. But in essence Level III learning is the capacity to engage in what we have already seen described as 'dual function and attention'[24] and arrive at a 'deeper' understanding as a result of having to reconcile maybe what is logically *unreconcilable* (a common state in most organizations!). In its way the example we discussed in section 7.4 of the Accounts Department being transformed into an information Systems Department is a case in point.

The process began with some Level I learning (single loop) – forms, procedures being completed in an unorthodox way. Single loop learning would be to correct the practice and return to normal. Level II learning (double loop learning), on the other hand, encourages a questioning of the norms as a result of which procedures are changed. Level III learning occurs when *someone* in the organization begins to use outcomes of Level I and Level II learning as what Hawkins calls 'spectacles through which we view the world'.[28] As a result, once one is free of the specific and the particular, the question begins to be asked – what is the purpose of the Accounts Department anyway? Level III is seen by Bateson as a state of enlightenment but, as Hawkins points out:

> The other more useful way of viewing this level is that it provides temporary access to a higher logical level of awareness, where we have the space to become free enough of our normal perspectives and paradigm constraints to see through them rather than with them, and thus create the space to change them (p. 177).[28]

He adds that by definition 'it is possible to change the way one double loop learns only if there is some temporary access to Learning Level III'. His point is that valuable though double learning is, it can 'lead to survivor mentality', i.e. keeping one ahead in the game. But what is the game? What is it that Senge calls 'the larger story'? It is only when we begin to contemplate the *possibility* of not being able to survive that we can take a broader and more creative view of our current position. But Hawkins is not

> advocating that we give up strategic thinking or that we move into a fatalistic acceptance of organizational mortality, but rather that if somewhere within an organization there is some treble loop learning, then there will be a higher quality of double loop learning (p. 179).[28]

So who do we look to in the organization to engage in such learning? If you go back to Chapter 5 you will see that this is just the role we were advocating managers should take on board as part of their development. The more senior the manager the more widely they should engage in Level III learning culminating in the senior manager who 'has to embody the self-consciousness of the institution'.[29]

In my view, the MBA of the future will be less and less about teaching more and advanced techniques and theory related to functional strategems that worked in the past and much more concerned with developing senior managers of the future to engage in Level III learning. The programme would be a systematic critique of every theory and practice that has worked *so far.* The measure of success would be how such learning and thinking contribute to the transformation of the organizations of the future.

7.6 Moving from competence to capability

In Chapter 6 we explored the arguments for and against a 'cost-benefit' approach to evaluation and in Figure 6.5 summarized the hypothetical financial consequences of achieving a particular training objective. We also added another far more speculative column headed 'What added value might accrue from these consequences which have a financial payoff?' What I am describing as corporate capability I see as the equivalent organizational version of this second column, which could be headed 'What added value might accrue to the organization as a result of questioning, changing the procedures, experience, outcomes listed in Column One?' (Column One would summarize the organization's achievements to date using the kind of approaches we have advocated for investing in its human capital.)

In Figure 7.9 I have summarized the themes from each chapter of the book into two columns. Column One is headed 'Improving current competence' and lists ideas, techniques that might be appropriate. Column Two summarizes what approaches (often based on upside-down thinking) might build on Column One to bring about 'improved organizational capability'. Between them they represent the 'dual focus of attention' in which everyone in your organization should be engaged to transform individual competence into organizational capability. This is the ultimate goal of investing in people.

Improving current competence	Extending corporate capability
Chapter 2	
1 Use local TEC's expertise, facilities	Invest resources in TEC as a clearing bank
2 Use BS5750 as a framework for auditing current performance	Identify 'variety' of customers for business in future and capacity of staff to respond to their needs
3 Use 'Investors in People' self-diagnostic pack to review how well staff are able to meet business needs and provide support as necessary	Find out each employee's 'image' of the company and its future, compare with company view and modify as necessary

Figure 7.9 *Summary of key themes of the book that contribute to improving existing competence on the one hand and potentially adding to corporate capability on the other*

Chapter 3

| 4 Use competences to confirm current standards of performance | Identify contingency and task management skills and job environment skills |

5 Use NVQ standards for occupations in company as a framework for auditing current performance and giving accreditation

Use evidence of such skills as basis for building a picture of corporate capability for the future

Use the 11 dichotomies as basis for 'dialectical inquiry' and indicator of capability

Chapter 4

6 Design individual development programmes to meet identified competences

Make available details of learning resources (including skills, expertise of individuals) widely throughout organization and encourage individuals to use rich mix to build up capability for future and also to record details of which have been used

7 Use mix of learning resources that best meets need using 'Learning Mix' matrix as a guide

Encourage each employee to be a resource to each other and accredit such development activity

Chapter 5

8 Use MCI management competences as a framework to review current management performance

Use each competence as a 'direction of inquiry' as to the kind of competences needed for the future

9 Design individual development programme to achieve necessary competences

Use seven modes from MSC study to identify quality of managing required for the future

Encourage managers to identify,and add value to their own subordinates and reward such activity

Chapter 6

10 Choose combination from eight models of evaluation to collect information about a given development programme and current level of contribution to organization

Use evaluation as a process for adding value to each development activity and feeding back the result so that the whole organization can see how its corporate capability has been enhanced

Chapter 7

Always be on the look out for 'changes of potential' within the organization and encourage individuals and groups to question norms and practices

Provide the necessary organizational support and mechanisms to reinforce and make public the outcome from such a questioning process

Figure 7.9 (*continued*)

References

1 Schon, D. (1971) *Beyond the Stable State*, Temple Smith
2 Garratt, R. (1987) *The Learning Organization*, Fontana
3 Pedler, M., Boydell, T., and Burgoyne, J. (1988) *Learning Company Project*, Manpower Services Commission
4 Garratt, R. (1990) *Creating a Learning Organisation*, Director Books
5 Senge, P. (1990) *the Fifth Discipline; The Art and Practice of the Learning Organization*, Doubleday
6 Lessem, R. (1991) *Total Quality Learning: Building a Learning Organization*, Basil Blackwell
7 Pedler, M., Burgoyne, J. and Boydell, T. (1991) *The Learning Company*, McGraw Hill
8 Argyris, C. and Schon, D. (1978) *Organizational Learning: A Theory of Action Perspective*, Addison Wesley
9 Dixon, P. (1990) Creating a learning organization. MBA dissertation, Middlesex Business School
10 Argyris, C. and Schon, D. (1978) *Organizational Learning: A Theory of Action Perspective*, Addison Wesley
11 Bateson, G. (1973) *Steps to an Ecology of Mind*, Paladin
12 Morgan, G. (1986) *Images of Organization*, Sage
13 Hedberg, B., Nystrom, P. and Starbuck, W. (1976) Camping on Seesaws: Prescriptions for a Self-designing Organization. *Administrative Science Quarterly*, **21**(1) 41–65
14 Kanter, R. M. (1983) *The Change Masters*, Unwin Paperbacks
15 Handy, C. (1989) *The Age of Unreason*, Hutchinson
16 Lawler, E. E. (1990) *Strategic Pay: Aligning Organizational Strategies and Pay Systems*, Jossey Bass
17 Thomson, K. (1990) *The Employee Revolution – The Rise of Internal Corporate Marketing*, Pitman
18 Checkland, P. and Scholes, J. (1990) *Soft Systems Methodology (SSM) in Action*, Wiley
19 Kohn, A. (1986) *No Contest – The Case Against Competition*, Houghton Mifflin
20 Holland, G. (1986) Excellence in industry: Developing managers a new approach. Speech given at the Dorchester Hotel, London, 11 February 1986
21 Peters, T. (1988) Restoring American competitiveness: looking for new models of organizations. *The Academy of Management Executive*, **II**(2), 103–109
22 Peters, T. (1987) *Thriving on chaos*, AA Knopf
23 Weick, K. E. (1979) *The Social Psychology of Organizing*, Addison Wesley
24 Smircich, L. and Stubbart, C. (1985) Strategic management in an enacted world. Academy of Management Review 1985, reprinted in *Creative Organization Theory – A resource Book* (1989) (ed. Gareth Morgan), Sage

25 Marsick, V. J. and Watkins, K. E. (1990) *Informal and Incidental Learning in the Workplace*, Routledge
26 Lindblom, C. E. (1966) The science of muddling through. In *Business Strategy – Selected Readings* (ed. I. Ansoff), Penguin
27 Prospect Centre (1990) *Strategies and People – 1990*, Prospect Centre, Kingston
28 Hawkins, P. (1991) The spiritual dimension of the learning organization. In *Joining Forces: Working with Spirituality Organizations* (ed. R. Snell, J. Davies, T. Boydell and M. Leary), *Management Education and Development*, **22**(3), 172–187
29 Beer, S. (1979) *The Heart of Enterprise*, Wiley

Index